Geography and the Wealth of Nations

Geography and the Wealth of Nations

Sherif Khalifa

LEXINGTON BOOKS

Lanham • Boulder • New York • London

Published by Lexington Books
An imprint of The Rowman & Littlefield Publishing Group, Inc.
4501 Forbes Boulevard, Suite 200, Lanham, Maryland 20706
www.rowman.com

6 Tinworth Street, London SE11 5AL, United Kingdom

British Library Cataloguing in Publication Information Available

Library of Congress Cataloging-in-Publication Data

Names: Khalifa, Sherif, author. Title: Geography and the wealth of nations / Sherif
   Khalifa.
Description: Lanham : Lexington Books, [2022] | Includes bibliographical references and
   index. | Summary: "In Geography and the Wealth of Nations, Sherif Khalifa argues
   that geography influences the factors that determine economic performance, such as
   the quality of institutions, the adopted cultural values, the systems of governance, the
   likelihood of conflict, the historical experiences, and the integration into the global
   economy" —Provided by publisher.
Identifiers: LCCN 2022005016 (print) | LCCN 2022005017 (ebook) | ISBN
   9781666900521 (cloth) | ISBN 9781666900538 (epub) | ISBN 9781666900545 (pbk.)
Subjects: LCSH: Economic geography. | Environmental economics.
Classification: LCC HF1025 .K46 2022 (print) | LCC HF1025 (ebook) | DDC 330.9—
   dc23/eng/20220222 LC record available at https://lccn.loc.gov/2022005016 LC ebook
   record available at https://lccn.loc.gov/2022005017

To my son, Yusef Khalifa
May he grow up to understand why we live in a world with huge
differences in living conditions, to have the compassion to care for
those who are not as fortunate, to have the desire to do something about
these differences, and to have the courage to stand for what is just.

Contents

Introduction

In ancient Greek mythology, Prometheus is a Titan, a hero and a trickster who defies the Olympian gods by stealing fire and offering it to humanity. This was considered an act that enabled civilization. Prometheus was, hereinafter, known as a champion of mankind and a larger-than-life figure who defined humans' striving for advancement. Zeus, king of the Olympian gods, was infuriated by Prometheus' theft. He punished Prometheus by having him chained to a rock and sent an eagle to feed on the Titan's liver. To make matters worse, the liver grew back every night and the eagle returned every day to perpetually torment Prometheus. In the words of Cyrano de Bergerac, "Prometheus heretofore went up to Heaven, and stole fire from thence. Have not I as much Boldness as he?"

Contemplating about this story, one but wonders what was in Prometheus fire that enabled human civilization. Some would argue that Prometheus offered humans the warmth of fire without which humanity would not have survived. In this book, however, we take a metaphorical approach to Prometheus fire. In other words, this book is an attempt to explore the symbolism in the fire that made human progress possible. Thus, this book addresses the elusive question of why some nations prosper and thrive while others fail and languish in poverty. This question continues to attract lots of attention from social scientists, scholars, and the interested public.

In particular, this book examines the factors that have been identified by scholars as critical determinants of economic outcomes. These include the geographic, climatic, geological, and topographic features of a country; the quality of a country's institutions or the systems that are intended to impose a structure on our economic, political, legal and social interactions; the country's cherished cultural values and faith paradigms; the country's system of governance and the extent of political freedoms and political stability; the level of a country's ethnic and linguistic diversity and the likelihood of ethnolinguistic conflict; the extent of income inequality in a country and the degree of distributional conflict; the historical events that occurred a long time ago but continue to shape contemporary outcomes; and the integration of the country into the global economy.

The core argument of the book is that behind all these factors, geography looms large. In other words, geography has a clear effect on current economic outcomes directly or indirectly through these other factors. As will be seen in the book, geography affects productivity, the technology of production, and the accumulation of physical capital and human capital which are critical for economic performance. The reliance on natural resources could be a curse or potentially a blessing, while natural disasters could have a significant effect on stricken economies. While all these issues highlight the direct economic effect of geography, the book also emphasizes that the natural environment is behind all the other factors that we believe are critical for economic performance. In this context, this book discusses how certain geographic characteristics influence the political, economic and legal institutions that we observe today; how geography affects the cultural traits, the faith paradigms and the linguistic attributes that may shape our economic choices today; how the natural environment impact the likelihood of conflict within society between people and authority, between different groups of people, and between those in different income categories; and how the geographic location has a long lasting effect on the level of engagement in a globalized world. The book also looks into how some geographic features determined historical events that occurred a long time ago but continue to affect our economies today.

The arguments against a geographic narrative of economic outcomes include three primary points of view. The first is that geography only affects economic performance indirectly through its effect on other factors that are of more paramount importance, but has no direct effect. The second is that the argument in favor of a geographic contribution to current economic outcomes should not be taken seriously given the technological advances that allow humans to dominate their natural environment. The third is that conceding to a geographic contribution implies that humans have no control over their destiny given that they cannot choose their natural surroundings.

To respond to the first claim, this book posits that arguing that geography has an indirect effect does not discount the contribution of geography. As we will see between the two covers of the book, the origin of each critical determinant of economic prosperity can be traced back to one geographic factor or another. For instance, there is a consensus that the quality of institutions is indispensable for economic performance. But as much as it is essential to ascertain the economic effect of institutions, it is vital to know what caused institutions to be so different. As much as it is critical to know the economic consequences of some cultural traits, it is equally important to understand why people adopt different values and attitudes. As much as it is crucial to know the effect of historical events on current outcomes, it is also imperative to learn what brought these occurrences about in the first place. As much as it is valuable to know the effect of integration into the global economy on economic outcomes, it is also beneficial to discern why some communities are more engaged with other economies than others. This book argues that these differences can be traced back to one geographic feature or another.

As for the second claim on the potential of technology in allowing us to tame our surrounding environment, this book argues that the effect of geography was palpable in a period when technological knowledge was not developed enough to grant humans that power over nature. As such, geography influenced some of these factors whose effect persisted until the present day. For instance, we will see that some geographic features shaped the form and substance of these persistent institutional structures that we have to deal with nowadays. Technology is not likely to allow us to change that significantly. The book also shows that our cultural traits, the extent of our adherence to our articles of faith, and the linguistic structure of our speech has been affected by geographic features. It is not likely that technology is going to change these attributes drastically either. In the book, we also see that the extent of diversity in a society can be tracked to some natural elements. This degree of heterogeneity that continued until the present day affecting the likelihood of conflict and our political structures is not likely to be transformed by our technology. This book also investigates some historical events that took place centuries ago yet have a lingering effect on contemporary economies. These events were induced to a large extent by the geographic environment at a time when technology was not advanced enough for humans to have a say in the course of these developments.

As for the third claim that emphasizing geography's effect implies inevitable economic outcomes that we cannot change, we can argue instead that bringing to light the compelling effect of these geographic factors can guide decision makers in directions that can be overlooked otherwise. Accordingly, policy prescriptions could be directed to assist countries with unfavorable geographic conditions to overcome these specific shortcomings.

To achieve its objectives, the book is divided into several chapters. Each chapter attempts to survey the studies in the literature; to discuss the arguments, debates and controversies included in these studies; to demonstrate the analytical techniques used to address the question of interest; and to present their main findings and conclusions. This is, however, not intended to be an exhaustive overview of scholarly work in the pertinent literature. Alternatively, a selective approach is adopted to focus on some of these studies that contributed to the literature in one way or another. This is done in a manner that is hopefully engaging to those experts in this field of study in addition to those who have a general interest in the subject. This book is, thus, an effort to present the thought provoking and intellectually stimulating ideas developed by scholars from various fields of study.

In this context, the first chapter titled "The Fingerprint of Geography" highlights the signature of geography in our lives. This chapter defines the geographic features of a country in terms of climate, location, topography, abundance of natural wealth, and the incidence of natural disaster. The chapter is an overview of how the geographic feature of a country affects a nation's cultural traits, faith paradigms, gastronomical habits, fashion trends, artistic currents, architectural patterns, production technologies, communication modes, institutional structures, forms of governance, foreign policy, the likelihood of conflict, and outcomes of warfare. The chapter also discusses how geography can shed light on the causes of some significant historical junctures such as the transition to agriculture, the slave trade, the colonial expansion, and the age of discovery.

The second chapter titled "Climate, Crops, and Capital" discusses the direct effect of climate on agricultural productivity through its effect on the quality of the soil, the scarcity of water for irrigation, the pervasiveness of crop pests and parasites, and the photosynthetic potential of crops. The chapter also focuses on the effect of climate on the accumulation of capital that is critical for economic productivity, and on the development and diffusion of technology across ecological borders. The chapter also discusses how geographic isolation can allow for the development of specific cultures of innovation and technology creation.

The third chapter titled "Germs, Groups, and Gender" considers the effect of climate on the spread of infectious tropical diseases such as Malaria, Leishmaniasis, Schistosomiasis, Onchocerciasis, Filariasis, Helminths, Trypanosomiasis, Yellow fever, Dengue fever and others. Specifically, the book explores in this chapter how climatic, biological, ecological, and environmental factors encourage high levels of biodiversity in pathogens and vectors that cause these diseases to spread in the tropics, and their subsequent effect on economic outcomes. The chapter also focuses on the effect of climate on the spread of veterinary diseases in the tropics and their effect on livestock, farming, institutions, and culture.

The fourth chapter titled "Accursed Are the Blessed" focuses on the natural resource curse which refers to the fact that some countries that are endowed with natural wealth have worse economic outcomes. This curse is reflected in the lack of economic diversification, lower educational attainment, higher likelihood of conflict, higher income inequality, and the absence of democratic governance. The chapter also surveys the literature on whether resource abundance and dependence are a curse or a blessing.

The fifth chapter titled "The Wrath of Nature" concludes the discussion on the direct effect of geography on economic outcomes with an exploration of the consequences of natural disasters. The chapter focuses on the impact of the wrath of nature on overall economic outcomes, the accumulation of physical capital and human capital, agricultural productivity, health conditions, the degree of religiosity, the likelihood of conflict, and the system of governance. The chapter discusses the adverse effects of disasters in terms of the death toll and casualties; the destruction to property, infrastructure, and productive facilities; and the physical and psychological traumas that people suffer from due to their exposure to these calamities.

The sixth chapter titled "Determinism versus Determination" distinguishes between formal and informal institutions and focuses on the effect of the quality of these institutions on the incentives for investment and innovation. The chapter considers the institutional constraints dictated by the state and those imposed on the state to avoid an overreach by state representatives out of the purview of the law. This discussion includes the institutional structures to protect property, to enforce contracts, to maintain the rule of law, to regulate economic activity, to ensure competitiveness, to guarantee judicial independence, and to impose checks and balances. The chapter also includes an exposition of the scholarly work that studies the effect of institutional quality on economic outcomes, compares between the consequences of distinct types of institutions, explores the channels of transmission from institutions to economic outcomes, and explores whether institutions affect different countries differently.

The seventh chapter titled "On the Geographic Origins" delves into the roots of current institutions that evolved over time by the determined will of nations or their leaders. In this context, the chapter discusses the colonial origins of institutions, how the expansion of trade across the Atlantic affected the institutions of the countries engaged in it, how factor endowments and crops impact the quality of institutions, how climatic factors affect institutions, how reliance on irrigation agriculture determines the form of institutions, and how the topographic features of a country influence its institutional structures as well.

The eighth chapter titled "Sand or Grease" discusses the effect of different forms of corruption on economic outcomes. The extent of corruption is a component of the quality of the institutional structure in a country. The chapter starts with a geographic explanation of the differences in corrupt practices across countries. This chapter also discusses whether corruption hurts investment activities, creates an unjustified level of inequality in opportunity and income that can fuel frustration and discontent, causes an inefficient allocation of talents and resources, and diminishes the quality of public officials. The chapter also explores whether corrupt transactions are a means of circumventing pervasive red tape, a convenient device for overcoming hurdles that distort incentives, greases the wheels of a cumbersome bureaucracy and a rigid government administration, and as a trouble saving device to entrepreneurs and businesses to speed the issuance of licenses and permits.

The ninth chapter titled "Nature's Democratic Dividend" focuses on political institutions. The chapter starts with a discussion on the geographic origins of democratic transitions. The book also discusses in this chapter whether democratic practices stimulate economic performance by imposing constraints on the executive, by allowing the voters to elect politicians who can represent their interests, and by changing governments that could not fulfill their promises. The chapter examines whether democracy can enhance the quality of policy making by submitting politicians to public scrutiny and by promoting viable alternatives in the form of opposition parties. The chapter elaborates on how democracy affects political stability, institutional quality, government size, income inequality, trade liberalization, human capital, physical capital, social capital, and technology adoption. The chapter surveys some studies that examine the effect of democracy on economic outcomes, compares the effect of democracy to that of democratization and democratic capital, contrasts the effect of different forms of democratic governance, and distinguishes between the consequences of different types of democratic transitions as well.

The tenth chapter titled "Elixir or People's Opium" discusses the influence of religious beliefs, religious practices, and religious affiliation on economic outcomes. The chapter discusses the geographic origins of religiosity and then elaborates on the effect of religiosity on cultural traits, consumption patterns, resource allocation, institutional quality, political participation, religious conflict, income inequality, human capital, physical capital and social capital. The chapter concludes with a comprehensive survey of scholarly studies that examine the influence of the degree of religiosity on economic outcomes, on cultural traits, on attitudes toward science and innovation, on income inequality and on institutional quality as well.

The eleventh chapter titled "In (Trust) We Trust" discusses other aspects of culture besides faith, such as social capital. The chapter starts with the geographic origins of trust and surveys the literature on the effect of trust on economic performance, on investment and innovation, on government intervention in the economy, on economic reforms, on economic exchange and international flows, and on democratic governance. The chapter also discusses the effect of civic engagement and associational activities as components of social capital.

The twelfth chapter titled "Me, Myself, and Society" discusses the debate on whether we should emphasize an individualistic approach on the expense of the collective, or alternatively stress social solidarity between individuals, for better economic outcomes. Thus, the chapter discusses the virtues of individualism versus collectivism, the merits of cooperation, cohesion and social solidarity, and the economic and social benefits of tolerance. The chapter finishes with an overview of the economic consequences of specific linguistic structures that allow for different forms of expression about self worth and connection to society. The chapter also explores the geographic origins of individualism, collectivism, and the features of our languages.

The thirteenth chapter titled "The Wrath and Wealth of Nations" focuses on the effect of conflict on economic outcomes and explores the climatic effect on the likelihood of conflict. The chapter focuses on conflict between people and the authorities, which undermines political stability. Thus, this chapter explores the effect of political instability, or the likelihood of government change or collapse, on economic outcomes. The chapter surveys the arguments and the findings of some scholarly work on the effect of political instability on economic performance, policy uncertainty, policy quality, institutional quality, physical capital and human capital.

The fourteenth chapter titled "Heterogeneous We Stand" focuses on conflict between different groups of people and how certain geographic characteristics contributed to the extent of heterogeneity in a society. In this context, the chapter addresses whether diversity along ethnic, linguistic and religious dimensions affects the likelihood of conflict, income inequality, social capital, political partisanship, policy quality, and institutional quality. The chapter discusses whether a heterogeneous society along these lines has difficulty agreeing on public policies that are growth promoting, has difficulty coordinating to influence politicians and policymakers, will be prone to violent conflict, and will be prey to distrust, corruption, and favoritism. The chapter also distinguishes between the concepts and economic effects of ethnic fractionalization, ethnic polarization, ethnic inequality, ethnic favoritism, ethnic exclusion, and ethnic segregation.

The fifteenth chapter titled "Climbing the Social Ladder" explores the effect of distributional conflict, due to high levels of income inequality, on economic outcomes. The chapter starts with highlighting some ideas on the climatic origins of income distribution. The chapter also discusses the arguments on how income inequality can hinder economic growth if egalitarian conditions allow the poor to overcome the credit constraints to invest in human capital. The chapter covers the political economy arguments that conclude that inequality can lead to distributional conflict, to a higher support for redistribution, and to lower social solidarity. The chapter also presents the counter arguments that inequality can enhance economic growth through the concentration of income and wealth in the hands of those who have a higher propensity to save which is essential for investment. The chapter illustrates the scholarly efforts to reconcile these two approaches and the ample empirical evidence in support of one or the other of these hypotheses. The discussion also addresses the question of whether the inequality of opportunity differs from the inequality of outcomes in their impact on economic performance.

The sixteenth chapter titled "Echoes of the Past" covers some historical events that had a persistent and lasting impact on the countries' ability
to improve their living conditions in the present. This chapter focuses on
the effects on current economic outcomes of some of the significant events
in human history, such as the timing of the transition to agriculture or the
Neolithic Revolution, state history or the extent of experience within state
institutions, and the Protestant Reformation. The chapter also includes a discussion on the effect of the slave trade on current economic outcomes, social
capital, income inequality, ethnic stratification, and conflict. The geographic
origins of these historical events are also covered in this chapter.

The seventeenth chapter titled "The Big Scramble, the Great Loot" discusses whether colonialism and the colonial heritage have an adverse effect
on the ability of currently independent countries to improve their lot. The
chapter discusses whether the identity of the colonial power, the duration of
colonization, and the degree of penetration and exploitation of the colonies
have an impact on the post-colonial economic potential of these countries.
In addition, the chapter covers how the extraction of resources, draining the
wealth of colonies through excessive taxation, the enslavement of the indigenous population through the slave trade or forced labor, and the distortion of
the educational policies hampered the colonies' growth potential. The chapter
discusses the arguments of the favorable effect of colonialism by promoting modernization in the colonies, building infrastructures, and enhancing
the integration of the colonies into the international economic system. The
chapter also discusses the precolonial and post-colonial institutions, and the
effects of the so-called Columbian exchange.

The eighteenth and final chapter titled "In a Flat World" discusses the
effect of globalization and economic integration on economic outcomes. The
chapter starts with the economic consequences, and the extent of involvement in commercial exchange, of the proximity to the coast, to navigable
waterways, and to core markets. The chapter discusses the classical work on
the economic gains from trade. The chapter also presents the latest findings
on the effect of trade liberalization on economic outcomes and whether trade
barriers hinder economic growth.

As can be clearly seen, this book is a comprehensive account of the determinants of economic outcomes that have been identified in scholarly, literary, and academic works. Thus, this book can serve as a complete reference
for those who continue to explore the effect of these factors and those who
question the disturbing differences in incomes and living conditions that we
observe across countries in our world today. The book, however, does not
only serve as an overview of the pertinent literature but also proposes an argument that all these factors can be traced to one geographic feature or another.
Thus, this narrative can serve as a guide for us to comprehend the impact of

our natural environment on every aspect of our lives, and for policy makers who continue to wonder about the best policies to implement to change their country's economic performance given these specific challenges. This is particularly important and pertinent as our world faces unprecedented natural challenges nowadays that include climate change and global warming, the increase in the severity of natural disasters, the depletion of natural resources, soil degradation, deforestation, the loss of biodiversity and others. This implies that we will not be able to respond appropriately to these imminent threats to our existence unless we understand their potential implications on our political, economic, legal, institutional, social, and cultural structures. As we come to understand that any alterations to our natural surroundings have serious implications, then we can admit that these challenges are consequential and that we need to react accordingly. This book is, hopefully, a small contribution in that direction.

Chapter One

The Fingerprint of Geography

THEATRUM ORBIS TERRARUM[1]

Some countries are famous for their unique natural attributes and singular geographic features. Other countries are often referred to by one or more of their conspicuous territorial elements, prominent natural wonders, or salient earthly formations that evolved naturally over time. These sites attract visitors, travelers, tourists, sightseers and pilgrims for their awe-inspiring landscape and scenery.

Some communities are defined by their surrounding environment. We occasionally distinguish between the people of the mountains and those of the lowlands, between those who live in the hills and those who inhabit the valleys, between those who are located in furrowed terrain and those who occupy flat lands, between those who settle in coastal areas and those trapped in the hinterland, between riparian nations and those who dwell away from a river valley, between nomadic people who wander around and sedentary ones who settle permanently, between those who reside in an island and those of the mainland, between those who live in the tropics and those in the temperate zone, and between those who endure harsh climate and those who live in agreeable conditions.

The personality and character of some societies have continued to be shaped by their uninterrupted interaction with their natural milieu. These everlasting experiences contributed to their way of life, cultural traits, revered values, cherished customs, communal norms, social traditions, and societal taboos. Some communities even incorporated familiar geographic features into their faith paradigms and belief systems. Throughout history, societies worshipped a deity that is found pervasively within their natural perimeter such as a common plant, a wild beast, or some notable landmark. Other societies adopted nature worship deemed by some as a variety of devotional credos which underscores the spiritual connection with some aspects of the natural world and idolizes the spirits behind the natural phenomena discernible throughout. Some societies also perceived an ominous natural event as a way of divinity to chastise and punish them for their wrongdoings, while others considered an auspicious one as a way of providence to award them for their piety and adherence to their supreme being. Humans have also huddled for their faith in face of hardships, such as those climatic shocks which cause rainfall fluctuations that catch farm communities off guard or increase the frequency of natural-induced disasters that struck those who happen to be in their way.

Geography also had a substantial influence on our gastronomical habits, fashion trends, artistic streams, and architectural patterns. Culinary delights are usually inspired by ingredients available to a community in its territory. Cuisines are influenced by the plants that can be cultivated, and the animals that can be bred, in their surrounding environment. Domestic dishes became an assortment of the local nature's offerings. People also designed their costumes to allow them to operate with ease within their natural habitat. Clothes were woven with fabrics abundantly available in the environmental neighborhood, and attires and apparel were designed for people to be comfortable with the weather, the terrain, and other natural features. Architectural blueprints and construction designs are also affected by our geography. The erection of dwellings, domiciles, edifices, and temples aimed to cater to human needs for safety and shelter from the natural elements particular to that area. The design of a structure considered the need to moderate the temperature for the occupants, to dispense with precipitation, and to overcome the terrain asymmetries. Artistic trends also used natural elements within reach to find an aesthetic expression of our experience with nature. These artistic statements, that stood the test of time, survived as a testament to humans' incessant desire to narrate their adventure using the natural ingredients at their disposal.

Societies also used the natural components available to them to create tools, instruments, and devices to produce their needs. Nature also influenced the production modes that societies adopted, as it paved the way for the development of technologies that are suitable for their specific environment. The diffusion of these geography-specific technologies from one society to another also depended on whether these societies shared similar environmental conditions. Jared Diamond adroitly observes that[2]

> Another reason for the higher local diversity of domesticated plants and animals in Eurasia than in the Americas is that Eurasia's main axis is east/west, whereas the main axis of the Americas is north/south. Eurasia's east/west axis meant that species domesticated in one part of Eurasia could easily spread thousands of miles at the same latitude, encountering the same day-length and climate to which they were already adapted.

Nature also influenced societies' means of communication and interaction with others. Some natural features afforded a bridge between communities or acted as a pathway between human settlements. This facilitated trade transactions, commercial exchange, and cultural flows. Societies that enjoyed these features were more amenable to cultural assimilation, technological dissemination, and the mercantile spirit. Other geographic characteristics acted as barriers to communications and a hindrance to the conduct of commerce with other communities. Societies impaired by these features were isolated from trade routes, migration trails, knowledge webs, and exploration thoroughfares. Some of these societies even lived in what seems like a solitary confinement or a complete seclusion from cultural spillovers and commercial networks.

Societies' interaction with nature in some cases expedited state formation and the establishment of specific sorts of political institutions and particular forms of governance. State formation signifies the emergence of a centralized government structure within a territory. Some attributed this notable stride in organizing human societies to some geographic features. For instance, Karl Wittfogel argues that farmers in arid land were confronted by the limitations of small-scale irrigation systems. Thus, farming communities would join to create a state apparatus with a centralized government that could construct and administer large-scale irrigation projects. Wittfogel suggests in his *Oriental Despotism: A Comparative Study of Total Power* that the[3] "prime necessity of an economical and common use of water, which, in the Occident, drove private enterprise to voluntary association . . . necessitated in the Orient . . . the interference of the centralizing power of Government."

Governments who were able to control the critical resources, without which their citizens cannot survive, were also capable of imposing their will on the entire populace. The rulers of ancient Egypt, who controlled the Nile and the distribution of its water for irrigation, are said to have established the first dictatorship in history. The complete and utter dependence on the Nile water created a strong state with a huge bureaucratic structure. This is because the state controlled the citizens' livelihood through a centralized system of flood control, access to water, and irrigation canals. Egyptian geographer Gamal Hamdan in his *Personality of Egypt* states that[4] "Egypt is the first political unit, the first unified state in history, but also probably the world's first tyranny, and the oldest and most deep-rooted centralized state to emerge on Earth." Geography, thus, paved the way for state formation and authoritarianism in ancient Egypt. Historian William McNeill discusses how other geographic characteristics defined ancient Egypt as[5] "Deserts gave the land of Egypt clear-cut and easily defensible boundaries; while the Nile provided it with a natural backbone and nervous system. Frontier defense against outlanders was seldom a serious problem for the king of Egypt." Historian Sir Halford Mackinder also points out that the Nile valley civilization was protected on the east and west by deserts, and never suffered from Mediterranean piracy because of the marshlands of the Nile Delta.[6] These natural bequests provided Egyptian kingdoms with an extraordinary level of security and stability. Thus, was civilization able to dawn and to continue in Egypt for centuries. In contemporary times, other natural attributes continue to have their indelible mark on Egypt's destiny. As the country is bereft of natural wealth and as the population is densely settled in a narrow Nile valley surrounded by deserts, Egypt continues to languish in a state of economic distress with a contemporary version of Pharaonic despotism.[7]

On the other hand, some societies came to experience other forms of shared political participation and collective governance, especially where access to resources was less restricted. In addition, communities that were geographically isolated from the heavy handedness of the government enjoyed a wider margin of freedom compared to others who were not as protected by natural barriers. These isolated communities are known for their defiant spirit and their unwillingness to submit to a centralized authority.

Abundance and dependence on natural wealth also influenced the likelihood of conflict and the outcome of warfare. Robert Kaplan states that[8] "For maps are a rebuke to the very notions of equality and unity of humankind, since they remind us of all the different environments of the earth that make men profoundly unequal and disunited in so many ways, leading to conflict." Nicholas Spykman also asserts that[9]

> Because the geographic characteristics of states are relatively unchanging and unchangeable, the geographic demands of those states will remain the same for centuries, and because the world has not yet reached that happy state where the wants of no man conflict with those of another, those demands will cause friction. Thus, at the door of geography may be laid the blame for many of the age-long struggles which run persistently through history while governments and dynasties rise and fall.

In support of this view, some point out the fact that nations went to war, in so many occasions in human history, due to the scarcity of natural endowments or in pursuit of the others' natural bounty. No better example than the term "Lebensraum" or "living space" which refers to the geopolitical goal of territorial expansion embraced by Germany in the late nineteenth century and the early twentieth century. The term was used to describe the expediency for Germany to expand eastward to control resources that are not abundantly available within borders.[10] This was the excuse used to instigate the two world wars when millions were vanquished, dreadful horrors were committed, and appalling atrocities were perpetrated. Similarly, Japan delved into the Second World War with its expansion in the East Asian provinces to seek a supply of raw materials badly needed for the home islands. Japan's imperial ambitions were intended to gain control over the East Indies' oil, Manchuria's iron and coal, and Indochina's rubber. This dragged Japan to what historians would eventually call the "Valley of Darkness." The detonation of the first and last atomic bombs in human history would be the unfortunate final chapter of that lamentable blunder.

Outcomes of armed conflict were also altered by the abundance of some natural endowments. No better exposition than the one afforded by Daniel Yergin on how oil turned the direction of the two world wars as he states that[11]

> The battlefields of World war I established the importance of petroleum as an element of national power when the internal combustion machine overtook the horse and the coal-powered locomotive. Petroleum was central to the course and outcome of World War II in both the Far East and Europe. The Japanese attacked Pearl Harbor to protect their flank as they grabbed for the petroleum resources of the East Indies. Among Hitler's most important strategic objectives in the invasion of the Soviet Union was the capture of the oil fields in the Caucasus. But America's predominance in oil proved decisive, and by the end of the war German and Japanese fuel tanks were empty.

On the other hand, countries blessed with raw materials are otherwise cursed to be the most prone to internal conflict. This paradox of plenty is the puzzle that countries abundant with natural wealth tend to have worse outcomes than those with fewer supplies.[12] This is because countries that are well endowed with natural assets usually endure an internal armed conflict over the control of these resources. In these occasions, the return on resource extraction acts not only as a catalyst to instigate a civil war but also serves as a lucrative source of funding for the insurgents to continue being embroiled in conflict.

In international relations, the geostrategic significance of a country is said to be influenced by its geographic location on the map and its position in the global political arena. Robert Kaplan makes clear that[13] "the only thing enduring is a people's position on the map. Thus, in times of upheaval, maps rise in importance. With the political ground shifting rapidly under one's feet, the map, though not determinative, is the beginning of discerning a historical logic about what might come next." Thus, geography sometimes bestows strategic significance on a country even if its people inadvertently diminish it with their actions. Countries have geopolitical weight because they control a route that is important for international trade, because they occupy a core location that lies in the intersection of the spheres of influence of superpowers, or because their territory contains resources that are critical to the world economy. Thus, a country's prominence in the international arena could be amplified by its endowment of essential natural assets that are crucial to the economies of other nations in the production process or in the generation of energy.

Geography also influences a country's foreign policy, its sphere of influence, its labyrinth of neighboring allies, and the cobweb of foes in its vicinity. Napoleon Bonaparte is known to have said that "If you know a country's geography, you can understand and predict its foreign policy." Nicholas Spykman also asserts that[14] "In such a world, the geographic area of the state is the territorial base from which it operates in time of war and the strategic position which it occupies during the temporary armistice called peace. It is the most fundamentally conditioning factor in the formulation of national policy because it is the most permanent. Ministers come and ministers go, even dictators die, but mountain ranges stand unperturbed."

Imperial expansion was also attributed to geographic and ecological factors. For instance, Robert Kaplan argues that Europe came to dominate large parts of the world during colonial times because[15]

> Europe lay in a "congenial" ecozone between the deserts of Africa and the ice sheets of the Arctic, with a climate moderated by the Gulf stream. Europe was rich in resources, with wood, stone, metals, and furs. Most crucially, Europe has a deviating and shattered coastline, indented with many good natural harbors, and cluttered with islands and half islands. This coastline is 23,000 miles long—an epic length equal to the circumference of the earth. In fact, Europe has a higher ratio of coastline to landmass than any other continent or subcontinent. Europe borders on no fewer than four enclosed and semi-enclosed seas that squeeze the subcontinent, so to speak, into a relatively narrow peninsula: the Mediterranean, the Black, the Baltic, and the North seas; even as Europe has an advantageous riverine topography blessed with cross-peninsula routes-the Rhine, the Elbe, and above all the Danube.

Kaplan concludes that "This very elaborate interface between land and water, and the fact that Europe is protected from—and yet accessible to—a vast ocean, has led to maritime dynamism and mobility among Europe's peoples." On the other hand, historian Peter Turchin begs to differ with a poignant comment on empire formation as he states that[16]

> In fact, it is not Europe that is exceptional, it is China. No other region in the world had had such a long history of imperial rule. Perversely enough, the reason, ultimately, is geographic or, more precisely, ecological. The distribution of rainfall within eastern Asia creates a sharp ecological boundary between the drier steppe and wetter agricultural regions. Ever since humans learned predatory nomadism, this ecological boundary coincided with a metaethnic frontier between nomadic pastoralists and settled agriculturalists. Under pressure from the steppe, Chinese agriculturalists built one empire after another. On the steppe side, the nomads united in one imperial confederation after another. The Chinese made forays into the nomad territory, but never could make it their own, because they could not grow crops there. Nomads repeatedly conquered China, but in

the process assimilated and merged into the Chinese. The fault line between the Chinese and nomadic civilizations was anchored by the geography of eastern Asia. That is why one universal empire repeatedly followed another in China. A universal empire is a state that unifies all, or virtually all, of a civilization.

Large scale historical developments were also driven by geographic factors. Robert Kaplan asserts that[17] "Geography is the backdrop to human history itself," and that[18] "geography is the preface to the very track of human events." A plethora of examples in human history support this view including such events as the agricultural transition, the colonial expansion, the slave trades, and the age of discovery.

One of the most critical milestones in human history is the Neolithic Revolution. This refers to the wide scale transition of human societies from a lifestyle of hunter-gatherers whose sustenance depended on foraging, or collecting wild plants and pursuing undomesticated animals, to one of agriculture. Small groups of hunter-gatherers that had hitherto dominated human history were, thus, transformed into sedentary societies. These societies changed their way of life through the cultivation of domesticated species which allowed the production of surplus food. This decisive development provided the basis for densely populated settlements, specialization and division of labor, trade and commerce, centralized administrations, political structures, hierarchical ideologies, property ownership, writing alphabets, mathematics and astronomy, and other significant human achievements.

There are competing theories that aim to ascertain the factors that drove societies to adopt that consequential change about 12,000 years ago. Some ascribe this to a fundamental shift in climate in a certain period that made farming easier, or to the observation that the development of agriculture coincided with an increasingly stable climate at the beginning of the Holocene, or to the fact that societies stretched to the carrying capacity of the local environment which created the need for more food supplies than could be gathered. All these ideas are variants of the same theme; that drastic departures in the environmental pulse can lead to significant detours in the trajectory of humanity.

Another historical event that geography can shed some light on is colonialism. Colonialism was an instrument to extricate the natural wealth of the conquered countries and to extract the resources of the subjugated nations. Colonial powers found that the most efficacious way to secure the steady flow of vital natural supplies is to have them in their possession. This is referred to as "exploitation colonialism," where colonies were governed by colonial administrators who directed the local economies to divert the available resources to supply the metropole with food, raw materials, and finished goods. This type of exploitation was often justified by geographers of the imperial powers who introduced theories of environmental determinism which suggested warmer climates produced less civilized people. These theories helped legitimize the expansion of colonial powers into overseas territories. On the other hand, "settlement colonialism" took place when imperial powers oversaw the migration of their people to other lands. In lots of cases, the location of that ultimate destination was determined, to a large extent, by favorable geographic conditions to the settlers. Settlers who faced climatic and ecological challenges opted to relocate to a more habitable spot. These decisions had long term consequences for the areas they inhabited, and far-reaching ramifications for the ones they did not.

Slavery is another episode in human history that cannot be fully examined without the acknowledgment of the contribution of geography. Some scholarly work finds that the tragedy of the slave trade had a toll, which persisted until the present day, on the areas stricken by this adversity.[19] In this context, trans-Atlantic slave traders selected the areas to raid and capture their human prey where the climate and the terrain allowed such pursuits without inflicting heavy losses on themselves. The whereabouts of the slave castles were determined by geographic conditions according to some studies.[20] The human cargo was, then, transported from trading posts in the African coast to be sold to plantation owners across the Atlantic Ocean to work their crops. The demand for slaves in the other side of the ocean was attributed to a combination of soil and climate that allowed for crops that can be cultivated in enormous plantations with unwavering need for cheap labor.

In the age of discovery, explorations were sponsored and voyages were funded by monarchs, traders, merchants, and other patrons in hopes of finding natural riches beyond the unknown. In the words of historian Niall Ferguson,[21] "These extraordinarily ambitious and hazardous voyages created a network of new oceanic trade routes that would rapidly transform the global economy from a patchwork of regional markets into a single world market." In this context, Ferdinand Magellan led the Spanish expedition to the East Indies that culminated in the first circumnavigation of the globe. This endeavor was intended for the Spice Islands.[22] Vasco da Gama was the first to connect Europe and Asia by an ocean passage. His expedition offered access to the Indian spice routes.[23] Niall Ferguson explains the rationale for such risky enterprise:[24] "Why, then, did the Portuguese run such large risks? The answer is that the rewards to be earned from establishing—and then monopolizing—a new route for trade with Asia were worth the risk. It is well known that European demand for Asian spices such as pepper, ginger, cloves, nutmeg and mace grew rapidly in the sixteenth century." Christopher Columbus completed four voyages across the Atlantic to establish new trade routes to the East Indies by sailing westward. This was intended to allow the Spanish crown to enter the spice trade through this new route.[25] Sir Francis

Drake, who was dispatched by Queen Elizabeth I, became the first captain to successfully circumnavigate the earth with an audacious expedition that led him to the Spice Islands among other places.[26]

Waves of human migration were also driven by geographic circumstances. Whether to escape from dire natural conditions or in search of greener pastures, humans over the course of history found an excuse to leave one place for another. People chose to be displaced from their habitat in search of better food supply, finer climate, and more desirable living conditions in general. In an insightful literary prose, Nobel laureate José Saramago writes,[27] "Let him who has not a single speck of migration to blot his family escutcheon cast the first stone . . . if you didn't migrate then your father did, and if your father didn't need to move from place to place, then it was only because your grandfather before him had no choice but to go, put his old life behind him in search of the bread that his own land denied him."

The intensity of environmental and natural disasters also served as stimulus for societies. Thus, natural hardships acted as a catalyst for human breakthroughs, scientific advances, and technological discoveries. Historian Arnold Toynbee posits that[28] "ease is inimical to civilization" and that "the greater the ease of the environment, the weaker the stimulus toward civilization." According to this view, natural challenges nudge humanity to its full potential. In this context, James Fairgrieve discusses how natural conditions trigger human hard work and labor.[29] He states that because of the lack of solar energy compared to the tropics, humans in the temperate zones must work harder to deal with greater varieties of weather.

ON THE BACKDROP OF HISTORY

These observations led social scientists, historians, economists, and those curious about human progress to wonder if geography determines economic outcomes. This question was triggered by the observation that some economies have, one way or another, been affected by their geographic attributes. Geography has furnished some countries with advantages that catapulted their economies to a world of plenty and was a favorable factor in other countries' quest for economic growth. Other distinctive geographic features were, nevertheless, an impediment to some societies' pursuit of economic prosperity and a hurdle to their endeavors to be delivered from the poverty trap. Henry Kissinger claims, on the cover of *Revenge of Geography* by Robert Kaplan, that "Geography has been the predominant factor in determining the fate of nations, from Pharaonic Egypt to the Arab Spring."

In this context, some analysts argue that geography is the most influential factor and perhaps the sole determinant of the level of economic development in a country. The proponents of this view insist that there is a clear association between those indicators that capture the geographic features of a country and its achieved level of economic development. For these advocates, geography's effect is not necessarily predestination or an inevitable outcome. To them, bringing to light the compelling effect of these geographic factors can guide decision makers in directions that can be overlooked otherwise. Accordingly, policy prescriptions could be directed to assist countries with unfavorable geographic conditions to overcome these specific shortcomings.

Others do not go that far, but do not deny completely the argument that geography matters in our attempt to comprehend the economic plight of some countries. They propose, instead, that geography has an indirect effect through its influence on other factors that could directly boost economic performance. In their view, geography is considered an accomplice rather than the main culprit.

The detractors, however, contend that conceding to the notion that geography matters is tantamount to a complete admission of the inevitability of economic outcomes due to factors that are beyond human control. If geography is a deep determinant of economic development, impoverishment is preordained in countries doomed with adverse natural conditions. This implies a level of determinism that contradicts the comforting notion that a nation can endeavor to determine its own destiny. The advocates of this view also argue that advancing the geographic factor is commensurate with the logic of environmental determinism, which is a sort of fatalism that asserts that geography predisposes societies and states toward specific development trajectories. These ideas were criticized and even accused, at times, of legitimizing supremacy, ethnocentrism, imperialism, and colonialism. According to this logic, the notion that geography is of consequence should be abandoned and even condemned.

This book is an account of some of these debates, an exposition of the pertinent discussions, and a description of the academic, scientific, scholarly, historic, and literary work that argues in favor of one side or the other. The coming chapters will also discuss the indicators used to capture these geographic features in the literature, in addition to the findings of the studies that attempted to explore whether geography influence economic performance directly or indirectly.

The core argument of this book is to propose that our inquiry into the factors that affect economic outcomes cannot escape the fingerprint of geography. This natural imprint can be seen in its direct impact on economic outcomes, or its indirect one through other channels which cannot be fully comprehended without acknowledging their geographic origin. In the words of Boris Pasternak, "The ancient world was settled so sparsely that nature was not yet eclipsed by man. Nature hit you in the eye so plainly and grabbed you so fiercely and so tangibly by the scruff of the neck that perhaps it really was still full of gods."

Before delving into this venture, it is crucial to define geography. Geography comes from Greek "Geographia" or the description of earth. Our discussion will be confined to five natural dimensions: the climate, the location, the topography, the abundance of natural wealth, and the incidence of natural disasters. Climate comes from the Greek "Klima" meaning "inclination" and refers to the weather patterns over a long period of time in terms of the fluctuations of temperature, the degrees of humidity, the extent of frost, the strength of wind, the recurrence of storms, the intensity of precipitation and the frequency of rainfall.

Location refers to the proximity or nearness to something that can confer upon a country an economic advantage or a disadvantage of some sort. This can be closeness to core markets, to coastal areas, to rivers, to navigable waterways, or others. Location can also be captured by geographic isolation which can affect a country in so many ways. Topography refers to the shape of the surface of the Earth, the description of the terrain and the landscape, in addition to the identification of specific landforms. Topography also comes from the Greek word "Topos" meaning place, and "Graphia" meaning writing, which translates into "writing about a place."

The abundance of natural endowments refers to the preponderance of environmental assets, natural resources, geological deposits, and mineral reserves in a country. These geographic features, in one way or another, influence economic outcomes in countries around the world. Finally, natural disasters are adverse and calamitous events that are caused by the natural processes of the Earth. These can cause loss of life, destruction to property and infrastructure, and lots of devastation in their wake.

Even though the following account is intended to be a comprehensive coverage of the literature, it is more of an attempt to highlight the fundamental ideas with reference to a sample of scholarly contributions that represent a larger body of intellectual work which cannot possibly be incorporated in its entirety in these few chapters.

NOTES

1. Theatre of the World.
2. Diamond. "Why Did Human History Unfold Differently on Different Continents for The Last 13,000 Years?" The Haskins Lectureship on Science Policy.
3. Wittfogel. *Oriental Despotism: A Comparative Study of Total Power*.
4. Nagasawa. "Inventing the Geography of Egyptian Nationalism." *Mediterranean World*: 271–318.

5. McNeill. *The Rise of the West. A History of Human Community.*

6. Mackinder. *Democratic Ideals and Reality.*

7. Khalifa. *Egypt's Lost Spring: Causes and Consequences.*

8. Kaplan. *The Revenge of Geography* (p. 28).

9. Spykman. "Geography and Foreign Policy." *The American Political Science Review*: 28–50.

10. Shirer. *The Rise and Fall of the Third Reich: A History of Nazi Germany.*

11. Yergin. *The Prize: The Epic Quest for Oil, Money and Power* (p. 13).

12. Venables. "Using Natural Resources for Development." *Journal of Economic Perspectives*: 161–184. Frankel. "The Natural Resource Curse: A Survey." The National Bureau of Economic Research Working Paper 15836.

13. Kaplan. *The Revenge of Geography* (p. xviii).

14. Spykman. "Geography and Foreign Policy." *The American Political Science Review*: 28–50.

15. Kaplan. *The Revenge of Geography* (p. 137).

16. Turchin. *War and Peace and War: The Rise and Fall of Empires* (p. 200).

17. Kaplan. *The Revenge of Geography* (p. 28).

18. Ibid. (p. 30).

19. Meltzer. *Slavery: A World History.*

20. Eltis, Richardson, Blight, and Davis. *Atlas of the Transatlantic Slave Trade.*

21. Ferguson. *The Square and the Tower* (p. 71).

22. Bergreen. *Over the Edge of the World: Magellan's Terrifying Circumnavigation of the Globe.*

23. Cliff. *Holy War: How Vasco da Gama's Epic Voyages Turned the Tide in a Centuries-Old Clash of Civilizations.* Cliff. *The Last Crusade: The Epic Voyages of Vasco da Gama.*

24. Ferguson. *The Square and the Tower* (p. 73).

25. Bergreen. *Columbus: The Four Voyages, 1492–1504.*

26. Bergreen. *In Search of a Kingdom: Francis Drake, Elizabeth I, and the Perilous Birth of the British Empire.*

27. Saramago. *The Notebook.*

28. Kaplan. *The Revenge of Geography* (p. 44).

29. Fairgrieve. *Geography and World Power.*

Chapter Two

Climate, Crops, and Capital

Economists usually argue that the most direct way to quantify economic activity is to consider the value of production. This chapter considers the effect of some geographic features such as climate, topography, and location on production and on factors that determine productivity, such as the accumulation of capital and technological progress.

CLIMATE (FOR) CHANGE

Climate is one of the critical components of a country's geography. To identify the effect of climate on economic outcomes, scholars had to use several indicators that reflect different climatic dimensions. For instance, a country's climate can be captured by long term average weather indices of temperature, humidity, wind, atmospheric pressure, and precipitation. Some scholars, however, prefer to use latitude as an indicator for climate. Latitude is the angular distance north or south of the equator of a point on the earth's surface. Closeness to the equator indicates a more tropical climate, while areas far from the equator are more temperate in nature. Other studies use the share of the country's population, or the proportion of a country's land, located in a climatic zone which is an area with particular climate patterns.

These indicators are used in the literature to examine the association between climate and economic outcomes. In these studies, the claim that climate has a compelling effect on economic performance is motivated by the fact that the economies of the tropics, that include the area between the Tropic of Cancer and the Tropic of Capricorn, lagged those in the temperate zone. This pattern can also be seen within continents and countries that straddle climate zones. For instance, northern Europe industrialized half a century ahead of southern Europe, while the American south trailed the temperate American north in industrialization. Nicholas Spykman asserts that[1] "in general, history is made in the temperate latitudes, and, because very little of the land mass of

23

the Southern Hemisphere lies in this zone, history is made in the temperate latitudes of the Northern Hemisphere."

Prominent economist Jeffrey Sachs, with other collaborators, made some contributions toward our understanding of the economic effects of climate. Jeffrey Sachs shows that the share of population in the temperate zone is positively associated with higher economic growth, higher agricultural productivity, higher life expectancy, lower infant mortality, and lower fertility rates.[2] Jeffrey Sachs, John Luke Gallup, and Andrew Mellinger examine the effect of climate and location on economic development and income growth.[3] The authors show that the level and growth of income per capita have a negative association with the share of land in the tropics, the spread of malaria which is a tropical disease, and the distance to one of the core markets. Jeffrey Sachs, David Bloom, Paul Collier, and Christopher Udry find a statistically significant negative effect of the share of a country's land in the tropics, and a statistically significant positive effect of the coastal population density, on economic growth.[4] Jeffrey Sachs and Andrew Warner show that geographic factors such as the lack of access to the sea, the abundance of natural resources, and the tropical climate have contributed to Africa's slow economic growth.[5]

Besides the share of population or land in the tropics, some studies use latitude as an indicator of closeness to the tropics. These studies find that closeness to the tropics is associated with a lower level of economic development. A very insightful approach to understand this finding is proposed by Thomas Andersen, Carl-Johan Dalgaard and Pablo Selaya who examine the association between the latitude gradient and comparative economic development.[6] The authors show that the tropics have the highest intensity of ultraviolet radiation which increases the prevalence of cataracts that impair vision. The authors argue that eyesight is essential in high-skilled occupations where the ability to read and write is crucial. Therefore, the high incidence of eye disease in the tropics lowers the return to human capital accumulation, decreases the level of investment in human capital and adversely affects economic growth.

Other studies explore the economic effects of specific climate elements, such as temperature, precipitation, and frost. For instance, William Masters and Margaret McMillan explore the effect of the absence of frost in the tropics on economic growth.[7] The authors argue that frost constrains the transmission of disease, lowering morbidity and mortality. In addition, frost improves agricultural productivity by curbing plant diseases and by allowing for the build-up of fertile soils. The authors provide evidence that the number of frost days per month is positively associated with high population density, high cultivation intensity and high economic growth.

Some studies compare the effect of temperature with that of precipitation. For instance, Matteo Lanzafame finds supportive evidence of an adverse effect of temperature on economic growth in Africa, while the effect of rainfall seems to be less statistically significant.[8] Melissa Dell, Benjamin Jones, and Benjamin Olken also show a negative effect of temperature on income within countries and across countries, while the effect of precipitation is not statistically significant.[9] Benjamin Jones and Benjamin Olken compare the effect of temperature and precipitation shocks on exports.[10] The authors find a substantial adverse effect of higher temperatures, but little effect of precipitation, on the exports of poor countries. Wealthier countries, nonetheless, may also be affected by the decline in their imports from poor countries.

After this overview, the chapter continues to discuss in detail how geographical factors affect agricultural productivity, the accumulation of capital, and the evolution of a technological paradigm that is propitious for the process of industrialization.

CROPS

There is a consensus that climate affects the capacity of the agricultural sector.[11] Agricultural productivity, captured by the value added per worker or by yield per hectare, for the main crops is observed to be considerably higher in the temperate zone than in the tropics. Agronomists, ecologists, biologists, and economists identified several factors that affect agricultural productivity in the tropics that include the availability of water for irrigation, the quality of the soil, and the health of the crops.[12]

The first factor that contributes to low agricultural productivity in the tropics is water scarcity. Water availability depends on precipitation net of potential evapotranspiration which is the sum of evaporation and plant transpiration. Evaporation accounts for the vaporization of water to the air from the soil, canopy interception, and water bodies. Transpiration is the dissipation of water through plant stomata to the atmosphere as vapor. Due to the high temperature in the tropics, evapotranspiration occurs intensely and at a fast pace. Therefore, water scarcity can be a serious problem in tropical climates even with plentiful rainfall.

The second factor is the degraded quality of the soil. Soil quality refers to the capacity of the soil to function as a vital living ecosystem to sustain plants, animals, and humans. This depends on soil texture, ability to hold water, nutrient content, and other factors. In this context, tropical soil is poor in nutrients and deficient in organic matter compared to that of the temperate zone. This is because the soil is weathered intensely by heavy precipitation, which can be year-round in the tropics. This incessant rainfall can cause erosion, leaching, and compaction. Erosion is the wearing away of the top-soil by the sheer force of water. Leaching is the loss of water-soluble plant nutrients which strips the soil of minerals needed by the above ground vegetation. Precipitation also causes compaction when the stress applied to the soil leaves little space for air and water which are essential for root growth. Soils exposed to these factors lose their fertility and experience deterioration in crop output potential.

In addition to the adverse effects of exorbitant precipitation in the tropics, soil quality is also degraded by high temperature and absence of frost. Mineralization of organic compounds can be exacerbated by sweltering temperatures in the tropics. In soil science, mineralization is the decomposition of the chemical compounds in organic matter discharging the nutrients into soluble inorganic forms. This deprives the soil of essential nutrients. Winter frost forestalls this process and allows for a build-up of healthier topsoil over time. Thus, frost improves agricultural productivity in temperate zones while its absence in the tropics has the opposite effect.

The third factor that contributes to the low agricultural productivity in the tropics is the pervasiveness of crop pests and parasites. This is because the tropics are teeming with a high degree of biodiversity. The high temperature in the tropics and the absence of winter frost that kill parasites and pests are, thus, fundamental causes of plant diseases and the ensuing crop failure. The fourth factor that contributes to the meager agricultural yield in the tropics is the fact that the photosynthetic potential of crops in warmer climates is curtailed due to higher rates of plant respiration and shorter hours of sunlight per day. Crop yields depend on the net photosynthetic output which plants use to support their own metabolic processes. Respiration occurs at higher levels in hot temperatures and incurs a high cost on net photosynthesis. In addition, plants trap sun light energy with their leaves during photosynthesis to change water and carbon dioxide into glucose to generate energy. However, sunlight hours during the growing season are shorter in the tropics compared to the temperate zone, which limits the plants' ability to grow.

The fifth factor is the spread of veterinary diseases such as the sleeping sickness that delayed the introduction of cattle breeding and animal husbandry in the tropics. Domesticated livestock increases agricultural yield by providing fertilizers and as a source of draft power. Thus, the disease environment frustrated the practice of intensive farming and did not allow the use of the plough which is one of the most consequential technological advances in agriculture. The final factor pertains to the effect of high temperature on human labor in farming activities. As David Landes argues,[13] "the law of exhaustion applies to all, and few manage to work at full capacity when hot and wet."

Building on this intuition, some studies explore the connection between climate and agricultural productivity. For instance, Jeffrey Sachs and John Luke Gallup examine the effect of tropical climate on crop yields.[14] The authors find that tropical countries have significantly lower agricultural yields controlling for inputs such as labor per hectare, capital proxied by tractors, and fertilizers. Salvador Barrios, Luisito Bertinelli, and Eric Strobl examine the effect of rainfall fluctuations on economic performance in Africa through its effect on agriculture and hydro-energy supply.[15] The authors find that lower rainfall has an adverse effect on economic growth in sub-Saharan African countries, which are more dependent on rain-fed farming and more reliant on hydropower for electricity generation.

Agricultural productivity can also be affected by the topographic features of the land. Topography is a characterization of a country's landscape in terms of elevation, the degree of steepness of inclines and slopes, and the degree of terrain ruggedness. These features can be captured by the average standard deviation of elevation, the average uphill slope of the surface area, or the share of a country's land area that is rugged. Rugged and irregular terrain is tough to farm and harvest as this topographic feature increases the cost of cultivation. On steep slopes, erosion becomes a potential problem and the control of water for irrigation is more cumbersome. According to the Food and Agriculture Organization, when slopes are greater than 2 degrees the benefits of cultivation often do not cover the costs, and when slopes are greater than 6 degrees cultivation and agricultural activities become untenable.

Some natural disasters can also cause devastation to the harvest and the livestock, while others enhance soil fertility and agricultural productivity. For example, hurricanes, storms, and winds could wash or blow away topsoil, which decreases soil fertility and agricultural yields. Richard Hornbeck draws our attention to the[16] "large and permanent soil erosion during the 1930s that became widely known as the 'American Dust Bowl.'" Hornbeck states that the "Large dust storms swept topsoil from the land such that, by the 1940s, many Plains areas had cumulatively lost more than 75 percent of their original topsoil." Similarly, droughts can cause soil degradation which lowers agricultural yields. However, the effect of natural disasters on agriculture is not exclusively unfavorable. For instance, floods provide sediments that increase agricultural productivity in the surrounding plains. Volcanic eruptions deposit ash which has special chemical properties that enriches soil quality.

This implies that geographic factors such as climate, topography and the incidence of natural disasters can affect economic outcomes directly by lowering agricultural productivity.

CAPITAL

Certain climatic conditions may have also promoted a culture of thrift in primitive economies. Economies in higher latitudes are characterized by cold winters. During frost days there is no harvest, energy is vital, and survival demands more work and effort. People react to these challenges by saving during the warmer days to be able to endure the cold season. The stronger and longer the winter, the higher the level of savings needed to survive during the harsh winter days. This causes the evolution of a culture of savings that allows these economies to start a process of capital accumulation which enhances economic growth. This is not the case in the tropics, where there are no frost days. To test if this intuition is supported by evidence, Hernando Zuleta examines the effect of the average number of frost days per unit of land area on the saving rate.[17] The author finds that there is a statistically significant positive association between frost and saving.

TECHNOLOGY

Geographic factors can also affect the technology of production. Technology comes from Greek "techne" or "art, skill, and craft," and "logia" or the "study of," which translates to the "science of craft." Thus, technology is the application of science to practical purposes or the integration of scientific insights into the production process. The stock of technological knowledge depends on both the level of innovation within an area and the diffusion of technology across areas. Climatic conditions affect both indigenous technological innovation and knowledge dissemination. For instance, technological innovation is observed to be higher in the temperate zone than in the tropics. On the other hand, technological diffusion between the two zones was constrained. This is because critical technologies could not cross the climatic divide due to the inherent difficulties in the transfer of technologies, developed for a specific environment, to another area with different climatic characteristics.

In this context, some studies provide evidence that the temperate zone has a higher rate of technical innovation than the tropics, which lag in the number of patents and on the amount of spending on research enterprises. This observation could be attributed to the fact that the temperate zone has had larger population densities settled in urban areas than the tropics. This was due to the larger potential for food production in the temperate zone, which allowed societies to settle and grow over time. On the other hand, low food productivity in the tropics could not support large urban concentrations. In addition, scant agricultural productivity can also trap workers in farming until food availability per worker increases, while higher agricultural productivity leads to a decline in the share of the labor force engaged in farming since the same amount of food can be produced with fewer workers. There are some studies that document the association between climate and urbanization. For instance, Mesbah Motamed, Raymond Florax, and William Masters test whether urbanization occurs sooner in places with higher agricultural potential.[18] The authors find a robust association between earlier urbanization, agro-climatic suitability for cultivation and having seasonal frost which is absent in the tropics.

It is in urban centers with settled communities where craftsmanship flourished as a surplus of food from farming allowed some the freedom to explore and create. This led eventually to technological advances. Higher population densities also increased the potential compensation of an innovation due to the larger pool of potential consumers. The low level of population density and urbanization in the tropics, due to the anemic agricultural productivity, had the opposite effect on innovation.

In terms of diffusion, the tropics could not attract technologies developed specifically for the temperate zone. Some critical technologies are ecologically specific in areas such as health, agriculture, horticulture, agronomy, construction, energy, and others. These technologies are developed with specific climatic features in mind, and do not diffuse easily across ecological borders. For instance, farming and agricultural technologies are dependent on local weather patterns, the prevalence of water, and the quality of soil in a specific area. Innovations in public health are overwhelmingly directed at the prevention from, and the containment of, diseases widespread locally. Construction technology made use of local common materials and had the surrounding territorial landscape and climatic anomalies in mind. Energy generation was influenced by prevalent sources of energy available in a specific location. There is indeed a plethora of other examples of technologies that are developed to satisfy the needs of areas with specific geographic characteristics but could not serve others in different climatic zones. In this context, some studies show evidence that patent citations, which are an indicator of technological spillovers, are highest in neighboring countries but tend to decline with distance.[19]

In a similar vein, Jared Diamond suggested that the geographic axes of continents determined the diffusion of technology.[20] Thus, technological diffusion works most effectively in an east-west direction along the same latitude rather than in a north-south direction across different latitudes. These geographic axes favored the Eurasian civilizations. Eurasia's east-west orientation allowed for the dissemination of technologies across a shared ecological space. Accordingly, temperate zone countries easily shared the technological advances with other economies that dealt with analogous ecological conditions. This east-west orientation made it easier for crops, livestock, cultivation practices, farming techniques, construction technologies, and health systems to spread. Alternatively, Africa's and the Americas' north-south orientation frustrated technological diffusion by cutting across a swath of distinct ecological spheres. Thus, tropical countries, which did not have significant advances in technological innovation, could not benefit either from a technology transfer from the temperate zone innovators. Accordingly, these areas were cut off from technology, inventions, innovations, ideas, varieties, and trade that permeated the Eurasian steppe.

This was problematic to the tropics since the historical adoption of technologies is argued to have a lasting impact on current economic outcomes. Some studies argue that the earlier the adoption of technology, the sooner the society is able to absorb this technology, to incorporate it into its production modes, and to use it to increase their productivity and income. In this context, Diego Comin, William Easterly, and Erick Gong assemble a dataset on technology adoption at different points in time for the predecessors to current nation states.[21] The authors find an association between technology adoption in 1500 C.E. and current income per capita and technology adoption. This effect is stronger when the technology adoption indicator is adjusted to a population-weighted average of the technology adoption of the places of origin of the current population. In another pertinent study, Diego Comin and Bart Hobijn use data on the diffusion of technologies in countries over the last two centuries to examine the effect of adoption lags, defined as the length of time between the invention and the adoption of a technology.[22] The analysis shows that variations in technology adoption account for at least a quarter of income per capita differences.

Another geographic factor, besides climate, that may have affected technological progress is isolation. Some scholars argue that geographically isolated societies are less able to benefit from the latest advances in the world technological frontier. This may, however, foster a cultural environment that is conducive to an independent process of technological innovation. Geographically isolated societies also face a lower threat of predation. This promotes the protection of property rights, which in turn creates incentives for investment and innovation. To test these proposals, Quamrul Ashraf, Oded Galor and Omer Ozak explore the effect of the degree of geographical isolation, prior to the advent of sea-faring and airborne transportation, on economic development in the Old World.[23] The authors introduce an isolation index that reflects "the average time required to travel from the capital of a country to each square kilometer of land on the surface of the earth, along land routes that minimize travel time in the absence of maritime and airborne transportation technologies." Their analysis shows that prehistoric geographic isolation has generated a persistent beneficial effect on the contemporary standard of living across countries. Omer Ozak focuses on the effect of the distance to the pre-industrial technological frontiers on comparative economic development.[24] The author proposes that while remoteness from the frontier limited imitation, it fostered a culture conducive to innovation which may have persisted into the modern era. The analysis confirms this intuition by demonstrating that countries distant from these frontiers have higher contemporary levels of innovative and entrepreneurial activities.

Geographic isolation may also determine the diversity in cultural traits overtime which may shape the evolution of technological progress. Individuals in a society are subjected to two forces that generate different effects on the evolution of diversity in cultural traits: cultural assimilation or the homogenization of cultural traits within a society that decrease the level of diversity, and cultural diffusion or the spread of cultural attributes from one society to another that increase diversity through the introduction of new cultural traits.

Cultural values are transmitted from one generation to another. In the absence of any encroachment on these traits, individuals will continue to cherish their parental cultural heritage. Thus, cultural assimilation diminishes diversity by standardizing cultural attributes in society. This, however, improves the effectiveness of the transmission of society-specific human capital across generations. Thus, it enhances the ability of the society to operate with the available production technologies. On the other hand, cultural diffusion is characterized by the emergence of alternative modes of behavior in society. This generates greater cultural fluidity and flexibility that enhances the accumulation of knowledge of a widely applicable human capital. This expands the economy's ability to adapt to a new technological paradigm. Thus, the lack of cultural diffusion in geographically isolated societies could have delayed the onset of their industrialization. Quamrul Ashraf and Oded Galor examine these ideas and find that geographic isolation in pre-industrial times had a negative effect on the extent of contemporary cultural diversity, a positive effect on economic development in the agricultural stage, and a negative effect on income per capita during the process of industrialization.[25]

NOTES

1. Spykman. *America's Strategy in World Politics: The United States and the Balance of Power.*

2. Sachs. "Tropical Underdevelopment." National Bureau of Economic Research Working Paper 8119.

3. Gallup, Sachs, and Mellinger. "Geography and Economic Development." *International Regional Science Review*: 179–232.

4. Bloom, Sachs, Collier, and Udry. "Geography, Demography, and Economic Growth in Africa." *Brookings Papers on Economic Activity*: 207–295.

5. Sachs and Warner. "Sources of Slow Growth in African Economies." *Journal of African Economies*: 335–76.

6. Andersen, Dalgaard and Selaya. "Climate and the Emergence of Global Income Differences." *Review of Economic Studies*: 1334–1363.

7. Masters and McMillan. "Climate and Scale in Economic Growth." *Journal of Economic Growth*: 167–186.

8. Lanzafame. "Temperature, Rainfall and Economic Growth in Africa." *Empirical Economics*: 1–18.

9. Dell, Jones, and Olken. "Temperature and Income." *American Economic Review*: Papers and Proceedings: 198–204.

10. Jones and Olken. "Climate Shocks and Exports." *American Economic Review*: Papers and Proceedings: 454–459.

11. Schenkler, Eyer, and Roberts. "Agronomic Weather Measures in Econometric Models of Crop Yield with Implications for Climate Change." *American Journal of Agricultural Economics*: 236–243. Schenkler, Fisher, Hanemann, and Roberts. "The Economic Impacts of Climate Change." *American Economic Review*: 3749–3760. Schenkler, Lobell, and Costa–Roberts. "Climate Trends and Global Crop Production since 1980." *Science*: 616–620. Schenkler and Roberts. "Nonlinear Effects of Weather on Corn Yields." *Review of Agricultural Economics*: 391–398. Schenkler, Hanemann, and Fisher. "The Impact of Global Warming on U.S. Agriculture." *Review of Economics and Statistics*: 113–125.

12. Sachs. "Tropical Underdevelopment." National Bureau of Economic Research Working Paper 8119. Gallup and Sachs. "Agriculture, Climate, and Technology" *American Journal of Agricultural Economics*: 731–737.

13. Landes. *The Wealth and Poverty of Nations: Why Some Are So Rich and Some So Poor* (p. 15).

14. Gallup and Sachs. "Agriculture, Climate, and Technology." *American Journal of Agricultural Economics*: 731–737.

15. Barrios, Bertinelli, and Strobl. "Trends in Rainfall and Economic Growth in Africa." *The Review of Economics and Statistics*: 350–366.

16. Hornbeck. "The Enduring Impact of the American Dust Bowl." *American Economic Review*: 1477–1507.

17. Zuleta. "Seasonal Fluctuations and Economic Growth." *Journal of Economic Development*: 1–27.

18. Masters, Motamed, and Florax. "Agriculture, Transportation and the Timing of Urbanization." *Journal of Economic Growth*: 339–368.

19. Jaffee, Trajtenberg, and Henderson. "Geographic Localization of Knowledge Spillovers as Evidenced by Patent Citations." *Quarterly Journal of Economics*: 577–598. Jaffee and Trajtenberg. "International Knowledge Flows: Evidence from Patent Citations." *Economics of Innovation and New Technology*: 105–136.

20. Jared Diamond. *Guns, Germs, and Steel: The Fate of Human Societies*. W. W. Norton & Company, 1999.

21. Comin, Easterly, and Gong. "Was the Wealth of Nations Determined in 1000 BC?" *American Economic Journal*: *Macroeconomics*: 65–97.

22. Comin and Hobijn. "An Exploration of Technology Diffusion." *American Economic Review*: 2031–2059.

23. Ashraf, Galor, and Ozak. "Isolation and Development." *Journal of the European Economic Association*: 401–412.

24. Ozak. "Distance to the Pre–industrial Technological Frontier and Economic Development." *Journal of Economic Growth*: 175–221.

25. Ashraf and Galor. "Cultural Diversity, Geographical Isolation, and the Origin of the Wealth of Nations." The National Bureau of Economic Research Working paper 17640.

Chapter Three

Germs, Groups, and Gender

CLIMATE AND PATHOGENS

Another essential factor of production is human capital, which captures the level of knowledge and health conditions in an economy. Overall health conditions are affected by the disease environment which is, in turn, influenced by climate. For instance, the burden of disease is considerably higher in the tropics than in the temperate zone. This is due to tropical diseases, which occur solely, or principally, in the tropics. According to the World Health Organization, the term often refers to infectious diseases that thrive in hot and humid conditions such as Malaria, Leishmaniasis, Schistosomiasis, Onchocerciasis, Filariasis, Helminths, Trypanosomiasis, Yellow fever, Dengue fever and others. These are endemic in the tropical zone and nearly absent elsewhere.[1]

The prevalence of infectious diseases in the tropics is attributed to biological, ecological, and environmental factors that encourage high levels of biodiversity in pathogens, vectors, and hosts. A pathogen is anything that can cause disease and comes from the Greek "Pathos" or "suffering," and "Genes" or "producer of," which translates to "producer of suffering." The term is used to describe an infectious agent such as a virus, bacterium, protozoa, fungus, or some other microorganism. In epidemiology, a vector is any agent that carries a pathogen into another living organism. Humans and animals act as host in these cases.

One of the best illustrations of tropical diseases is Malaria. The epidemiology of this disease involves the interaction between Plasmodium parasites as pathogen, mosquitos as vector and humans as host. In this context, there are four species of the Plasmodium parasite that cause Malaria: *Plasmodium falciparum*, *Plasmodium malariae*, *Plasmodium ovale*, and *Plasmodium vivax*. On the other hand, the vectors include species of the *genus Anopheles* mosquito, such as *Anopheles Gambiae* and *Anopheles funestus*. The former is found exclusively in sub-Saharan Africa and shows a preference for absorbing blood from humans as opposed to animals.

Malaria is inherently a disease of a warm environment that creates amenable conditions for the encounter between the pathogen, the vector, and the host. Some studies concluded that the[2] "development and survival rates of both the Anopheles mosquitoes and the Plasmodium parasites that cause malaria depend on temperature, making this a potential driver of mosquito population dynamics and malaria transmission."

This is attributed to the fact that a central component of the lifecycle of the Plasmodium parasite and the Anopheles mosquito depends on temperature and precipitation. Intense precipitation in the tropics creates pools of water, puddles, and cisterns, which provide favorable breeding conditions for mosquitos. In these sites, mosquito eggs are deposited, larvae emerge from the eggs and transform into pupae that develop into adulthood. The survival of the adult mosquito is also dependent on warm temperatures, which is the case in the tropics.

The transmission of Malaria also depends on vector longevity compared to the life cycle of the parasite within the mosquito. Encyclopedia Britannica states that[3] "Plasmodium species exhibit three life-cycle stages—gametocytes, sporozoites, and merozoites. Gametocytes within a mosquito develop into sporozoites. The sporozoites are transmitted via the saliva of a feeding mosquito to the human bloodstream. From there they enter liver parenchyma cells, where they divide and form merozoites. The merozoites are released into the bloodstream and infect red blood cells." Once ingested by a vector, the parasites transform over a period of days into sporozoites. The vector must survive long enough to allow the parasites they harbor to complete this growth cycle. Warmer temperature shortens the duration of this cycle and, thus, increases the chances of transmission.

Climate also alters the behavior of the human host in a way that increases the chances of contracting the disease. For instance, hot weather encourages people to sleep outdoors and discourages them from using bed nets. This may increase contact with the mosquitos which are typically active between dusk and dawn. When an infected mosquito bites someone, it may transmit the parasite. If an uninfected mosquito bites an infected person, it may imbibe the parasite and later transmit the disease to another human host. Thus, tropical climate provides favorable conditions for the transmission of the disease. Those who contract Malaria gradually acquire partial immunity. Thus, Malaria may only become fatal to those without immunity such as children and adults who grew up elsewhere. Acquired immunity, however, is short lived if the individual leaves the Malaria area.

Some of the exposed groups also develop a genetic defense against Malaria known as the sickle cell trait.[4] Individuals with sickle cell trait acquire some resistance to Malaria. This genetic trait can be inherited from one or both parents. The allele inherited from both parents leads to sickle cell anemia which causes these individuals to die before the childbearing or reproductive age. On the other hand, the allele inherited from one parent comes without serious health complications which allow these individuals to survive to adulthood. However, individuals of this genotype are more likely to see their children die of sickle cell disease.

According to the World Health organization, even though nearly half of the world population is at risk of contracting Malaria a large number of cases are in sub-Saharan Africa. Malaria[5] "has plagued English kings and as many as eight U.S. presidents—including George Washington and Abraham Lincoln—and may have helped kill Genghis Khan. It causes wracking fever and chills, headaches and muscle pain, and can lead to severe anemia."

Malaria can also cause acute diseases in pregnant women, their fetus, and the newborn child. Exposed households react by increasing their fertility to compensate for the loss caused by the disease. This increases the dependency ratio, which is an indicator that assesses the number of dependents to those in the labor force who are in their productive age. High dependency implies more pressure on the working population which could diminish economic capacity. High fertility also decreases the share of saving devoted to capital deepening or increasing the amount of capital per person, and lowers the investment in human capital per child which has a long-lasting effect on the level of educational attainment. In addition, Malaria has lifelong effects on the cognitive development and the learning potential of children. This is because of time lost or wasted away from the classroom due to illness.

Malaria also became a leading barrier against integration into the world economy through foreign investment and international travel. Foreign investors avoid Malaria areas if the disease prevalence increases the cost of attracting domestic labor. Foreign investors also lack the immunity acquired by those who have endured repeated bouts of Malaria. In addition, tourism cannot prosper in areas of immense Malaria transmission. Conversely, Malaria is a problem for adults from Malaria areas who travel abroad for prolonged periods since their acquired immunity will abate if not boosted by recurrent infection. The transmission of ideas, the transfer of technologies, and the expansion of transportation systems may, thus, be stunted by Malaria.

Settlement in Africa by Europeans was also influenced by the spread of Malaria. Until the advent of quinine, Europeans could barely survive in coastal settlements because of Malaria, much less venture into the hinterland of the African continent.[6] The effect of Malaria is also best exemplified by the efforts to construct the Panama Canal. The failure of the French to complete the project was attributed to Malaria mortality, and the American efforts were only effective after the successful containment of the disease.[7] James Gilbert, the poet of the Isthmus of Panama, described his experiences there in a poem called "Beyond the Chagres River."[8]

> Are paths that lead to death
> To the fever's deadly breezes,
> To malaria's poisonous breath!

On the other hand, geographer Ray Hughes Whitbeck praises the efforts to contain the disease to be able to build the Panama Canal:[9]

> Today the swamps are filled, the mosquitoes are gone, the streets are paved and clean, and the zone is as healthy as Massachusetts. This is what man has done at a place where geographical conditions induced him to build an interoceanic canal. It is an inspiring example of man's conquest of adverse nature; not man's response to a hostile environment, but his defiance of it and his subjugation of it; an example of so-called geographic control upon which is superimposed a still more impressive example of man's control.

In this context, several studies attempt to explore the economic consequences of Malaria. For instance, Jeffrey Sachs and John Luke Gallup examine the effect of a disease prevalence index on income per capita.[10] The index captures the proportion of the population at risk of Malaria multiplied by the fraction of fatal falciparum cases. The authors find that this index has a negative effect on income levels after controlling for other factors that influence economic development. The authors argue that "the geographical specificity of malaria, the wide biological variation in the capacity of mosquito vectors, the inability to control malaria in Africa under experimental conditions, and the persistence of fatal blood diseases as a defense all point to a causation from malaria to poverty." In another contribution, Jeffrey Sachs tests the hypothesis that Malaria transmission has an explanatory power on the level of income per capita even after controlling for the quality of institutions.[11] The author uses the proportion of a country's population at risk of Malaria transmission as one measure, and the index of Malaria prevalence as another. The author finds that both low quality institutions and the Malaria indicators have statistically significant adverse effects on economic development. Jeffrey Sachs and John McArthur investigate the connection between the proportion of a country's population at risk of falciparum Malaria and economic development.[12] The authors conclude that the evidence strongly suggests that both institutional quality and Malaria contribute to the determination of income per capita.

Kai Carstensen and Erich Gundlach examine whether Malaria prevalence can explain the observed levels of economic development.[13] The authors use the proportion of population at risk of falciparum infection, and the prevalence of nonfatal species of the pathogen, as indicators. After controlling for institutional quality, the Malaria indicators are found to have direct adverse effects on income. Matteo Cervellati, Elena Esposito, and Uwe Sunde study the effect of long-term Malaria exposure on contemporary economic development using grid-cell data for sub-Saharan Africa.[14] Their evidence shows a negative correlation between Malaria, captured by the clinical incidence of falciparum Malaria, and night lights per capita.[15] Emilio Depetris-Chauvin and David Weil consider the prevalence of the mutation that causes sickle cell disease at the level of ethnic groups to examine the effect of Malaria on economic development in Africa.[16] The authors find no evidence on the adverse effect of Malaria on historical population densities, political institutions, and the intensity of agriculture. The study attributes this finding to the fact that the deaths caused by Malaria were among the very young, in whom society had invested very little.

Malaria may also trigger behavioral norms that are effective in limiting its circulation. The exposure to Malaria is known to increase disproportionately with the size of the susceptible population and interbreeding with surrounding groups. These factors made it prudent for the separation of vulnerable societies to contain the spread of the disease. Thus, social isolation, consanguineous inbreeding and limited contact between endogamous groups became an effective survival strategy against local strains of Malaria.[17] This helped define the boundaries of ethnic homelands and accentuate ethno-linguistic identities. Along the lines of this intuition, Matteo Cervellati, Giorgio Chiovelli, and Elena Esposito examine the effect of long-term exposure to Malaria in pre-modern times on the emergence of ethnic groups and the persistence of ethno-linguistic diversity.[18] Their study suggests that, even in the absence of a direct effect from Malaria in the present, ancestral exposure to Malaria continues to affect the persistence of ethnic identities and active endogamy.

The tropics are also replete with other infectious diseases besides Malaria. Another common tropical disease is Trypanosomiasis, or the sleeping sickness. This is a vector-borne disease caused by protozoan parasites of the *genus Trypanosoma* species. The parasite is transmitted to humans by a vector, the tsetse fly, which lives only in the tropical sub-Saharan Africa. This disease can cause the human host to experience swollen lymph, bloody urine, muscle ache, headaches, fever, neurological changes, slurred speech, and seizures. The host dies if these problems are not treated in time. According to the Center of Disease Control and Prevention, over 95 percent of the cases are found in sub-Saharan Africa.[19]

Leishmaniases are another group of diseases caused by protozoan parasites of the *genus leishmania* species. The parasite is transmitted to humans by the bite of infected female *Phlebotomine* sandflies which are prevalent in areas with temperatures above a certain level for at least quarter of the year. Otherwise, sand flies enter a dormant state to survive winter which diminishes the breeding population. Humidity is also an essential factor in egg survival. The factors of heat and humidity cause the tropics to be ideal for the transmission of the disease which presents with ulcers of the skin, mouth, and nose, and later with fever, low red blood cells, and enlarged spleen and liver. According to the Center of Disease Control and Prevention, the disease is found in countries in the tropics, subtropics, and Southern Europe.[20]

Schistosomiasis, also known as bilharzia, is a disease caused by parasitic flatworms of the *genus Schistosoma* species. Transmission occurs when those who carry the disease contaminate freshwater with their feces that contain parasite eggs. Larvae hatch from these eggs, spend a period in freshwater snails and then get discharged to the water column. Then, the worm penetrates the skin and enters the blood vessels of another host. For weeks, the worm develops into adulthood and their eggs are deposited after mating at maturity. Eggs enter the bladder and intestine to be excreted, and the process repeats. The disease causes abdominal pain, diarrhea, bloody stool, or bloody urine. Those who have been infected for a long time may experience liver damage, kidney failure, infertility, or bladder cancer. The disease is found in tropical countries in Africa, the Caribbean, South America, Southeast Asia, and the Middle East.[21]

Onchocerciasis, also known as river blindness, is a disease caused by the parasitic worm *Onchocerca volvulus*. The worm is spread and transmitted to humans through the bite of blackflies of the *genus simulium*. This disease is considered the second common cause of blindness after Trachoma. According to the Center of Disease Control and Prevention, the main burden is in thirty countries in sub-Saharan Africa.[22]

Filariasis, also known as elephantiasis, is a disease caused by three species of filariae worms, *Wuchereria bancrofti*, *Brugia malayi* and *Brugia timori*. These are spread to humans by black flies and mosquitoes. The worms form nests in the lymphatic system which is an essential component of the immune system. Lymphatic filariasis is a leading cause of permanent disability worldwide. Some patients develop a syndrome called elephantiasis marked by swelling in the arms, legs, or genitals. The disease affects over 120 million people in countries throughout the tropics, and the subtropics of Asia, Africa, the Western Pacific, and parts of the Caribbean and South America.[23]

Yellow fever is another disease caused by the virus of the *flavivirus genus* which is spread by the bite of an infected female mosquito of the *Aedes aegypti* that is found throughout the tropics and subtropics. For some, this condition begins causing yellow skin. If this occurs, bleeding and kidney failure problems become more likely. Dengue fever is a disease caused by the *dengue* virus which is spread primarily by a mosquito of the *Aedes aegypti*. In a small proportion of cases, the disease develops into the life-threatening dengue hemorrhagic fever, causing bleeding, low levels of blood platelets, blood plasma leakage, and low blood pressure.

The spread of these diseases in the tropics is accompanied by personal economic costs that include the expenditure on medical care and medicine, treatment fees, transportation to health facilities, and the cost of prevention. These tropical diseases also have public health costs on prevention and treatment of the disease, absenteeism from the workplace, extended absence from schools, adverse effects on children's cognitive development and long run learning potential, in addition to lost time due to illness or caring for a sick family member. All these factors affect aggregate economic outcomes.

CLIMATE AND LIVESTOCK

In addition to human diseases, various veterinary ones are also widespread in the tropical zone. This caused lots of areas in the tropics to be off limits to cattle breeding for a long period of time. A primary cause is Trypanosomiasis, known as sleeping sickness, which is transmitted by the tsetse fly. Some parasite species of the *genus Trypanosoma* such as *Trypanosoma brucei rhodesiense* and *Trypanosoma brucei gambiense* are pathogenic to wild and domestic animals. These parasites cause animal Trypanosomiasis, called Nagana. Pulitzer Prize winner Jared Diamond asserts that[24]

> the spread southward of Fertile Crescent domestic animals through Africa was stopped or slowed by climate and disease, especially by trypanosome diseases carried by tsetse flies. The horse never became established farther south than West Africa's kingdoms north of the equator. The advance of cattle, sheep, and goats halted for 2,000 years at the northern edge of the Serengati Plains, while new types of human economies and livestock breeds were being developed. Not until the period A.D. 1–200, some 8,000 years after livestock were domesticated in the Fertile Crescent, did cattle, sheep, and goats finally reach South Africa.

Some scholars argue that tropical veterinary diseases had far reaching ramifications on agricultural productivity, animal husbandry, farming technology, human settlement, state formation, and cultural traits as well. In this context, the disease environment in communities afflicted by the sleeping sickness inhibited the spread of pastoralism, hindered the formation of settled farming communities, impeded the ability to stockpile food surplus, delayed state formation, contributed to the spread of slavery, and did not allow for the transportation of agricultural products from one area to another.

Domesticated animals are a critical element in agricultural production. Livestock increases agricultural yield by providing compost for fertilizer, by using legumes as fodder which improves soil fertility, and by serving as a source of draft power. In this context, the sleeping sickness frustrated the practice of intensive farming that is reliant on the use of animal manure to replenish the soil if depleted of nutrients due to frequent cultivation. In addition, the use of draft animals allows for the adoption of more productive farming practices. For instance, the plough is one of the most consequential agricultural devices used to break up the soil, to control weeds and to bury crop residues. However, a plough is hard to use without draft animals. Thus, agricultural technology did not advance in many areas afflicted with the sleeping sickness. By circumscribing the use of domesticated animals to carry agricultural goods overland, transportation costs also increased. The immobility of food crops did not allow the agricultural communities to support a large nonagricultural workforce. This hindered the establishment of dense human settlements and urban centers.

The survival of wildlife over domesticated livestock, due to the sleeping sickness, also supported the persistence of a lifestyle of hunting and gathering. These societies continued to function as isolated groups and did not develop into densely settled hierarchical societies with strong states and centralized authority. Surplus crops and settled populations also form the tax base to support a central bureaucracy. Without such surplus, state formation was delayed in these areas due to the spread of the disease.

Finally, veterinary diseases may have contributed to the spread of slavery and the dependence on human porterage, or the carriage of goods by humans. When the use of pack animals was precluded by the sleeping sickness, societies depended on human carriers for transportation and other laborious tasks which encouraged the growth of slavery. The entomologist John Philip Glasgow conjectured that the practice of indigenous slavery and the presence of the tsetse fly were interconnected:[25] "Nearer the equator the use of draught or pack animals was impossible, and such trade as occurred depended on transport by human carriers. This circumstance, we may suppose, encouraged the growth of slavery."

Given these arguments, Marcella Alsan examines how the sleeping sickness affected African development using a tsetse suitability index from laboratory experiments on tsetse physiology.[26] The author provides evidence that the sleeping sickness is associated with lower intensive farming, lower plough use, lower population density, lower political centralization, higher levels of slavery, less dependence on animal husbandry, more engagement in hunting and gathering, and worse current economic outcomes.

The sleeping sickness disease may have also caused certain cultural traits to persist. Some scholars argue that agricultural practices influenced the gender-based division of labor and the evolution of gender standards. In this context, using the plough to prepare the soil is hard without animal power. To pull the plough, or to control the animal that drags it, requires immense upper body strength and a strong grip. In societies that used the plough, men who had a bodily advantage tended to work in the fields while women specialized in activities within their domestic sphere. Societies where veterinary diseases stymied the use of the plough embraced the opposite norms that persisted over time. To provide evidence for this intuition, Alberto Alesina, Paola Giuliano, and Nathan Nunn show that historical plough use is predictive of today's gender norms.[27] The authors find that the descendants of societies that traditionally practiced plough farming today have less equal gender standards.

NOTES

1. http://www.who.int/topics/tropical_diseases/en/

2. Beck-Johnson, Nelson, Paaijmans, Read, Thomas, and Bjørnstad. "The Effect of Temperature on Anopheles Mosquito Population Dynamics and the Potential for Malaria Transmission." *PLOS*: 1–12.

3. https://www.britannica.com/science/Plasmodium–protozoan–genus#ref200404

4. Allison. "The Discovery of Resistance to Malaria of Sickle-cell Heterozygotes." *Biochemistry and Molecular Biology Education*: 279–287.

5. Vogel. "The Forgotten Malaria." *Science*: 684–687.

6. Hugon. *The Exploration of Africa: From Cairo to the Cape.*

7. McCullough. *The Path between the Seas: The Creation of the Panama Canal, 1870–1914.*

8. Moore. "Mosquitoes, Malaria, and Cold Butter." *Panorama: Journal of the Association of Historians of American Art*, https://doi.org/10.24926/24716839.1603. Gilbert. *The Fall of Panamá: And Other Isthmian Rhymes and Sketches.*

9. Whitbeck. "Geography and Man at Panama." *Bulletin of the Geographical Society of Philadelphia*: 8.

10. Gallup and Sachs. "The Economic Burden of Malaria." *American Journal of Tropical Medicine and Hygiene*: 85–96.

11. Sachs. "Institutions Don't Rule: Direct Effects of Geography on Per Capita Income." National Bureau of Economic Research Working Paper 9490.

12. McArthur and Sachs. "Institutions and Geography: Comment on Acemoglu, Johnson and Robinson (2000)." National Bureau of Economic Research Working Paper 8114.

13. Carstensen, and Gundlach. "The Primacy of Institutions Reconsidered." *The World Bank Economic Review*: 309–339.

14. Cervellati, Esposito, and Sunde. "Long Term Exposure to Malaria and Development." *Journal of Demographic Economics*: 129–148.

15. An estimate of subnational economic activity as suggested by: Henderson, Storeygard, and Weil. "Measuring Economic Growth from Outer Space." *The American Economic Review*: 994–1028. Henderson, Storeygard, and Weil. "A Bright Idea for Measuring Economic Growth." *American Economic Review: Papers & Proceedings*: 194–199.

16. Depetris-Chauvin and Weil. "Malaria and Early African Development: Evidence from the Sickle Cell Trait." *The Economic Journal*: 1207–1234.

17. Consanguineous inbreeding is mating between related people. Endogamy is the practice of marrying within a specific social group. Endogamy, as distinct from consanguinity, may lead to the transmission of genetic disorders.

18. Cervellati, Chiovelli, and Esposito. "Bite and Divide: Malaria and Ethnolinguistic Diversity." Center for Economic and Policy Research Discussion Paper DP13437.

19. www.cdc.gov/parasites/sleepingsickness/epi.html.

20. www.cdc.gov/parasites/leishmaniasis/epi.html.

21. www.cdc.gov/parasites/schistosomiasis/epi.html.

22. www.cdc.gov/parasites/onchocerciasis/epi.html.

23. www.cdc.gov/parasites/lymphaticfiliariasis/epi.html.

24. Diamond. *Guns, Germs, and Steel: The Fates of Human Societies* (p. 186).

25. Glasgow. *The Distribution and Abundance of Tsetse* (p. 3).

26. Alsan. "The Effect of the Tsetse Fly on African Development." *American Economic Review*: 382–410.

27. Alesina, Giuliano, and Nunn. "On the Origins of Gender Roles: Women and the Plough." *The Quarterly Journal of Economics*: 469–530.

Chapter Four

Accursed Are the Blessed

One of the geographical factors that we cannot ignore is the endowment of natural resources which refer to substances present in nature that can be utilized for economic gain. These include forests, water, soil, hydrocarbons, precious gems, metal ores and others. The abundance of these resources endows the country with critical elements needed in the production process or in the generation of energy. A plentiful natural bounty also allows the country to increase its income by exporting some of these resources to the rest of the world. The export earnings can finance its expenditure on products supplied by other countries or can be used for other purposes essential for the economy.

On the other hand, some scholars argue that the abundance of natural endowments can be a curse. Scholars refer to this as the[1] "resource curse" or the "paradox of plenty." As an example, Daniel Yergin in his panoramic exposition of the saga of oil states that[2] "petroleum remains the motivating force of industrial society and the lifeblood of civilization that it helped create" and "an essential element in national power, a major factor in world economies, a critical focus for war and conflict, and a decisive force in international affairs." He concludes that "over almost a century and a half, oil has brought out the best and worst of our civilization. It has been both boon and burden." Some argue this also applies, to a large extent, to other natural resources.

In this context, studies distinguish between resource abundance, resource dependence, resource rents and resource prices. Resource abundance refers to whether a country is well endowed with a stock of minerals, metal ores, hydrocarbons, geological deposits, or some other resource. Resource dependence reflects the degree to which countries have access to alternative sources of income other than resource extraction and exports. This can be measured by the ratio of resource exports to total exports or to some estimate of national income. Resource rents indicate the flow of income derived from the resource at some point in time. Finally, resource prices reflect the market price per unit of the resource in international markets.

The seminal papers by Jeffrey Sachs and Andrew Warner provide evidence for the resource curse. In their study, the authors show that natural resource exports to Gross Domestic Product is negatively related to economic growth.[3] In another study, Jeffrey Sachs and Andrew Warner also show that economies with high natural resource exports to Gross Domestic Product in the early seventies of the twentieth century tended to have slower economic growth in subsequent periods.[4] In yet another contribution, Jeffrey Sachs and Andrew Warner present evidence from Latin America showing that primary product exports to Gross Domestic Product have a negative association with economic growth, and that natural resource booms are sometimes accompanied by declining income per capita.[5]

After these initial contributions to the literature, subsequent studies focus on the effect of resource reliance on different indicators of economic development, or on the economic effects of alternative measures of resource reliance. Erwin Bulte, Richard Damania, and Robert Deacon find that resource abundance is associated with a lower human development index, lower life expectancy, higher proportion of people who are undernourished, higher percentage of people who lack access to safe water, worse institutional quality, and governments that perform poorly along several dimensions.[6] On the other hand, there are studies that concluded that the resource curse is a red herring. For instance, Christa Brunnschweiler uses alternative indicators such as mineral production, subsoil wealth and natural capital.[7] The author finds a positive association between these measures and economic growth, that diminishes as institutional quality improves. Christa Brunnschweiler and Erwin Bulte critically evaluate the basis for the resource curse.[8] The authors find that resource abundance positively affects both economic growth and institutional quality, while resource dependence is not significantly associated with either.

Other studies find that better quality institutions can turn the resource curse into a blessing. For instance, Markus Brückner shows that using a real measure, not a nominal one, for the share of primary products exports in Gross National Product yields a larger negative economic effect especially in societies characterized by high levels of corruption and sluggish checks and balances in the political system.[9] Halvor Mehlum, Karl Moene and Ragnar Torvik claim that the distinct experiences of countries that are well endowed with natural wealth are ascribed to differences in the quality of institutions.[10] The authors provide evidence that natural resources are a curse on income when institutions are "grabber friendly" but a blessing with "producer friendly" institutions. Minoo Farhadi, Rabiul Islam, and Solmaz Moslehi examine whether institutions that promote property protection and economic freedoms can change the resource curse into a blessing.[11] The authors find that the negative growth effects of resource rents may turn positive in countries with greater economic freedom.

Some studies focus on the economic effect of oil abundance and whether there is an oil curse.[12] For instance, Kevin Tsui and Anca Cotet find that there is a positive association between oil abundance and economic growth, as oil-abundant countries benefit from health improvements reflected in gains in longevity.[13] These effects are more pronounced in countries with non-democratic systems of governance, with initial poor health conditions, and where oil wealth is concentrated in the hands of the ruling elite. Michael Alexeev and Robert Conrad examine the effect of a large endowment of oil and other minerals on economic growth.[14] The authors use hydrocarbon deposits per capita, the value of oil output per capita, and the oil to Gross Domestic Product ratio as alternative indicators. Their analysis demonstrates that oil and other resources enhance income per capita especially in countries with weak institutions.

This curse manifests itself when the endowed economies suffer from lack of diversification in economic activities, an increase in the likelihood of conflict, the authoritarian tendencies of their governments, in addition to some adverse effects on human capital accumulation. These issues are discussed in detail in the following sections.

THE DUTCH DISEASE

The Dutch Disease is the putative effect of the expansion of a sector specialized in resource extraction on the expense of the other sectors of the economy.[15] This is because the resource sector attracts larger net capital inflows, which leads to a lower supply of a country's currency. This shortage causes the country's currency to appreciate compared to those of other countries. The currency appreciation causes the country's other exports to become less affordable to foreigners and accordingly less competitive in world markets. On the other hand, the currency appreciation makes imports cheaper which leads domestic consumers to prefer purchasing foreign products. Thus, the employment and the productive capabilities of the non-resource sector deteriorate.

The abundance of natural wealth can have an adverse effect on the diversification of a country's economic structure as well. Economic diversification may be delayed or neglected altogether considering the high earnings that can be obtained from resource extraction. Thus, any attempt to diversify the economy is hindered because resource extraction is more lucrative compared to other types of production. Therefore, these countries often become increasingly dependent on extraction industries and become less diverse over time. The utter dependence on natural endowments leaves the economy vulnerable to market volatility and more susceptible to sudden fluctuations in the value of the natural prize.

THE DRILL AND THE SCRIBE

The reliance on the resource sector has repercussions on the allocation of talent between sectors in the economy, and on the accumulation of human capital and skill acquisition. The resource extraction sector tends to pay more generous salaries than elsewhere in the economy, especially in developing countries. Lured by better compensation, skilled workers flock to the resource sector from every corner of the economy. This tends to attract the best talents from both the private sector and the government agencies, depriving them of their most capable workers.

Resources can also be a curse due to their adverse effect on the accumulation of human capital and educational attainment. Countries that rely on resource extraction and exports tend to neglect education because they see low added value from the accumulation of human capital given their abundance in another factor of production. Economies bereft of these natural endowments, by contrast, may spend enormous resources on the accumulation of human capital. This is because the increase in human capital can compensate for the scarcity of the natural endowment that can be used in the production process.

To test these proposals, Thorvaldur Gylfason examines the effect of the share of natural capital in national wealth on human capital and economic development across countries.[16] The author finds that public expenditure on education, expected years of schooling for girls, and gross secondary-school enrollment are inversely associated with the share of natural capital in national wealth. Thus, natural capital crowds out human capital which adversely affects economic development.

THE ECOLOGY OF WAR

Raw materials, minerals, metal ores and geological deposits are lucrative sources of income and economic rent for those who own or control them. Some studies argue that the abundance of these natural assets is considered a potential cause of armed conflict.[17] Conflicts cause political instability, human adversity, loss of life, ruptures in the social fabric, destruction to infrastructure, devastation to productive facilities, and damage to property. Conflict can also take the form of internal discord between government agencies for access to budgetary allocations, which erodes the government's ability to function effectively and undermines the quality of its agencies. Natural wealth, thus, can instigate conflict over the control of these resources. The access to resource earnings can also prolong ongoing conflicts. Thus, natural wealth can influence the onset, duration, and intensity of conflicts.

Resource reliance can increase the likelihood of the onset of conflict. Resource earnings are both a source of funding for insurgency and an instigator of grievances. If rebels can extract and sell resources, or extort money from those who do, then they are more likely to afford to launch a civil war.[18] Natural resource extraction is also tied to a location. Thus, it is easier for rebels to extort money from resource extraction companies since the latter cannot relocate if their production facilities are held hostage. Rebels use looted resources in the prewar phase to buy arms, procure weapons, and recruit soldiers. Thus, resource rents fund the cost to initiate a rebellion and to challenge government forces.

On the other hand, production in the resource extraction sector is capital-intensive. This implies that the extraction process relies more on capital than labor. Thus, an increase in resource prices promotes capital-intensive production activities. This decreases dependence on labor in the production process, which frees up the unemployed to be recruited for rebellion.

Resource extraction also creates grievances among the local population, because of land expropriation, environmental hazards, and the social disruptions created by this type of economic activity. Resource wars are caused in part because mining interests are ravaging the environment, driving away those who inhabit the resource abundant area, or depriving them of any benefits from the appropriation of their traditional lands. These grievances, in turn, can lead to civil war. If natural wealth is located on a country's periphery in an area populated by a minority, residents will try to secede to create a separate state increasing the likelihood of a civil war.[19]

Proceeds from resource extraction relieve governments from the need to levy taxes, which in turn produces a state that is more repressive and less responsive to its people. This increases grievances toward a government that does not take the needs of its citizens into consideration and makes the state more susceptible to be engaged in civil war and less effective in counterinsurgency.[20]

Not only does it serve as a catalyst, but natural wealth can also prolong a conflict as it enables the rebels to continue funding the war effort instead of being defeated or forced to the negotiating table. Resource abundance also makes it harder for negotiators to enforce a binding ceasefire or a peace settlement if wartime looting is sufficiently profitable for soldiers and their commanding officers that they have no incentive to put an end to it.

The likelihood that insurgents will settle a conflict, through an agreement with the government, depends on whether they believe the latter will adhere to it. If the conflict was over an area that is blessed with resources, the government is more likely to renege on any such agreement to gain access to the resource earnings. Even if the government does not plan to retract, the rebels are more likely to expect it never to abide by the agreement and hence will prefer to continue being embroiled in conflict.

There are various studies that examine the effect of natural resource abundance and dependence on conflict. For instance, Dominic Rohner, Nicolas Berman, Mathieu Couttenier, and Mathias Thoenig combine data on mining extraction with information on conflict events in Africa.[21] The authors find a positive effect of mining on conflict at the local level, and that an increase in mineral prices increases the probability of conflict in producing areas. Dominic Rohner, Francesco Caselli, and Massimo Morelli assess the role of resources in interstate conflict.[22] Their analysis shows that the presence and location of oil are significant predictors of interstate conflicts after World War II. The authors also find that country pairs where only one country has oil near the border are more likely to engage in conflict than country pairs with no oil, or where oil is very far from the border, or when both countries have oil near the border. Dominic Rohner and Massimo Morelli examine whether conflict is more likely if an ethnic minority is in an area that is particularly endowed with oil.[23] The authors compute a novel indicator of the unevenness of oil field distribution across ethnic groups, called the Oil Gini coefficient. The authors find that this variable has a positive association with conflict which is more likely when the group out of power has an ethnic homeland that is abundant in oil. Christa Brunnschweiler and Erwin Bulte challenge the stylized fact that natural endowments lead to conflict.[24] The authors find that the ratio of primary exports to Gross Domestic Product does not have a statistically significant effect on conflict, while conflict increases dependence on resource extraction.

Other studies examine the effect of discoveries of natural wealth on the likelihood of conflict. For instance, Yu-Hsiang Lei and Guy Michaels use data on giant oilfield discoveries to identify their effect on economic and political outcomes across countries.[25] The authors find that these giant oilfield discoveries increase oil production per capita, oil exports, and the incidence of internal armed conflict especially in countries that had experienced armed conflicts or coups in the decade prior to discovery. Kevin Tsui and Anca Cotet examine the effect of oil wealth on political violence using a dataset of oil discoveries.[26] The authors find that the statistical association between oil wealth and civil war onset disappears once country-specific factors are controlled for, but that oil wealth is significantly correlated with defense spending in nondemocratic countries.

THE DRILL AND THE SCEPTER

Some scholars argue that the abundance of natural endowments has an adverse effect on democratic governance.[27] In economies that are not dependent on resource extraction, governments collect taxes from citizens who demand efficient and effective governance in return. This bargain establishes a social contract between leaders and citizens where the former is accountable before the latter. In economies dominated by resource extraction, governments do not need to tax their citizens because they have a guaranteed source of income from resource extraction and exports. Thus, they feel less obligated to gratify their citizens.

As the country's citizens are less taxed in countries abundant in natural resources, they also have less incentive to be watchful of how their government spends from its coffers. Consequently, the government has less of an incentive to provide the services needed by citizens. If people complain, the surplus from resource extraction and exports enables authorities to pay for a well-equipped police apparatus and armed forces to keep their disgruntled subjects in check. In addition, the ruling elite who benefit from their undeterred control over natural wealth may perceive a watchful civil society as a threat to the perks and perquisites they secured. Thus, those elite may take serious steps to thwart any effort to establish entities that can act as a watchdog over their political actions.

Some studies investigate the effect of natural resource abundance on democracy. For instance, Leonard Wantchekon and Nathan Jensen show evidence of a negative association between the size of the natural endowment sector and the level of democracy in Africa.[28] The authors conclude that in authoritarian political systems, resource rents allow incumbent politicians to consolidate their hold on political power which makes democratic transition less likely to unfold. In another contribution, Leonard Wantchekon argues that natural wealth windfalls empower an entrenched authoritarian and generate an incumbency advantage.[29] The author finds a strong and statistically significant association between authoritarianism and the ratio of fuel and mineral exports out of total exports.

Some studies focus on the association between oil and the system of governance. Kevin Tsui attempts to identify the effect of oil wealth and discoveries on democracy.[30] The author finds that discovering 100 billion barrels of oil pushes a country's democracy level almost 20 percentage points below trend after three decades. Markus Brückner and Rabah Arezki find that an increase in oil rents promotes corruption and civil liberties but limits political rights.[31] The authors conclude that these findings can be attributed to the presence of political elite who have an incentive to extend civil liberties on the expense of political rights to avoid any redistribution of oil windfalls.

Other studies suggest a resource blessing when it comes to the effect of natural wealth on democratic governance. For instance, Markus Brückner, Antonio Ciccone, and Andrea Tesei examine the effect of oil price fluctuations on democratic institutions and practices.[32] The authors show that countries with greater net oil exports to Gross Domestic Product see improvements in democratic governance following spikes in international oil prices. Stephen Haber and Victor Menaldo examine the relationship between resource reliance and political regime.[33] The authors find that increases in reliance on oil and minerals are not associated with authoritarianism.

THE DRILL AND THE LADDER

The abundance of natural wealth can have serious implications on the distribution of income in a country. If the resources are controlled by an elite or a ruling clique who appropriate the earnings of resource extraction, the distribution of income is expected to be skewed in favor of resource owners. On the other hand, if the earnings from resource extraction and exports are used to finance public spending on infrastructure, schooling, and health, we expect to see a lower level of income inequality. In this context, Osiris Parcero and Elissaios Papyrakis show[34] "that oil is associated with lower income inequality with the exception of the very oil-rich economies." Dong-Hyeon Kim, Ting-Cih Chen, and Shu-Chin Lin find that oil abundance increases human capital investment and enhances institutional quality which lower income inequality.[35] The authors, however, find that oil volatility has the opposite effect.

NOTES

1. Venables. "Using Natural Resources for Development." *Journal of Economic Perspectives*: 161–184. Venables and van der Ploeg. "Natural Resource Wealth: The Challenge of Managing a Windfall." *Annual Review of Economics*: 315–337. Ross. "What Have We Learned about the Resource Curse?" *Annual Review of Political Science*: 239–259. Ross. "The Political Economy of the Resource Curse." *World Politics*: 297–322.

2. Yergin. *The Prize: The Epic Quest for Oil, Money and Power.*

3. Sachs and Warner. "The Curse of Natural Resources." *European Economic Review*: 827–838.

4. Sachs and Warner. "Natural Resource Abundance and Economic Growth." National Bureau of Economic Research Working Paper 5398.

5. Sachs and Warner. "The Big Push, Natural Resource Booms and Growth." *Journal of Development Economics*: 43–76.

6. Bulte, Damania, and Deacon. "Resource Intensity, Institutions, and Development." *World Development*: 1029–1044.

7. Brunnschweiler. "Cursing the Blessings? Natural Resource Abundance, Institutions, and Economic Growth." *World Development*: 399–419.

8. Brunnschweiler and Bulte. "The Resource Curse Revisited and Revised." *Journal of Environmental Economics and Management*: 248–264.

9. Bruckner. "Natural Resource Dependence, Non–Tradables, and Economic Growth." *Journal of Comparative Economics*: 461–471.

10. Mehlum, Moene, and Torvik. "Institutions and the Resource Curse." *The Economic Journal*: 1–20.

11. Farhadi, Islam, and Moslehi. "Economic Freedom and Productivity Growth in Resource-rich Economies." *World Development*: 109–126.

12. Ross. *The Oil Curse: How Petroleum Wealth Shapes the Development of Nations*.

13. Tsui and Cotet. "Oil, Growth, and Health: What Does the Cross-Country Evidence Really Show?" *The Scandinavian Journal of Economics*: 1107–1137.

14. Alexeev and Conrad. "The Elusive Curse of Oil." *The Review of Economics and Statistics*: 586–598.

15. Van Wijnbergen. "The 'Dutch Disease': A Disease After All?" *The Economic Journal*: 41–55.

16. Gylfason. "Natural Resources, Education, and Economic Development." *European Economic Review*: 847–859.

17. Ross. "A Closer Look at Oil, Diamonds, and Civil War." *Annual Review of Political Science*: 265–300. Ross. "What Do We Know About Natural Resources and Civil War?" *Journal of Peace Research*: 337–356. Ross. "How Do Natural Resources Influence Civil War? Evidence from Thirteen Cases." *International Organization*: 35–67.

18. Collier and Hoeffler. "On Economic Causes of Civil War." Oxford Economic Papers: 563–73.

19. Le Billon. "The Political Ecology of War: Natural Resources and Armed Conflicts." *Political Geography*: 561–84.

20. Fearon and Laitin. "Ethnicity, Insurgency, and Civil War." *American Political Science Review*: 75–90.

21. Berman, Couttenier, Rohner, and Thoenig. "This Mine is Mine! How Minerals Fuel Conflicts in Africa." *American Economic Review*: 1564–1610.

22. Caselli, Morelli, and Rohner. "The Geography of Interstate Resources Wars." *The Quarterly Journal of Economics*: 267–315.

23. Morelli and Rohner. "Resource Concentration and Civil Wars." *Journal of Development Economics*: 32–47.

24. Brunnschweiler and Bulte. "Natural Resources and Violent Conflict: Resource Abundance, Dependence, and the Onset of Civil Wars." *Oxford Economic Papers*: 651–674.

25. Lei and Michaels. "Do Giant Oilfield Discoveries Fuel Internal Armed Conflicts?" *Journal of Development Economics*: 139–157.

26. Cotet and Tsui. "Oil and Conflict: What Does the Cross–Country Evidence Really Show?" *American Economic Journal: Macroeconomics*: 49–80.

27. Ross. "Does Oil Hinder Democracy?" *World Politics*: 325–61.

28. Jensen and Wantchekon. "Resource Wealth and Political Regimes in Africa." *Comparative Political Studies*: 816–41.

29. Wantchekon. "Why Do Resource Dependent Countries Have Authoritarian Governments?" *Journal of African Finance and Economic Development*: 57–77.

30. Tsui. "More Oil, Less Democracy: Evidence from Worldwide Crude Oil Discoveries." *The Economic Journal*: 89–115.

31. Brückner and Arezki. "Oil Rents, Corruption, and State Stability: Evidence from Panel Data Regressions." *European Economic Review*: 955–963.

32. Brückner, Ciccone, and Tesei. "Oil Price Shocks, income, and Democracy." *The Review of Economics and Statistics*: 389–399.

33. Haber and Menaldo. "Do Natural Resources Fuel Authoritarianism? A Reappraisal of the Resource Curse." *American Political Science Review*: 1–26.

34. Parcero and Papyrakis. "Income Inequality and the Oil Resource Curse." *Resource and Energy Economics*: 159–177.

35. Kim, Chen, and Lin. "Does Oil Drive Income Inequality? New Panel Evidence." *Structural Change and Economic Dynamics*: 37–152.

Chapter Five

The Wrath of Nature

NATURE'S MOOD SWINGS

We cannot conclude our discussion on the direct effect of geography on economic outcomes without touching upon the consequences of natural disasters. These expressions of the wrath of nature are determined by geographic factors. The climatic, hydrological, and geological environment can determine the occurrence of a disaster, its location, its type, its severity, and its duration. Climate change is known to have increased the frequency of natural disasters as well. The United Nations states that[1] "from 1970 to 2019, these natural hazards accounted for 50 per cent of all disasters, 45 per cent of all reported deaths and 74 per cent of all reported economic losses. There were more than 11,000 reported disasters attributed to these hazards globally, with just over two million deaths and $3.64 trillion in losses. More than 91 per cent of the deaths occurred in developing countries." The effect of these natural calamities on economies obviously cannot be understated. Thus, we cover these consequences in detail in this chapter.

As some countries experience the benevolent hand of mother nature, others endure its fury. Natural disasters were, and continue to be, a common occurrence in human history. In lots of cases, little were humans able to do to avert these disasters or to contain their consequences. Despite the notable strides in science and technology, humans continue to be susceptible to the sudden swings in the mood of nature. These adverse natural events can take the form of floods, tsunamis, droughts, severe heat waves, wildfires, storms, hurricanes, tornadoes, blizzards, cyclones, typhoons, avalanches, landslides, volcanic eruptions, earthquakes and others. These disasters continue to have a tremendous economic impact costing the stricken countries billions in damages, and scores of casualties and human suffering. They can also have a long-lasting effect that varies depending on the country's ability to absorb the initial shock, to contain its aftermath, and to recuperate from its repercussions.

The effect of a natural disaster naturally depends on the type, the epicenter, the intensity, and the duration of the event. Disasters of moderate magnitude are easier to deal with compared to severe ones. In the former case, government agencies and private organizations can redeploy their emergency personnel, supplies and resources to compensate for the losses and resuscitate the economy. However, if the disaster is of such degree that it overwhelms public and private agents its effect is likely to be more detrimental.

Lots of research in social studies and natural sciences has been devoted to advancing our ability to predict disasters, to prepare for them, to contain them or to lessen their damage. In this context, some scholars focus on the effect of natural disasters on the economy.[2] Despite the obvious catastrophic and tragic consequences of disasters, some studies argue that there is also a potential favorable effect of these natural events. This favorable effect can be seen in the context of the desire to believe that adversity strengthens its victims, and that the resilience of those who were exposed to calamitous episodes can lift the economy. John Stuart Mill eloquently states that[3] "What has so often excited wonder, the great rapidity with which countries recover from a state of devastation; the disappearance, in a short time, of all traces of the mischiefs done by earthquakes, floods, hurricanes, and the ravages of war." In a similar vein, the insight of "stimulus and response" proposed by historian Arnold Toynbee in understanding the history of civilizations can also guide us in comprehending the argument that disasters can have a positive effect on economic outcomes. The prominent historian argues that civilizations arose in response to some set of extreme challenges. When a civilization reacts creatively to these challenges it survives, and when it does not it stagnates and disintegrates. Toynbee adroitly declares that[4] "Now civilizations, I believe, come to birth and proceed to grow by successfully responding to successive challenges. They break down and go to pieces if and when a challenge confronts them which they fail to meet." Natural disasters can be perceived as a challenge of sorts. Maybe the sort of challenge that Friedrich Nietzsche was referring to when he said "That which does not kill us, makes us stronger."

The following sections discuss in detail the effect of natural disasters on the economy, on physical capital, on human capital, on technological progress, on cultural attitudes, on agricultural production, on the likelihood of violence, and on the system of governance.

DISASTERS AND THE ECONOMY

There are several studies that explore the effect of natural disasters on economic growth, compare the effects of distinct types of natural disasters, contrast the effect of disasters on different categories of countries, and determine the effect of disasters on various sectors of the economy.

For instance, Ilan Noy finds that natural disasters, captured by property damage, have a statistically significant negative economic effect especially in the more vulnerable developing countries and smaller economies.[5] On the other hand, countries with higher literacy rates, better quality institutions, larger income per capita, greater degree of trade openness, and higher levels of government spending are found to be better able to withstand the initial disaster shock and to prevent further spillovers into the economy. Ilan Noy, Eduardo Cavallo, Sebastian Galiani, and Juan Pantano find that significantly large disasters have an adverse effect on output only when the disastrous event was followed by political revolutions.[6] Once the authors control for these events, even large disasters are shown not to display any significant effect on economic growth.

Mark Skidmore and Hideki Toya examine the association between disasters, capital accumulation, total factor productivity, and economic growth.[7] Their study demonstrates that climatic disasters allow for a substitution from physical capital accumulation toward human capital investment. Disasters are also shown to provide an incentive to update the capital stock and adopt new technologies, leading to improvements in total factor productivity and economic growth. In another contribution, Mark Skidmore and Hideki Toya examine the degree to which the losses from natural disasters are curtailed as economies develop.[8] The authors find that countries with higher income, higher educational attainment, greater openness, developed financial systems, and smaller government experience fewer losses from disasters.

Other studies investigate the effect of different varieties of natural disasters on various sectors of the economy. For instance, Norman Loayza, Thomas Fomby, and Yuki Ikeda examine the effect of different natural disasters on income growth, and on its agricultural and non-agricultural components.[9] The authors show evidence that droughts have an adverse effect on economic growth, which is immediate for agricultural growth and with some delay for non-agricultural growth. Floods tend to have a positive effect one year after, while the effect on non-agricultural growth appears later. Finally, earthquakes have a positive effect on non-agricultural growth, while storms tend to have a negative effect on non-agricultural growth the same year of the event. Norman Loayza, Eduardo Olaberria, Jamele Rigolini, and Luc Christiaensen show that economic growth in developing countries is more sensitive to natural disasters than in developed ones.[10] The authors also find that droughts have a negative effect mainly on agricultural growth in developing countries, storms lower agricultural growth but enhance industrial growth in developing countries, earthquakes bring about higher industrial growth in developing countries, and moderate floods have a positive effect on various sectors of the economy.

Another stream of literature focuses on the effect of these disasters on different countries. This is because poor countries are more susceptible to the effects of disasters as they are the least prepared to absorb the shock, the least equipped to deal with its consequences, and the least able to fund recovery. In this context, Zeb Aurangzeb and Thanasis Stengos examine whether the effect of natural disasters on the economy is uniform across countries.[11] The authors find that countries with higher income, higher government spending, more trade openness, less fiscal imbalances, and greater financial stability, are better able to withstand the disaster shock. Matthew Kahn finds that wealthier nations, democracies, and countries with better institutions sustain a lower level of fatalities from natural disasters.[12] Gabriel Felbermayr and Jasmin Gröschl provide evidence of a substantial adverse effect of natural disasters on economic growth driven by very large earthquakes, that poor countries are more affected by geophysical disasters, that rich countries are more affected by meteorological events, and that international openness and democratic institutions lower the unfavorable effect of disasters.[13]

Some studies focus on Central America and the Caribbean countries that are particularly stricken by hurricanes. For instance, Eric Strobl shows that hurricane strikes cause output losses in Central America and the Caribbean.[14] Eric Strobl, Preeya Mohan and Luisito Bertinelli examine how hurricanes can cause catastrophic destruction that can hamper economic growth in the Caribbean.[15] The authors show that the expected property damage and subsequent economic effects are non-negligible, with large variations across islands depending on their size. Eric Strobl and Preeya Mohan undertake a hurricane wind risk and loss assessment in Caribbean island economies.[16] Their analysis indicates that expected wind losses are large especially in smaller islands which are more likely to be adversely affected. Eric Strobl, Preeya Mohan and Bazoumana Ouattara explore the effects of hurricane strikes on the components of Gross Domestic Product in the Caribbean.[17] The authors find that after a hurricane strike, exports are negatively affected two years after, imports and investment spending tend to initially expand after the event and then contract, government consumption increases in the year of the event while private consumption reacts negatively three years later. The authors conclude that these findings jointly suggest that Gross Domestic Product may initially increase after a hurricane and then decrease later.

DISASTERS, CAPITAL, AND TECHNOLOGY

Natural disasters can cause substantial physical damage to the stricken area. Destruction to property, infrastructure and manufacturing plants lowers the stock of physical capital which may impair a country's productive potential. Natural disasters can also have an adverse effect on technological progress by tightening the budgets allocated for research, innovation, and invention. These calamitous events strain resources, and the recovery efforts in their aftermath divert these scarce resources away from research and development.

On the other hand, the aftermath of disasters is a rare opportunity to repair the damage, to rebuild the infrastructure, to reconstruct factories, to overhaul the demolished capital, to adopt new technologies and to prepare better for future disasters. Disasters, thus, offer the afflicted economy a chance to replace the obsolete equipment with the leading cutting-edge technology. This would have advantageous future consequences on the economy's productivity. Thus, disasters that are followed by upgrading the older damaged equipment with newer ones that embodies the latest technology can have favorable effects on the productive capacity of the economy. These actions also generate economic activity and employment opportunities that may compensate for the losses and offset the direct damage caused by the natural disaster.

Reconstruction, however, can be more complicated in countries with fewer resources, bureaucratic barriers, rampant corruption, worse institutions, and lower rates of insurance. Disaster inflicted countries could, however, get a substantial flow of emergency aid. This could assist these countries in dealing with the devastation caused by these disasters. Nevertheless, corrupt officials can horde foreign aid, or divert it to fund their pet projects rather than ones that would aid the entire country in its calamity.

DISASTERS, EDUCATION, AND HEALTH

Human capital refers to the level of educational attainment and health conditions in a country. Natural disasters can either have an adverse or a favorable effect on human capital accumulation. The former comes from the loss of life, the disruption of the educational process and the destruction of school facilities. The latter manifests itself through a lower opportunity cost to educational attainment.

Natural disasters decrease human capital if there is a substantial loss of life due to epic disastrous events that hit without warning. However, these categories of disasters are infrequent and uncommon. Other milder ones do not lead to substantial casualties as people can either brace themselves for the incoming harm or escape altogether from harm's way. Another potential impact on human capital accumulation comes from the damage disasters cause to educational facilities. Destruction of school campuses and instructional institutions can force students out of classrooms and make them lose out on the learning opportunities that they otherwise would have obtained. In addition, when families lose a source of income due to a disaster, some children will drop out of school to work to decrease the household expenses and to compensate for the decline in the family's income. This increases the incidence of child labor.

On the other hand, natural disasters can also have a favorable effect on human capital as school attendance, especially by older students, increases following economic crises. Students are more likely to attend school if the opportunity cost of that choice is low. The opportunity cost of education includes the earnings you forsake as you choose to attend school. If real wage decreases following a disaster, the opportunity cost for students to attend school falls. Thus, the decline in real wages due to disasters would prod them back into school. In addition, the damage to physical capital due to natural disasters makes investment in human capital more worthwhile. Households and governments increase investment in educational attainment and job training, which would increase human capital accumulation.

Human capital is about health conditions as well. The emotional, psychological, and physical effects continue to have their toll on people well after the occurrence of a natural disaster. Some survivors suffer permanent physical disabilities. Disasters could also psychologically handicap those who experience them. Some people suffer from post-traumatic stress disorders in these situations, and the trauma can continue to affect them for a long time. This can create psychological syndromes that can cripple their ability to perform well in the workplace. Workers who suffer from these psychological side effects of disasters may not be as productive as they were before their traumatic experience. This, in turn, affects productivity and economic growth.

In this context, Germán Daniel Caruso examines the persisting effects of exposure in childhood to natural disasters that occurred in Latin America in the last 100 years.[18] The author shows that children in utero and young children suffer long-lasting adverse effects from natural disasters. These effects include lower human capital accumulation, diminished health, and fewer assets in adulthood. The evidence also indicates that children born to mothers who were exposed to natural disasters have less education and higher levels of child labor.

DISASTERS AND DEBT

The recovery efforts in the aftermath of a natural disaster incur a steep cost to society. Governments must foot the bill, and sometimes must borrow to fulfill this financial obligation. Thus, disasters can lead to the exacerbation of sovereign debt and the worsening of the public finances of a country. This is because stricken countries either tend to borrow more to finance recovery after a disaster, or to repudiate on its debt obligations due to the fiscal burden in the aftermath of a disaster. Jeroen Klomp shows that large-scale natural disasters significantly increase the likelihood of a sovereign debt default.[19] The author also finds that earthquakes and storms in particular increase the likelihood of a default due to the widespread damage they create which limits the debt servicing capacity of a country.

If governments cannot afford additional debt accumulation, public officials may pressure the central bank to print more money. The outcome of printing too much money is inflation. This is because the increase in money supply induces a spending spree which puts an upward pressure on prices. Inflation could also occur because of market forces. Prices may skyrocket as disasters disrupt the supply of products and commodities such as food, housing, and energy. Demand also increases because disasters strip people of their personal possessions and destroy their property. The decline in supply and the increase in demand for goods and services cause prices to soar and inflation to abound. In this context, Miles Parker studies how disasters affect consumer price inflation.[20] The author finds that the effect is negligible in advanced economies, while the impact can last for years in developing countries. The author also shows that storms increase food price inflation in the short-term, but the effect dissipates within a year, floods have a short-term effect on inflation, while earthquakes lower consumer price index inflation excluding food, housing, and energy.

Some sectors in the economy, such as tourism, can also be disrupted by the occurrence of disasters. No tourist wants to spend a vacation in a disaster-stricken area. For economies reliant on tourism, these incidents can drastically cut their indispensable source of foreign currency which affect their ability to repay their loans. On the other hand, tourism can also see an eventual boost from some disasters. Docile volcanoes attract tourists. Yellowstone in the United States, Toba in Indonesia, and Taupo in New Zealand are known as super volcanoes that are major tourist attractions. The mother of all disaster tourism sites is the ancient Roman city of Pompeii. When Mount Vesuvius erupted in 79 C.E., it buried Pompeii under mounds of ash and pumice. Nowadays, Pompeii is one of Italy's most popular tourist attractions and a continuous inspiration to many writers and poets. In the words of Marcel Proust,[21] "The features of our face are hardly more than gestures which force of habit made permanent. Nature, like the destruction of Pompeii, like the metamorphosis of a nymph into a tree, has arrested us in an accustomed movement."

DISASTERS AND FAITH

Natural disasters can also have an influence on religiosity. We observe that individuals hit by various adverse life events tend to become more religious. Religion provides individuals with a higher power to turn to in times of hardship. Individuals draw on religious beliefs and practices to deal with and to withstand unbearable situations. As disasters are adverse experiences, some observe that religiosity increases in afflicted areas. This can influence the entire economy since religiosity has been associated with decisions pertaining to fertility rates, labor force participation, educational attainment, gender equality, crime and violence, health conditions, in addition to aggregate economic outcomes. In this context, Jeanet Bentzen shows that individuals living in districts frequently hit by earthquakes, volcanic eruptions and tsunamis are more religious.[22] This finding applies to individuals belonging to all major denominations and those living in every continent.

DISASTER AND VIOLENCE

Some scholars argue that disasters can instigate violence. Disasters of moderate magnitude can expose the unpreparedness of the authorities. The inadequate reaction by the government can generate, or exacerbate, grievances by the people of the affected area. Since the destruction in these cases would be limited, the state retains some of its power of coercion. This diminishes the likelihood of full-fledged conflict but allows for the possibility of acts of terrorism. To examine this intuition, Jose Montalvo and Marta Reynal-Querol study the association between earthquakes and terrorism.[23] The authors show that the likelihood of domestic terrorist events increases with the previous occurrence of an earthquake. Claude Berrebi and Jordan Ostwald argue that natural disasters can strain a society creating vulnerabilities which terrorists can exploit.[24] The authors find a strong positive effect of disaster deaths on subsequent terrorism incidence and fatalities.

DISASTERS AND DEMOCRACY

Natural disasters can also influence the system of governance. Some scholars argue that disasters can have two contradictory effects on the political scene. On one hand, disasters can induce a democratic transition if citizens hold the incumbent government accountable for the lack of emergency preparedness or for the failure to react competently to a disaster. On the other hand, disasters can slow the transition into democratic governance because of the increase in incomes due to the flow of emergency aid and the recovery efforts. This increases the opportunity cost of contesting the incumbent authorities.

Building on this intuition, Muhammad Habibur Rahman, Nejat Anbarci, Prasad Sankar Bhattacharya and Mehmet Ali Ulubaşoğlu show that earthquake shocks open a new democratic window of opportunity, but this window is narrowed by improved economic conditions.[25] In another paper, the same set of authors study whether and how rainfall-driven flooding affects democratic conditions.[26] Their finding indicates that flooding leads to corrupt practices in relief efforts and post-disaster assistance distribution. This increases the demands for political reform and better democratic practices. On the other hand, flooding stimulates the suppressive tendencies of the autocratic authorities to ensure an efficient post-disaster administration without chaos or plunder. The authors find that the net effect is an improvement in democratic conditions.

In an intriguing contribution, Marianna Belloc, Francesco Drago and Roberto Galbiati exploit a unique historical experiment to explore the dynamics of institutional change in the Middle Ages.[27] The authors assemble a data set on political institutions for some Italian cities between 1000 C.E. and 1300 C.E. with detailed information on the earthquakes that hit the area at the time. The authors show that the occurrence of an earthquake retarded institutional transition from autocratic to self-government in cities where the political and ecclesiastical leaders were the same person. The findings are consistent with the notion that earthquakes, interpreted as manifestation of the wrath of God, represented a shock to people's beliefs. Therefore, earthquakes enhanced the ability of political-religious leaders to restore social order after a crisis.

NOTES

1. https://news.un.org/en/story/2021/09/1098662
2. Popp. "The Effects of Natural Disasters on Long Run Growth." *Major Themes in Economics*: 61–82. Stromberg. "Natural Disasters, Economic Development, and Humanitarian Aid." *Journal of Economic Perspectives*: 199–222.
3. Mill. *Principles of Political Economy.*

4. Toynbee. *Civilization on Trial* (p. 56).

5. Noy. "The Macroeconomic Consequences of Disasters." *Journal of Development Economics*: 221–231.

6. Cavallo, Galiani, Noy, and Pantano. "Catastrophic Natural Disasters and Economic Growth." *The Review of Economics and Statistics*: 1549–1561.

7. Skidmore and Toya. "Do Natural Disasters Promote Long Run Growth?" *Economic Inquiry*: 664–687.

8. Toya and Skidmore. "Economic Development and the Impacts of Natural Disasters." *Economics Letters*: 20–25.

9. Fomby, Ikeda, and Loayza. "The Growth Aftermath of Natural Disasters." *Journal of Applied Econometrics*: 412–434.

10. Loayza, Olaberria, Rigolini, and Christiansen. "Natural Disasters and Growth: Going Beyond the Averages." *World Development*: 1317–1336.

11. Aurangzeb and Stengos. "Economic Policies and the Impact of Natural Disasters on Economic Growth." *Economics Bulletin*: 229–241.

12. Kahn. "The Death Toll from Natural Disasters." *The Review of Economics and Statistics*: 271–284.

13. Felbermayr and Gröschl. "Naturally Negative: The Growth Effects of Natural Disasters." *Journal of Development Economics*: 92–106.

14. Strobl. "The Economic Growth Impact of Natural Disasters in Developing Countries." *Journal of Development Economics*: 130–141.

15. Strobl, Bertinelli, and Mohan. "Hurricane Damage Risk Assessment in the Caribbean." *Ecological Economics*: 135–144.

16. Strobl and Mohan. "A Hurricane Wind Risk and Loss Assessment of Caribbean Agriculture." *Environment and Development Economics*: 84–106.

17. Strobl, Mohan, and Ouattara. "Decomposing the Macroeconomic Effects of Natural Disasters: A National Income Accounting Perspective." *Ecological Economics*: 1–9.

18. Caruso. "The Legacy of Natural Disasters: The Intergenerational Impact of 100 Years of Disasters in Latin America." *Journal of Development Economics*: 209–233.

19. Klomp. "Flooded with Debt." *Journal of International Money and Finance*: 93–103.

20. Parker. "The Impact of Disasters on Inflation." *Economics of Disasters and Climate Change*: 21–48.

21. Proust. *Within a Budding Grove* (p. 291).

22. Bentzen. "Acts of God? Religiosity and Natural Disasters across Subnational World Districts." *Economic Journal*: 2295–2321.

23. Montalvo and Reynal-Querol. "Earthquakes and Terrorism: The Long-Lasting Effect of Seismic Shocks." *Journal of Comparative Economics*: 541–561.

24. Berrebi and Ostwald. "Earthquakes, Hurricanes, and Terrorism: Do Natural Disasters Incite Terror?" *Public Choice*: 383–403.

25. Habibur Rahman, Anbarci, Bhattacharya and Ulubaşoğlu. "The Shocking Origins of Political Transitions: Evidence from Earthquakes." *Southern Economic Journal*: 796–823.

26. Habibur Rahman, Anbarci, Bhattacharya and Ulubaşoğlu. "Can Extreme Rainfall Trigger Democratic Change? The Role of Flood-induced Corruption." *Public Choice*: 331–358.

27. Belloc, Drago, and Galbiati. "Earthquakes, Religion, and Transition to Self-Government in Italian Cities." *The Quarterly Journal of Economics*: 1875–1926.

Chapter Six

Determinism versus Determination

TAKING DESTINY INTO OUR HANDS

Geography typically casts its shadow on our endeavors to identify the determinants of economic outcomes. There is an encompassing presence to our surrounding nature as we have seen in the previous chapters. The signature of geography can be seen inscribed on the story of humanity and its stamp engraved on the course of human history. Despite the abundance of arguments in favor of a geographical account of the narrative of the human experience, some scholars found these claims not only unconvincing but even disturbing to their conviction that human destiny cannot be predetermined by factors out of our control. This is because geography has a deterministic connotation to it. Societies cannot choose the geographic features of their land. Some describe this as a battle between an unconditional surrender to determinism on one hand, and an inclination to affirm the power of human agency and to assert the clout of human determination on the other.

This inclination for human determination hinges on the observation that there are areas around the world that share similar geographic features but have very distinct living conditions. Daron Acemoglu and James Robinson in *Why Nations Fail: The Origins of Power, Prosperity and Poverty* point our attention to the different conditions in cities on both sides of the Mexican American border despite analogous geographic conditions. The authors state that[1]

> Life south of the fence, just a few feet away, is rather different. While the residents of Nogales, Sonora, live in a relatively prosperous part of Mexico, the income of the average household there is about one-third that in Nogales,

Arizona. Most adults in Nogales, Sonora, do not have a high school degree, and many teenagers are not in school. Mothers have to worry about high rates of infant mortality. Poor public health conditions mean it's no surprise that the residents of Nogales, Sonora, do not live as long as their northern neighbors. They also do not have access to many public amenities. Roads are in a bad condition south of the fence. Law and order is in worse condition. Crime is high, and opening a business is a risky activity. Not only do you risk robbery, but getting all the permissions and greasing all the palms just to open is no easy endeavor. Residents of Nogales, Sonora, live with politician's corruption and ineptitude every day.

This example, and others around the world, implies that there are possibly other elements besides geography that cause these differences in living conditions even with similar geographic characteristics. In this context, scholars explore how systems that humans designed to work within can have a decisive effect on our destiny. These systems are intended to impose a structure on our transactions and a framework for our interactions. These are what we refer to as "institutions" defined by historian Niall Ferguson as[2] "the structure within which we organize ourselves as groups."

Given the place that institutions take under the spotlight in this literature, it is imperative to dedicate few chapters for an elaborate exposition of this potential determinant of economic outcomes. In this and the few coming chapters, we will attempt to define institutions, to comprehend their potential effect on economic activity, to look at some scholarly evidence on how institutions affect economic outcomes, and to consider the origins of current institutional structures that will bring us back to the critical role of geography.

A concrete definition of institutions has been elusive despite a persistent effort by scholars to produce one. Douglass North offers a first stab at a definition as he states that[3] "Institutions are the rules of the game in a society or, more formally, are the humanly devised constraints that shape human interaction." He also defines institutions as[4] "a set of rules, compliance procedures and moral and ethical behavioral norms designed to constrain the behavior of individuals in the interests of maximizing the wealth or utility of principals."

One effective way of clarifying the concept of institutions is by distinguishing between the alternative varieties of institutional structures. In this context, the institutional framework comprises both formal and informal constraints. Formal ones include constitutions, laws, rules, and regulations. Informal ones include customs, traditions, and taboos. In the absence of formal institutions, social interactions lead to the development of societal arrangements that constitute an informal institutional structure. In this case, transactions occur typically between two parties belonging to the same group, economic exchange operates through social networks, contracts cannot be concluded without trust that can be established only with recurrent interaction, and cultural homogeneity facilitates enforcement. When a contract is broken, other group members may punish the party who did not honor the agreement with social sanctions. In a more formal context, there are constitutions and laws governing economic transactions and political processes. In these cases, contracts are protected through legislation and adjudication while enforcement takes a more formal shape.

In this context, Claudia Williamson compares the effects of formal institutions and informal arrangements on economic progress.[5] The author distinguishes between formal institutions that reflect well defined enforced constraints by the government, and informal institutions that capture private constraints and cultural traits. The study suggests that informal arrangements are a strong determinant of economic development, while formal institutions are only successful when embedded in informal constraints. The author concludes that codifying informal rules can, thus, lead to adverse unintended consequences.

NUMBERS BEAR WITNESS

Plenty of scholars assert the primacy of institutions in our attempt to ascertain the determinants of growth and stagnation. For instance, social scientist Douglas North underscores that[6] "That institutions affect the performance of economies is hardly controversial. That the differential performance of economies over time is fundamentally influenced by the way institutions evolve is also not controversial." He also states that[7] "I wish to assert a much more fundamental role for institutions in societies; they are the underlying determinant of the long-run performance of economies" and that[8] "the inability of societies to develop effective, low cost enforcement of contracts is the most important source of both historical stagnation and contemporary underdevelopment." Adam Smith also wrote that[9]

> Commerce and manufactures can seldom flourish long in any state which does not enjoy a regular administration of justice, in which the people do not feel themselves secure in the possession of their property, in which the faith of contracts is not supported by law, and in which the authority of the state is not supposed to be regularly employed in enforcing the payment of debts from all those who are able to pay. Commerce and manufactures, in short, can seldom flourish in any state in which there is not a certain degree of confidence in the justice of government.

In a similar vein, Niall Ferguson stresses that[10] "both stagnation and growth are in large measure the results of 'laws and institutions.'" These scholars not only underline the role of institutions, but also undermine the potential of other factors to provide us with guidance in our attempt to unearth the pillars of economic prosperity. For instance, Niall Ferguson states that[11] "institutions-in the broadest sense of the term-determine modern historical outcomes, more than natural forces like the weather, geography or even the incidence of disease." He also posits that[12]

> Explanations that emphasize the role of geography, climate, disease or natural-resource endowments are less convincing today than they seemed in the eighteenth century. Scientific knowledge, technological innovation and market integration have greatly reduced the significance of distance, weather and germs, while mineral wealth has been revealed to be as much a curse as a blessing.

There is also a consensus within the literature that institutional quality is a fundamental factor of economic performance.[13] A stream of this literature focuses on the overall effect of institutions on economic outcomes. For instance, Robert Hall and Charles Jones show that differences in capital accumulation, educational attainment, productivity, and output per worker can be ascribed to differences in institutions and government policies.[14] The authors conclude that "a country's long-run economic performance is determined primarily by the institutions and government policies that make up the economic environment within which individuals and firms make investments, create and transfer ideas, and produce goods and services." In another seminal contribution, Gerald Scully finds that institutions have significantly large effects on the efficiency and growth of economies.[15] The author concludes that "politically open societies, which subscribe to the rule of law, to private property, and to the market allocation of resources, grow at three times the rate and are two and one-half times as efficient as societies in which these freedoms are abridged."

Phillip Keefer and Stephen Knack argue that the ability of poor countries to catch up to wealthier ones is determined largely by the institutional environment in which economic activity is conducted.[16] To provide evidence for their argument, the authors use various indicators of institutional quality including the rule of law, the pervasiveness of corruption, the risk of expropriation and contract repudiation. The authors find that these institutional aspects are critical determinants of the ability of countries to converge to their advanced counterparts.

INSIGHTS INTO INSTITUTIONS

We can distinguish between institutions in terms of their ultimate purpose. Some of these institutions are intended to enforce the state power as a third party in transactions between private agents, while others are designated to tie the hands of the state itself to prevent it from encroaching on those private agents.[17] The former are those institutions that foster exchange by lowering transaction costs. The latter are those institutions that circumscribe the state and other powerful actors to protect property and persons, rather than to expropriate the former and subjugate the latter.

In this context, institutions refer to the constraints by a third party, usually the state, on transactions conducted between private agents. Sometimes, the state is endowed with the power to enforce contracts, to protect property, to ensure fair competition, and to assure stability and peace. These institutions lower transaction costs and curb the ascendancy of any single interest group in order to create widespread opportunities for private agents and organizations. Institutions also imply restrictions on the state's ability to stretch its powers on the expense of the rights of those private agents. Some countries formulate mechanisms to limit state power, through independent legislatures and judiciaries, checks and balances, constitutional provisions, and other means. This section focuses on the effects of these constraints, by the state and on the state, on economic performance.

PROPERTY PROTECTION

Protection of property rights is an essential component of institutions. These are defined as the rights of an individual or an organization to a specific allocation of resources and to the stream of income generated by these assets. These rights are secure as long as the political, economic, and legal institutions prohibit any unilateral decisions to reassign them. Protection of property rights also ought to be secured for a broad cross section of society. A society in which property rights are secure for a small fraction of those with economic wealth and political power may not be the ideal environment for investment and capital accumulation. In such society, some of those with the entrepreneurial abilities and investment initiatives can also be without property rights.

Protection of property rights is considered one of the pillars of economic success. Institutions that protect physical and intellectual property matter for economic performance because they shape the incentives of economic actors to invest in physical capital, in human capital, and in technological progress.

Institutions should ensure security of property, so that those with productive initiatives are encouraged to invest as they expect to earn some return on their venture. If individuals and organizations are not able to realize a return on their investment, they will refrain from capital accumulation to the detriment of the entire economy.[18] This is because capital accumulation is a condicio sine qua non of economic growth. In support of these ideas, Barry Weingast explains that[19] "The more likely it is that the sovereign will alter property rights for his or her own benefit, the lower the expected returns from investment and the lower in turn the incentive to invest. For economic growth to occur the sovereign or government must not merely establish the relevant set of rights, but must make a credible commitment to them."

Property rights must include physical assets and intellectual input as well. This is because innovators and inventors need to ensure the security of their original contributions and breakthroughs. Otherwise, there will be less incentive for creative work and technological advances to the detriment of the entire economy. Technology can also be either developed domestically or transferred from technological frontiers. Convergence between underdeveloped and advanced economies depends on the former taking advantage of the technological discoveries in the latter. The transfer of such technologies entails guarantees of intellectual property rights. The lack thereof prevents poor countries from taking advantage of a technology transfer from developed countries. Nobel laureate Paul Romer states that knowledge is not a public good because patents grant monopoly power to innovators.[20] Patents, therefore, serve as incentives for investments that eventually lead to knowledge creation. Romer emphasizes that[21] "good institutions contribute to facilitate the process of registering new patents, to disseminate ideas and promote cooperation across researchers, to speed up diffusion of scientific knowledge, to improve enforcement of property rights and to reduce the uncertainty of new projects; all factors that stimulate R&D activities."

Security of property and certainty about the legal claim on the stream of future income also lowers transaction costs. This encourages individuals and firms to engage in economic activities, to accumulate physical and human capital, and to choose more efficient technologies. Noble laureate Ronald Coase points out that the adverse effects of high transaction costs[22] "are pervasive in the economy. Businessmen, in deciding on their ways of doing business and on what to produce, have to take into account transaction costs. If the costs of making an exchange are greater than the gains which that exchange would bring, that exchange would not take place."

Where property is insecure and transaction costs are high, scarce resources will be channeled away from productive enterprises toward influence activities, such as paying bribes or purchasing security. In this environment, entrepreneurs succeed based on political connectedness rather than economic effectiveness. Thus, inefficient entrepreneurs can survive if they happen to have the personal ties and connections with state officials that are essential to protect their assets from expropriation.

In this context, there are studies that focus on the impact of property rights. For instance, Phillip Keefer and Stephen Knack examine the impact of property rights protection on economic growth.[23] The authors find property rights to have a significant effect on investment and economic growth, and that convergence to income levels of the United States increase significantly in countries that protect property rights. In addition, Daron Acemoglu and Simon Johnson compare the effects of "property rights institutions" which protect citizens against expropriation by the government and the powerful elite, and "contracting institutions" which enable private contracts between citizens.[24] For the former, the authors use the constraints on government power and protection of property rights, while contracting institutions are captured by a legal indicator which estimates the procedural complexity to collect on a nonpaying commercial debt. The authors find that "contracting institutions" have a limited impact while "property rights institutions" have a significant effect on economic growth, investment, and financial development.

CONTRACT ENFORCEMENT

Earlier communities depended largely on face-to-face trade between individuals who typically share kinship, ethnic, or other social ties. In this context, exchange is simultaneous, transactions clear instantly, and deals are enforced by social ostracism, coercion by others, or by holding valuables hostage. Parties to these contracts were able to depend largely on norms and networks to administer agreements between strangers. In these markets, reputation for honoring commitments is valuable and economic interaction relied on interpersonal trust which can be established over time through continuous cooperation. Nonetheless, reputation is of limited use for transactions in which agents deal with each other infrequently, and any deviation from the agreed upon stipulations or contractual covenants can lead to the dissipation of the sentiments of trust.

Over time, groups engaging in trade activities envisioned lucrative opportunities with people who live even farther away and do not belong to their social circle. Parties involved sought to devise contractual enforcement mechanisms with these new trading partners. Thus, these complex transactions needed to be secured through a third party, such as the state. This is because the benefits from these transactions can be reaped when the interested parties expect that the contracts they sign will be honored and not abrogated by anyone involved.

In this case, individuals will be more willing to specialize and invest, to undertake complex transactions, and to accumulate and share knowledge.

Complex transactions also include the ability to offer and receive promises about future actions. For instance, capital is lent in expectation of a later payoff. Thus, capital markets cannot prosper without contractual enforcement. Firms in societies without contract enforcement are, thus, constrained to capital obtained through personal saving or family connections. Thus, the absence of contract enforcement hinders the ability of firms to finance their investment. This is disadvantageous to capital accumulation and economic growth.

JUDICIAL INDEPENDENCE

One of the main entities in charge of securing property and enforcing contracts is courts of law. For courts to perform these functions properly, judicial independence ought to be guaranteed. Judicial independence ensures that the judiciary is not subject to influence from other branches of the government or private groups. There are three archetypical situations in which judicial independence is crucial: conflict between citizens, conflict between the government and citizens, and conflict between various government agencies.

In the first case of conflict between citizens, parties voluntarily enter into a contract. If these parties expect the judiciary to be nonpartisan and impartial, they can save on transaction costs while negotiating the contract. When these parties get into a disagreement, especially when one of the signatories believes that the other has not honored their part, the presence of an even-handed conflict resolution entity becomes imperative.

In the case of conflict between governments and citizens, the latter need an adjudicative organization that acts according to the laws and is not subject to any pressure from the executive branch. Thus, judicial independence has tremendous value when the government is itself a litigant. This is even more valuable in private disputes when one of the plaintiffs is politically connected and the government wants the court to favor its ally. In this case, there is a need for a separation between the executive and the judicial branches.

The last case is of conflict between various government branches. In the absence of an evenhanded arbiter, conflicts between government agencies are likely to spiral into power contests. An independent judiciary can keep these frictions within the boundaries laid out in the constitution. In this context, the judiciary will not only have to ascertain the constitutionality of newly passed legislations but will also have to check whether the agents of the state have acted within the purview of the law. If the judiciary is not independent from the executive and the legislature, citizens will not trust in the rule of law.

Thus, the principle of equal treatment and the consistent and non-discriminatory application of the law constitute the fundamental tenets of the rule of law as captured by the slogan of blind justice. If individuals and organizations cannot be confident of equal treatment before the judicial system, then the courts cease to be a dependable entity for conflict resolution. Encyclopedia Britannica defines the rule of law as[25] "the mechanism, process, institution, practice, or norm that supports the equality of all citizens before the law, secures a nonarbitrary form of government, and more generally prevents the arbitrary use of power."

Historian Niall Fergusson states that[26] "few truths are today more universally acknowledged than that the rule of law—particularly insofar as it restrains the 'grabbing hand' of the rapacious state—is conducive to economic growth." It is also insightful what Herodutus said about the effect of the rule of law on the Greeks in their confrontation with the Persian Empire:[27] "how noble a thing is equality before the law [*isonomia*], not in one respect only but in all; for while they were oppressed under tyrants they had no better success in war than any of their neighbors, yet, once the yoke was flung off, they proved the finest fighters in the world."

In this context, several studies investigate the effects of court efficiency and judicial independence on economic outcomes. For instance, Simeon Djankov, Rafael La Porta, Florencio Lopez-de-Silanes, and Andrei Schleifer construct an index of procedural formalism using information on the procedures taken by litigants and courts to evict a tenant for nonpayment of rent and the processes to collect a bounced check.[28] The authors find that such formalism is systematically greater in civil law than in common law countries and is associated with longer expected duration of judicial proceedings, higher corruption, and less consistency, less honesty, and less fairness in judicial decisions.

Stefan Voigt and Lars Feld compare the effects of two types of judicial independence on economic outcomes: de jure judicial independence which focuses on legal foundations, and de facto judicial independence which focuses on actual experiences.[29] The authors find that economic growth is not affected by the de jure variable but is positively associated with de facto judicial independence. They conclude that this comparison indicates that it does not suffice to state judicial independence in legal documents, it is more essential to append this by additional informal procedures that may be enforced by social sanctions. In a similar contribution, Stefan Voigt, Lars Feld and Jerg Gutmann confirm their previous findings that the de jure indicator is not systematically associated with economic growth, whereas the de facto one is significantly correlated with economic growth.[30] In addition, the authors show that the effect of the de facto judicial independence is reinforced by a high level of checks and balances and by having a semi-presidential form of government. Other studies also argue that the favorable economic effect of institutional quality can be only achieved in an environment that guarantees judicial independence. Stefan Voigt and Jerg Gutmann emphasize that the mere promise of secure property is not likely to have any effect on economic outcomes unless accompanied by some commitment to enforce these promises that is perceived as credible by private agents.[31] The authors provide evidence for a favorable effect of property rights on economic growth if the judicial system is independent enough to ensure their enforcement.

CHECKS AND BALANCES

Judicial independence is also secured in a system of checks and balances. Encyclopedia Britannica states that checks and balances is a[32] "principle of government under which separate branches are empowered to prevent actions by other branches and are induced to share power." Checks and balances are of fundamental significance in governments with tripartite systems which separate between the legislative, the executive, and the judiciary. This system aims to ensure that no branch becomes too powerful at the expense of the others, and that each branch can act to constrain the power of the other branches.

Checks and balances can be observed in different ways. First, the creation of laws is separated from the administration of justice. The legislature formulates laws, the independent judiciary apply the letter and spirit of the law without interference, while the executive branch enforces these laws. Second, the legislative branch formulates laws, but the process of lawmaking can be subject to inspection by constitutional courts for their compliance with the constitution. This process is known as judicial review. In this context, the executive and the legislature may wish to pursue policies and pass laws that benefit them or their cronies. By checking laws against a constitution, a supreme constitutional court can constrain such self-serving behavior. Third, elected law makers can monitor the performance of policy makers and constrain some of their actions that are considered not beneficial to the public. Law makers also have the power of the purse, as the legislative branch controls the coffers used to fund any executive actions.

In this context, Rafael La Porta, Florencio Lopez-de-Silanes, Cristian Pop-Eleches, and Andrei Schleifer compare the effects of two distinct types of checks and balances on the power of the parliament and the executive: judicial independence and constitutional review.[33] The authors find that judicial independence matters more for economic freedom while constitutional review matters more for political freedom.

Checks and balances also include those constraints imposed on the state, or those restrictions placed on its operatives and representatives, to avoid overreaching out of the purview of the constitutions or the laws. Barry Weingast clarifies that[34] "Thriving markets require not only an appropriately designed economic system, but a secure political foundation that limits the ability of the state to confiscate wealth. This requires a form of limited government, that is, political institutions that credibly commit the state to honor economic and political rights."

In societies with weak constraints on the executive, returns on economic activities can only be guaranteed if one acquires sufficient political clout. Thus, the lack of constraints on politicians and politically powerful groups implies that there are greater gains from holding power and commanding political authority. This environment leads agents to reallocate resources away from economic activity and into the political arena, which lowers productive investment and economic growth. In this environment, there will also be greater discord between various groups who clamor for power to enjoy these economic perks and perquisites. This may lead to political instability and social turmoil as these groups compete to take control over state affairs. On the other hand, a society where politicians are effectively constrained is expected to allocate more resources for productive activities and to experience less power contest.

In societies with few constraints on the executive, politically influential groups use their power to implement policies to expropriate assets and incomes. These policies will promote their interests on the expense of the entire populace and will lower the incentives to invest. In addition, politicians may also pursue policies to please some lobbies and interest groups to be able to remain in power. These types of policies usually lead to worse economic outcomes.

Governments not only have the power to renege on their commitments, but sometimes have strong incentives to do so. Given these incentives, the rule of law cannot be credible unless there are effective checks on executive discretion and sufficient constraints on the potential transgression of those in the government. Such checks and balances are essential because of the classic time-inconsistency problem.[35] This is a situation in which a policy maker prefers one policy in advance but later enacts another one. Institutions that restrict the ability of authorities to haphazardly change policies are also essential for economic performance. Arbitrary changes in economic policy increase uncertainty. In response to this, investors invest in safeguards against policy changes, demand higher and more immediate return, or not invest at all. This may hinder the accumulation of capital and economic growth.

LEGAL ORIGINS

Besides the maintenance of the rule of law that ensures that these laws are implemented without bias or partiality, the sources of laws and the content of laws also define the quality of institutions. Creating incentives for investment depends to a large extent on the ability to formulate, draft and promulgate laws that have the effect of promoting the economic activities of private agents. Scholars have produced a considerable body of work suggesting that the origin of a country's laws and the source of its legal traditions are highly correlated with a broad range of legal rules and regulations that affect economic outcomes.

The common feature of the dominant legal traditions worldwide is that they have been transplanted, during the era of colonization, from few countries to the remainder of the world.[36] Such transplantation includes the content of laws and legal codes, the legal outlook, the principles and philosophy of the legal system, the organization and the acquired human capital of the judiciary, as well as the expectations of the participants in the processes of law. Following the transplantation process, national laws changed, evolved, and adapted to local circumstances. Economic, political, social, and cultural conditions of every country came to be reflected in their national laws such that no legal systems of any two countries are literally identical. This individualization and domestic adjustment of laws, however, was lacking as the fundamental outlook of the transplanted legal tradition persisted even after independence. The theory of legal origins argues that these systems continue to exert substantial influence on the economic outcomes in these countries. In this context, scholars compare between two primary legal traditions: the English common law and the French civil law.

The common law has spread to, and is practiced in, British colonies and settlements. The common law is formed by appellate judges who establish precedents when handling legal disputes. Unlike statutory law, the body of common law is derived from these judicial precedents rather than statutes. If a similar dispute has been settled in the past, the common law court is bound to follow the reasoning used in the prior case. This principle is known as "stare decisis." If the court finds that the current dispute is fundamentally different from previous cases, and statutes are either silent or ambiguous on the question at hand, judges have the authority to resolve the issue. The common law developed because landed aristocrats and merchants wanted a system of law that would limit the crown's ability to interfere in markets and to expropriate property.

On the other hand, the civil law tradition is the oldest and most widely adopted around the world. Its preeminent feature is that the core principles are codified by legal scholars in statutes that serve as the primary source of law. This legal system traces its origin in the Roman law but is usually identified with the French Revolution and Napoleon's codes. The civil law developed because the revolutionary generation and Napoleon Bonaparte wished to use state power to alter property rights while ensuring that judges do not interfere.

In this context, some scholars examine whether the approach and content of these different legal traditions matter for economic outcomes. For instance, Rafael La Porta, Florencio Lopez-de-Silanes, and Andrei Schleifer argue that differences in legal rules and regulations that matter for economic outcomes are accounted for by legal origins.[37] The authors show that countries that adopted civil law have ineffective governments, less efficient courts, less investor protection, and more regulations compared to those that inherited the common law.

Other studies argue that the way in which the legal tradition was initially transplanted is a more critical determinant of economic outcomes than the adoption of law from a particular legal family. The argument is that for the law to be effective, it must be meaningful in the context in which it is applied. This allows citizens to have an incentive to use the law and to demand institutions that enforce it. Based on this intuition, Daniel Berkowitz, Katharina Pistor, and Jean-Francois Richard explore the effect of legality, or the effectiveness of legal institutions.[38] The argument is that legal effectiveness depends on whether the transplant adapted the law to local conditions or had a population that was familiar with the transplanted law. The authors show that countries that developed legal systems domestically, adapted the transplanted law, and had a population that was familiar with its basic principles have more effective legality than others. The authors also find that the transplanting process has a stronger indirect effect on economic development through its impact on legality, compared to the effect of originating from a particular legal tree.

GOVERNMENT REGULATIONS

Economies that enjoy a higher level of competitiveness are widely believed to grow faster than those that are not. Economic theory proposes that competition is conducive to higher productivity through the reallocation of market shares to efficient firms. In a competitive environment, firms that do not cater to the needs of consumers are replaced by others who do. Competition also provides greater opportunities for entrepreneurs to try out their initiatives, discoveries, and innovative ideas to see whether they can pass the market test. This ensures that those with better products can obtain higher earnings than others, which implies an efficient allocation of resources. Thus, competition drives away inept firms and rewards competent ones. This can be accomplished by the exit of inefficient firms from the market and by the entry of more efficient ones. Countries differ significantly in the way in which they regulate the entry of new firms into the market in terms of the legal stipulations that need to be fulfilled, the cost of fulfilling these prerequisites, and the time needed to satisfy these requirements. Some scholars argue that the legal framework that regulates entry to markets is a critical determinant of economic outcomes.

Markets also fail when the participants commit fraudulent acts or adopt any behavior that goes against the spirit of free competition.[39] Models of coordination failure and capital market imperfections make it clear that strategic government interventions may be needed in some cases to elicit desirable private investment actions. Therefore, market economies are sometimes overseen by regulatory agencies.

In this context, there are two main approaches to the effect of regulation on economic outcomes: the public interest theory and the public choice theory. The public interest theory postulates that regulation is beneficial since unregulated markets experience frequent failures in the form of low-quality products, monopoly power, consumer fraud, and pollution externalities. A government that aims at socially optimal outcomes, and aspires to protect the public, preempts these failures with regulation. In this context, the rules of market entry ensure that new companies must satisfy some standards to engage in transactions with the public. Thus, the government should screen these new entrants with the lens of strict standards of entry to ensure that consumers purchase quality products and are not exposed to fraud by some sellers. In the words of Richard Posner,[40]

> One assumption was that economic markets are extremely fragile and apt to operate very inefficiently (or inequitably) if left alone; the other was that government regulation is virtually costless. With these assumptions, it was very easy to argue that the principal government interventions in the economy—trade union protection, public utility and common carrier regulation, public power and reclamation programs, farm subsidies, occupational licensure, the minimum wage, even tariffs—were simply responses of government to public demands for the rectification of palpable and remediable inefficiencies and inequities in the operation of the free market. Behind each scheme of regulation could be discerned a market imperfection, the existence of which supplied a complete justification for some regulation assumed to operate effectively and without cost.

On the other hand, the public choice theory considers governments less benign and their regulations socially inefficient. According to this view, regulations are imposed primarily to the benefit of incumbent firms. Regulations erect barriers of entry to keep out the competitors and increase the incumbents' profits rather than offer benefits to the public. Incumbent firms are also able to promote regulations that create rents for themselves, since they face lower costs of organizing themselves than the dispersed consumers. In the words of George Stigler,[41] "as a rule, regulation is acquired by the industry and is designed and operated primarily for its benefit." He also adds that

> The state has one basic resource which in pure principle is not shared with even the mightiest of its citizens: the power to coercion. The state can seize money by the only method which is permitted by the laws of a civilized society, by taxation. The state can ordain the physical movements of resources and the economic decisions of households and firms without their consent. These powers provide the possibilities for the utilization of the state by an industry to increase its profitability.

This can occur through regulatory capture which implies that regulatory agencies in charge of acting in the public's interest can be dominated by the industries they are supposed to be regulating. Those special interests allocate their immense resources to secure the policy outcomes they prefer by capturing influence with the members of the regulatory agency. In this case, regulatory agencies act in the best interest of the industries they are supposed to regulate and prioritize the interests of these organizations and groups over the interests of the public. Another strand of the public choice theory argues that regulations are pursued to the benefit of politicians and bureaucrats.[42] Politicians use regulation to generate rents since licenses and permits exist only to bestow on the officials the power to deny them unless a bribe or a campaign contribution is paid. Thus, the regulation of entry enables the regulators to collect bribes from the potential entrants and serves no social purpose.

There are some studies that attempt to test these hypotheses. For instance, Simeon Djankov, Caralee McLiesh, and Rita Maria Ramalho examine the economic consequences of government regulation on starting a business, hiring and firing workers, registering property, securing bank credit, protecting equity investors, enforcing contracts in courts, and closing a business.[43] The authors find that countries with a better regulatory framework experience faster economic growth. Simeon Djankov, Rafael La Porta, Florencio Lopez-de-Silanes, and Andrei Schleifer introduce new data on the number of procedures, and the official time and cost that a start-up must bear before it can operate.[44] The authors show that countries with more regulation of entry have higher corruption, larger unofficial economies, and lower quality of public and private goods.

Other studies explore the relationship between government regulation and social trust, which is shown to be indispensable for economic success. For instance, Phillipe Aghion, Yann Algan, Pierre Cahuc and Andrei Shleifer predict that the lack of trust creates public demand for regulation, whereas regulation in turn discourages the formation of a culture of trust.[45] The authors test this hypothesis and show that distrust in others, distrust in civil servants, and distrust in companies have a positive effect on regulation of entry, regulation of labor market, and the demand for regulation.

NOTES

1. Acemoglu and Robinson. *Why Nations Fail: The Origins of Power, Prosperity, and Poverty* (pp. 30, 31).

2. Ferguson. *The Great Degeneration: How Institutions Decay and Economies Decay* (p. 12).

3. North. *Institutions, Institutional Change, and Economic Performance* (p. 3).

4. North. *Structure and Change in Economic History* (pp. 201–202).

5. Williamson. "Informal Institutions Rule: Institutional Arrangements and Economic Performance." *Public Choice*: 371–387.

6. North. *Institutions, Institutional Change and Economic Performance* (p. 3).

7. Ibid. (p. 107).

8. Ibid. (p. 54).

9. Smith. *Inquiry into the Nature and Causes of the Wealth of Nations* (p. 320).

10. Ferguson. *The Great Degeneration: How Institutions Decay and Economies Decay* (p. 10).

11. Ibid. (p. 21).

12. Ibid. (p. 136).

13. Barro. "Institutions and Growth, an Introductory Essay." *Journal of Economic Growth*: 145–148.

14. Hall and Jones. "Why do Some Countries Produce so much more Output Per Worker than Others?" *Quarterly Journal of Economics*: 83–116.

15. Scully. "The Institutional Framework and Economic Development." *Journal of Political Economy*: 652–662.

16. Knack and Keefer. "Why Don't Poor Countries Catch Up? A Cross National Test of an Institutional Explanation." *Economic Inquiry*: 590–602.

17. Rodrick and Subramanian. "The Primacy of Institutions." *Finance and Development*: 31–34.

18. Tebaldi and Elmslie. "Institutions, Innovation and Economic Growth." *Journal of Economic Development*: 1–27. Tebaldi and Elmslie. "Does Institutional Quality Impact Innovation?" *Applied Economics*: 887–900.

19. Weingast. "The Political Foundations of Democracy and the Rule of Law." *The American Political Science Review*: 245–263.

20. Romer. "Endogenous Technological Change." *Journal of Political Economy*: 71–102.

21. Ibid.

22. Coase, Ronald. 2005. "The Institutional Structure of Production." In the *Handbook of Institutional Economics*, edited by Claude Menard and Mary Shirley. New York: Springer.

23. Knack and Keefer. "Institutions and Economic Performance." *Economics and Politics*: 207–225.

24. Acemoglu and Johnson. "Unbundling Institutions." *Journal of Political Economy*: 949–995.

25. https://www.britannica.com/topic/rule-of-law.

26. Ferguson. *The Great Degeneration: How Institutions Decay and Economies Decay* (p. 84).

27. Pagden. *Worlds at War: The 2,500 Year Struggle between East and West* (p. 21).

28. Djankov, La Porta, Lopez-de-Silanes, and Schleifer. "Courts." *The Quarterly Journal of Economics*: 453–517.

29. Voigt and Feld. "Economic Growth and Judicial Independence: Cross–country Evidence Using a New Set of Indicators." *European Journal of Political Economy*: 497–527.

30. Voigt, Gutmann, and Feld. "Economic Growth and Judicial independence, a Dozen years on." *European Journal of Political Economy*: 197–211.

31. Voigt and Gutmann. "Turning Cheap Talk into Economic Growth: On the Relationship between Property Rights and Judicial Independence." *Journal of Comparative Economics*: 66–73.

32. https://www.britannica.com/topic/checks-and-balances

33. La Porta, Lopez-de-Silanes, Pop-Eleches, and Schleifer. "Judicial Checks and Balances." *Journal of Political Economy*: 445–470.

34. Weingast. "The Economic Role of Political Institutions: Market-Preserving Federalism and Economic Development." *Journal of Law, Economics, & Organization*: 1–31.

35. Kydland and Prescott. "Rules Rather Than Discretion: The Inconsistency of Optimal Plans." *Journal of Political Economy*: 473–491.

36. Watson. *Legal Transplants: An Approach to Comparative Law*. Watson. *Legal Origins and Legal Change*.

37. La Porta, Lopez-de-Silanes, and Schleifer. "The Economic Consequences of Legal Origins." *Journal of Economic Literature*: 285–332.

38. Berkowitz, Pistor, and Richard. "Economic Development, Legality, and the Transplant Effect." *European Economic Review*: 165–195.

39. Rodrick. "Institutions for High-Quality Growth: What They Are and How to Acquire Them." *Studies in Comparative International Development*: 3–31.

40. Posner. "Theories of Economic Regulation." *The Bell Journal of Economics and Management Science*: 335–358.

41. Stigler. "The Theory of Economic Regulation." *The Bell Journal of Economics and Management Science*: 3–21.

42. McChesney. "Rent Extraction and Rent Creation in the Economic Theory of Regulation." *The Journal of Legal Studies*: 101–118. Shleifer and Vishny. "Corruption." *The Quarterly Journal of Economics*: 599–617.

43. Djankov, McLiesh, and Ramalho. "Regulation and Growth." *Economics Letters*: 395–401.

44. Djankov, La Porta, Lopez-de-Silanes, and Schleifer. "The Regulation of Entry." *The Quarterly Journal of Economics*: 1–37.

45. Aghion, Algan, Cahuc and Shleifer. "Regulation and Distrust." *The Quarterly Journal of Economics*: 1015–1049.

Chapter Seven

On the Geographic Origins

Each country is endowed with certain geographic characteristics. Nations have very little say in their climate, their location, their topography, the abundance of natural wealth in their territories, or their exposure to naturally induced disasters. Institutions, however, are not predetermined fate or destiny. Institutions evolve by the determined will of nations or their leaders over a long period of time.

Institutions include the economic arrangements, the political constraints, the social organizations, and the legal codes that a society adopts to shape the interactions of different actors. In this context, political institutions may refer to the quality of the civic administration, the efficacy of the public sector, the extent of corruption in the public domain, the checks on executive power, the constraints on the government, the scope of government accountability, and the involvement of civil society. On the other hand, legal institutions may refer to the rule of law, the state's subordination to the letter and spirit of laws, the protection of property rights, the enforcement of contracts and the fulfillment of contractual obligations, the sophistication of laws and legal codes, the efficiency of the legal framework, the level of fairness in the adjudicative channels, the smoothness of litigation, the extent of judicial independence, resolving bona fide disputes without prohibitive cost or inordinate delay, the legislative environment and the smooth functioning of the courts of justice and tribunals. Finally, economic institutions may refer to the business-friendly atmosphere, the regulatory environment, the extent of red tape and bureaucracy, the degree of investor protection, the level of competition in the marketplace, and a dynamic free market economy.

Given that institutions evolve over time, it is essential to explore their sources. This chapter entertains some ideas on the origins and roots of the institutional structures that we observe worldwide today. Even though institutions are designed by nations and their leaders over time, looking into their origins brings us back to nature's eminent role. This is obvious in a stream of literature that conducts a horse race between geography, institutions, and other factors. Within this literature, some studies argue that the geographic features of a country matter for economic performance only in as much as they affect institutional quality. For instance, William Easterly and Ross Levine examine how the natural endowments can shape the institutions that ultimately impact economic performance.[1] The authors find that latitude and the cultivation of certain crops affect economic development through an institutional index that captures political rights, civil liberties, political stability, government effectiveness, regulatory burden, rule of law, and absence of corruption. The authors also find no evidence that these geographic variables affect national incomes directly other than through the institutional channel. Similarly, Dani Rodrik, Arvind Subramanian, and Francesco Trebbi compare the contributions of institutions, geography, and integration into the global economy in determining the variations in income levels across countries.[2] The authors find that the quality of institutions is more important than the other factors, while the typical geography indicators of a country have a weak direct effect on income but a strong indirect effect by influencing the quality of institutions. This chapter focuses on the geographic origins of current institutional structures.

FROM DISEASE TO INSTITUTIONS

European colonization of a large part of the globe from the fifteenth to the twentieth century provided scholars with some clues as to how the current institutions that we observe today evolved over time. Colonial powers imposed political, economic, social, cultural, and legal institutional structures on their colonies. These systems persisted even after these colonies gained independence. Thus, present day independent polities can be perceived as successors of the colonial era, inheriting its structures, systems, and practices. Thus, the era of colonialism comes close to a natural experiment that can be exploited by scholars to ascertain how various current institutions evolved over time. This is a particularly useful exercise since the institutions were not only largely shaped by the European colonizers, but there were also systematic variations in the institutions that Europeans introduced in these colonies. Therefore, the history of the era of colonialism can serve as a laboratory experiment that can be used to understand the effect of institutions on current economic performance.

In this context, Douglass North proposes that colonial powers created institutions that mirrored their own.[3] According to this argument, Spain transplanted in its new world colonies its system of centralized government, large bureaucracy, and restricted property rights. On the other hand, England brought its decentralized government and common law to its colonies in the new world. As a result, the United States and Canada were better positioned to curb state power, create more competitive markets, and industrialize faster than Latin America. This explanation, however, fails to explain why the English influence failed to benefit other British colonies around the world. This claim also falls short of explaining why Spain and England converged over time to a greater extent than their former colonies. These shortcomings, however, opened the door for other explanations about the possible connections between colonialism and current institutions that fare better with real world experiences. These explanations cannot evade the obvious contribution of geography.

Colonial Origins

Daron Acemoglu, Simon Johnson, and James Robinson assert that there were different types of colonial practices and policies, which produced distinct sets of institutions. There was "settler colonialism" when Europeans settled in their colonies, as opposed to "exploitation colonialism" in which Europeans extracted resources and exploited their colonies without permanent settlement.

Thus, the presence or absence of European settlers was a critical factor in the form of colonialism that the subjugated countries had to endure. The brand of colonialism that prevailed was ultimately predicated on the feasibility of settlement, which depended upon the disease environment that determined the ability of Europeans to survive in these far lands. Historians show that the European public was informed of settler mortality in the colonies. Philip Curtin documents how the press informed the public of mortality rates and the likelihood of survival in the colonies.[4] Curtin introduces his *Death by Migration: Europe's Encounter with the Tropical World in the Nineteenth Century* by stating that[5]

> From the beginning of European trade and conquest overseas, Europeans have known they died from the effect of the strange "climate." Later, they came to understand that it was disease, not climate, that killed, but the fact remained that every trading voyage, every military expedition beyond Europe, had its price in European lives lost. For European soldiers in the tropics at the beginning of the nineteenth century, this added cost in deaths from disease—the "relocation cost"—meant a death rate at least twice that of soldiers who stayed home.

Mortality in the colonies, in these cases, depended upon the prevalence of diseases such as Malaria. Thus, settler mortality influenced the decision to settle. In colonies where the early settlers faced substantial death prospects, there would be less incentive for new settlers to join. In colonies where early settlers did not face such hazards, they would be tempted to settle.

We also observe that colonies where Europeans did not settle permanently are today substantially poorer than those where they settled. The explanation is that settlement was a core determinant of early institutions. In colonies where the disease environment was not favorable to European settlement, European powers set up "extractive institutions." The main purpose of this institutional structure was to extract slaves and valuable commodities from the colony and to transfer them to the metropole. These institutions did not introduce protection of private property or constraints against expropriation. Thus, colonial powers set up authoritarian and absolutist states to solidify their control and to facilitate their plunder.

On the other hand, many Europeans settled permanently in several colonies which the historian Alfred Crosby calls the[6] "Neo-Europes." As Europeans settled in large numbers in these colonies, they wanted to proclaim the rights that they enjoyed in their homelands. In these cases, settlers tried to replicate those European institutions that emphasize protection of private property and checks on executive power. Therefore, their life in settler colonies was mod-eled after their home country. In this context, Donald Denoon argues that set-tler colonies had representative institutions which promoted freedom, law and order, protection of property and the ability to accumulate wealth by engaging in trade.[7] When the establishment of European institutions did not develop naturally, the settlers fought for them. An example is the American war of independence which was initiated by delegates from the British American colonies against Great Britain over their objection to the crown's taxation policies and lack of colonial representation.

These early institutions established by colonial powers or by European settlers persisted till the present day to form the basis of current institutions in these countries.[8] There are several factors that led to this institutional per-sistence. Setting up institutions that place checks on the executive and enforce protection of property is costly.[9] If the costs of creating these institutions have been sunk by the colonial powers, then it may not be worth the elite to switch to extractive institutions after independence. In contrast, when the elite inherit extractive institutions, they will likely opt to exploit the existing system to their own benefit. Thus, the small elite, to whom European powers delegated the administration of the state, had a greater incentive to continue being extractive to secure a large share of the economic and political pie.

Building on this intuition, Daron Acemoglu, Simon Johnson, and James Robinson examine the effect of institutions, captured by the protection against expropriation, on economic performance.[10] The authors find that there is a high correlation between settler mortality rates faced by soldiers, bish-ops, and sailors in the colonies and European settlement; between European settlement and early institutions; and between early institutions and current ones. The authors estimate large effects of institutions on income per capita, which are robust to the inclusion of latitude, climate, current disease environment, culture, natural endowments, soil quality, ethnolinguistic structure, and current racial composition. The implication is that climatic factors are pertinent only in as far as they affect institutions. However, this also means that we cannot explain the institutional structures that we observe without acknowledging the part that geography played in shaping them.

Other scholars argue that we are putting the institutional cart before the human capital horse. Their contribution offers an alternative to the idea that different institutions set by colonial powers explain the variations in living standards today. Instead, these studies suggest that Europeans brought primarily human capital to their colonies. In places where they brought more human capital, the economy flourished and society was organized differently. In this context, Edward Glaeser, Rafael la Porta, Florencio Lopez-de-Silanes, and Andrei Shleifer compare the effect of institutions and human capital on economic growth.[11] The authors find that human capital is a more basic source of economic growth than institutional quality. In response, Daron Acemoglu, Francisco Gallego, and James Robinson show that the impact of institutions on economic performance is robust, and that there is no support for the view that differences in human capital endowments of early European colonists have been a critical factor in the subsequent institutional development of former colonies.[12]

Reversal of Fortune

Daron Acemoglu, Simon Johnson, and James Robinson also observe that among countries colonized during the past 500 years, those that were more prosperous in the year 1500 C.E. are poorer today. For example, the Mughals in India, the Ottomans in the Middle East, and the Aztecs and Incas in the Americas were some of the wealthiest civilizations in 1500 C.E. Today, the countries that occupy these areas are underdeveloped. On the other hand, the communities that inhabited what is now known as the United States, Canada, Australia, and New Zealand were less developed. Today these countries are more advanced than the countries now occupying the territories of the older civilizations.

The explanation, in their opinion, is that there are two types of institutions that were transplanted by European imperial powers in their colonies and dominions. The first is referred to as "institutions of private property," and the other is "extractive institutions." The former are institutions ensuring secure property for a broad cross section of society. The latter are institutions where a large portion of the population encounters expropriation by the government, its agents, and the ruling elite.

European colonial powers developed institutions of private property in previously poor areas, and extractive institutions in formerly prosperous places. The cause of this institutional reversal is that the then poor areas were sparsely inhabited. This tempted and enabled Europeans to settle in large numbers. As they themselves were affected by these institutions, the European settlers demanded rights and protections similar to, or even better than, those they enjoyed in their homeland.

In the then wealthier areas where there was a large population and wide prosperity, extractive institutions were more profitable for the colonial powers. In these cases, high population density provided a supply of natives who could be forced to work in mining and plantations. For example, the presence of abundant Amerindian labor in Meso-America was conducive to the establishment of forced labor systems.[13] Similarly, the high population density in certain areas in Africa created a profit opportunity for slave traders from supplying labor to American plantations. Furthermore, in these densely populated areas there was also an existing system of tax administration or tribute. The large population made it profitable for Europeans to take control of these systems and to continue to levy hefty taxes on the inhabitants. These differences in population density are known to have been influenced by geographic conditions, to a large extent, as discussed earlier.

This reversal of institutions laid the seeds for the reversal of fortune. This is because the spread of industrialization entailed the participation of a broad cross section of society such as the small landlords, the middle class, and the entrepreneurs. The industrial revolution, therefore, created considerable advantages for societies with institutions of private property. Building on this intuition, Daron Acemoglu, Simon Johnson, and James Robinson attempt to provide evidence for this reversal of fortune.[14] To do so, the authors show a negative relationship between historical indicators of economic development, the urbanization rates and population density in 1500 C.E., and current income per capita and institutional quality. The authors also show that the quality of current institutions, predicted by urbanization rates and population density, has a positive association with current income.

On the other hand, Areendam Chanda, Justin Cook, and Loius Putterman examine the reversal of fortune using data on the origin of today's populations and the indicators for the level of economic development in 1500 C.E. used by the previous study.[15] The authors confirm a reversal of fortune for colonized countries as territories but find persistence of fortune for people and their descendants. The authors find that "for nations thought of as groups of people sharing linguistic and other features, and for their descendants, persistence rather than reversal is the rule."

FROM COASTS TO INSTITUTIONS

Some studies argue that the expansion of trade, and the immense wealth it created, contributed to the types of institutions developed in the old world. Between 1500 C.E. and 1800 C.E., Western Europe experienced an unprecedented period of sustained economic expansion especially in coastal countries with access to the Atlantic trade. Daron Acemoglu, Simon Johnson, and James Robinson argue that the Atlantic trade contributed to the growth of Western Europe, not only through its direct economic effects but also indirectly by inducing fundamental institutional change.

Their argument is that in countries where institutions placed constraints on the power of the monarchy before 1500 C.E., the Atlantic trade strengthened the traders who were able to enact further changes in the institutional structure to extend property rights and to allow free entry into profitable businesses. Thus, additional constraints on royal powers and prerogatives were imposed when groups that favored them became sufficiently powerful. In these countries, the expansion in Atlantic trade enriched merchants and strengthened commercial interests outside the royal circle and enabled them to introduce the institutional reforms that are beneficial to them. With their newly acquired powers, they took advantage of the opportunities offered by the Atlantic trade and fueled the growth that these countries enjoyed. These changes did not occur in countries with initial absolutist institutions. In these countries, the monarchy and the allied elite were the main beneficiaries of the early profits from the Atlantic trade. In this case, groups favoring change in political governance did not become powerful enough to induce them.

Based on this intuition, Daron Acemoglu, Simon Johnson and James Robinson find that the Atlantic trade contributed to European growth through an indirect institutional channel in addition to its direct effects.[16] The authors show that European countries that had access to the Atlantic trade, and with better initial institutions, had a higher portion of the population living in urban areas, higher income per capita, and more constraints on the executive.

FROM CROPS TO INSTITUTIONS

Stanley Engerman and Kenneth Sokoloff provide another perspective on the evolution of institutions in a series of studies that emphasize the contribution of the geographic factors.[17] Their argument is that soil and climate in the new world predisposed them to different degrees of inequality in wealth, human capital, and political power. These differences in inequality had profound and enduring effects on economic development because they contributed to systematic differences in the way institutions evolved. The quality of soil and climate in different areas allow for the cultivation of different crops. Some studies suggest that growing grains is better for institutional development than tropical cash crops. These differences can be seen between the northern and southern parts of the western hemisphere.

For example, climate and soil in the West Indies and parts of South America are more amenable to certain crops and commodities, such as sugar cane, tobacco, and coffee. These staple crops can be efficiently produced in large scale plantations featuring the use of slaves or indigenous labor. Therefore, the population of these countries came to be inhabited by slaves of African descent and Europeans who were lured by the opportunities to earn exceptionally high incomes from producing these valuable commodities. The extreme disparities in human capital between these two groups contributed to a high level of inequality. This inequality in wealth continued even after the abolition of slavery and was associated with a concentration of power in the hands of the plantation owners, landlords and mining interests. In this context, the elite created institutions that protected their power with limited suffrage. Thus, political institutions were less democratic, only the elite had access to economic opportunities, and investments in public goods and infrastructure were limited. In these cases, the elite were both inclined and able to establish systems that ensured them a disproportionate share of power and greater access to economic opportunities.

In contrast, soil and climate in North America were more amenable to the cultivation of wheat and grains. These types of crops can grow on smaller family farms with laborers of European descent who had comparably high levels of human capital. This promoted the growth of a broad middle class in which power and wealth were more equally distributed. In these societies, more democratic modes of governance were introduced, more institutions that offered broader access to economic opportunities evolved, and more investment in public goods and infrastructure was conducted. In these cases, the elite were either less inclined or less able to institutionalize systems that advantage them on the expense of others.

To summarize these historical trends, David Landes states in his book *The Unbound Prometheus* that[18]

> In some areas (notably Spanish America), the native was impressed into service; in others (the West Indies and the southern colonies of British North America), he proved unwilling or unable to do the work required, and the colonists killed him or drove him off and brought in black slaves from Africa to take his place. Farther north, the settlers did their own work, establishing in the New World societies that were in many respects replicas of what they had known at home.

FROM CLIMATE TO INSTITUTIONS

There were also some attempts to find an association between climate, civilization, colonialism, and slavery. For instance, Ellsworth Huntington attempts to propose a connection between climate and social institutions.[19] Huntington posits that the "nature of a nation's religious faith, its form of government, its social organization, its ease of intercourse with other nations, and various other conditions play a fundamental part in the distribution of civilization. Yet each is conditioned by the degree of energy possessed by a people. Energy, in turn, seems to depend upon climate, and thus climate becomes an essential element in determining the status of civilization."

Charles-Louis de Secondat, known as Baron de Montesquieu, also proposed that there is a connection between climate, biology, human behavior, and various social institutions. Montesquieu claims that people in colder climates are generally more vigorous, more disciplined, and more determined while people in hotter environments are by nature inactive and lethargic.[20] These prejudicial views on the climatic-induced differences in temperament led Montesquieu to argue that those in favorable climates can dominate those who are not. This explains the subjugation of the inhabitants of warmer climates through slavery and colonization. In a similar vein, David Landes states that[21] "It is no accident that slave labor has historically been associated with tropical and semitropical climes." He proposes that slavery can be explained by the fact that Europeans, who are not adapted to the discomfort of heat, were unable to work in colonial plantations in the tropics. Thus, these plantation owners depended on slaves to do the work.

FROM SOIL TO INSTITUTIONS

Institutions are also associated with the characteristics of the soil that, in turn, determine the nature of agricultural practices. For instance, Karl Wittfogel introduces the controversial concept of Oriental Despotism.[22] The argument is that riverine nations dependent on irrigation agriculture become highly stratified hydraulic societies. This is because river valleys with highly alluvial soils provide the ideal environment for irrigation agriculture. This was carried out on a scale that necessitated a high level of organization, a refined division of labor, a sophisticated administration of scarce water, and supervision of workers by the elite. Thus, Wittfogel's thesis proposes a causal connection between the presence of alluvial soils, arid river valleys, agricultural hydraulic technology, and institutions. In his *Oriental Despotism:A Comparative Study of Total Power*, Wittfogel states that the "prime necessity of an economical and common use of water, which, in the Occident, drove private enterprise to voluntary association . . . necessitated in the Orient . . . the interference of the centralizing power of Government." Lon Fuller in his exposition of Wittfogel's thesis states that[23]

> as one surveys the history of mankind and examines the archeological evidence from prehistoric times, one will find that irrigation is normally accompanied by tyranny. If we were to discover, for example, in some hitherto unexplored area of the world the remains of the dams, canals, and conduits essential for an agriculture based on irrigation, we could conclude with considerable assurance that the political system of the people inhabiting that area was one of despotism.

Indeed, there is a plethora of examples of authoritarian states that emanated along the Yangtze and Yellow rivers, in the Indus valley, on the banks of the Nile, and on the shores of the Euphrates and Tigris. Conversely, European farmers who had access to a steady supply of rainfall were not completely reliant on a water controlling tyrant. Thus, these distinct agricultural environments may offer an explanation to the differences we observe today in political and economic institutions.

FROM LANDSCAPE TO INSTITUTIONS

Some scholars argue that the topographic features of a country can influence the quality of its institutions. For instance, Eric Jones argues that the "European miracle" could be attributed to the fact that the continent is naturally fragmented by its mountains that act as barriers between its areas, its rivers that cut through its land, and its indented coastline with lots of peninsulas. These topographic features of the continent meant that no single core civilization could emerge, and no one power was sufficiently great to form an empire as occurred in the Orient.

Europe's fragmentation would eventually prove advantageous since it fostered competition between numerous small states. Eric Jones suggests that[24] "Against the economies of scale that large empires could offer, the decentralization of Europe's states-system offered flexibility and a family of experiments in government decision-making." Niall Ferguson also argues that[25] "The main institutional difference between the west and the east of Eurasia after 1500, however, was that networks in the west were relatively freer from hierarchical dominance than those in the east. No monolithic empire occurred in the west; multiple and often weak principalities prevailed."

In this context, if someone with a specific venture was not successful in one European country, that pioneer could always try to convince some other sovereign of the utility of the undertaking. This strategy could not be employed in the orient. An often-cited example is the sudden decision in 1433 C.E. by a Ming emperor to abandon China's ambitious sea-faring expeditions.[26] From 1405 C.E. to 1433 C.E., General Zheng He led enormous sailing vessels in seven ocean voyages that were unparalleled at the time. The abrupt ruling by the Ming court put an end to Chinese exploratory ambitions. Louise Levathes wrote in her *When China Ruled the Seas: The Treasure Fleet of the Dragon Throne, 1405–1433* that[27]

> China could have become the great colonial power, a hundred years before the great age of European exploration and expansion. But China did not. Shortly after the last voyage of the treasure fleet, the Chinese emperor forbade overseas travel and stopped all building and repair of oceangoing junks. Disobedient merchants and seamen were killed. Within a hundred years the greatest navy the world had ever known willed itself into extinction.

Only some decades later, the Genovese Christopher Columbus was able to convince the Spanish court to finance an expedition to take the maritime initiative from the Portuguese. Thus, the riches of the new world became spoils of the Europeans rather than the Chinese.

NOTES

1. Easterly and Levine. "Tropics, Germs and Crops: How Endowments Influence Economic Development." *Journal of Monetary Economics*: 3–39.
2. Rodrick, Subramanian, and Trebbi. "Institutions Rule: The Primacy of Institutions over Geography and Integration in Economic Development." *Journal of Economic Growth*: 131–165.
3. North. *Institutions, Institutional Change, and Economic Performance*.
4. Curtin. *Disease and Empire: The Health of European Troops in the Conquest of Africa*. Curtin. *Death by Migration: Europe's Encounter with the Tropical World in the Nineteenth Century*.
5. Curtin. *Death by Migration: Europe's Encounter with the Tropical World in the Nineteenth Century*.
6. Crosby. *Ecological Imperialism: The Biological Expansion of Europe, 900–1900*.
7. Denoon. *Settler Capitalism: The Dynamics of Dependent Development in the Southern Hemisphere*.
8. Acemoglu and Robinson. "De Facto Political Power and Institutional Persistence." *American Economic Review*: 325–330. Acemoglu and Robinson. "The Persistence and Change of Institutions in the Americas." *Southern Economic Journal*: 282–299.
9. Acemoglu and Verdier. "Property Rights, Corruption and the Allocation of Talent: A General Equilibrium Approach." *The Economic Journal*: 1381–1403. Acemoglu and Verdier. "The Choice between Market Failures and Corruption."

The American Economic Review: 194–211. Acemoglu, Robinson, and Verdier. "Asymmetric Growth and Institutions in an Interdependent World." *Journal of Political Economy*: 1245–1305.

10. Acemoglu, Johnson, and Robinson. "The Colonial Origins of Comparative Development: An Empirical Investigation." *The American Economic Review*: 1369–1401.

11. Glaeser, La Porta, Lopez-de-Salinas, and Schleifer. "Do Institutions Cause Growth." *Journal of Economic Growth*: 271–303.

12. Acemoglu, Gallego, and Robinson. "Institutions, Human Capital and Development." *Annual Reviews of Economics*: 875–912.

13. The Encomienda for example was a labor system applied during the Spanish colonization of the Americas. It rewarded conquerors with the labor of groups of subjected people. Conquered peoples were considered vassals of the Spanish crown which awarded an encomienda as a grant to an individual. The grants were a monopoly on the labor of particular groups of Indians, held by the grant holder, the encomendero, and his descendants.

14. Acemoglu, Johnson, and Robinson. "Reversal of Fortune: Geography and Institutions in the Making of the Modern World Income Distribution." *The Quarterly Journal of Economics*: 1231–1294.

15. Chanda, Cook, and Putterman. "Persistence of Fortune: Accounting for Population Movements, There Was No Post-Columbian Reversal." *American Economic Journal: Macroeconomics*: 1–28.

16. Acemoglu, Johnson, and Robinson. "The Rise of Europe: Atlantic Trade, Institutional Change, and Economic Growth." *The American Economic Review*: 545–579.

17. Engerman and Sokoloff. "Factor Endowments, Inequality, and Paths of Development among New World Economies." National Bureau of Economic Research Working Paper 9259. Engerman and Sokoloff. "Colonialism, Inequality, and Long Run Paths of Development." National Bureau of Economic Research Working Paper 11057. Engerman and Sokoloff. "Institutions, Factor Endowments, and Paths of Development in the New World." *Journal of Economic Perspectives*: 217–232. Engerman and Sokoloff. "Five Hundred Years of European Colonization: Inequality and Paths of Development." In *Settler Economies in World History*, edited by Christopher Lloyd, Jakob Metzer, and Richard Sutch. Netherlands: BRILL.

18. Landes. *The Unbound Prometheus: Technological Change and Industrial Development in Western Europe from 1750 to the Present* (p. 36).

19. Ellsworth. *Civilization and Climate* (p. 207).

20. de Montesquieu. *The Spirit of the Laws*.

21. Landes. *The Wealth and Poverty of Nations: Why Some Are So Rich and Some So Poor* (p. 7).

22. Wittfogel. *Oriental Despotism: A Comparative Study of Total Power*.

23. Fuller. "Irrigation and Tyranny." *Stanford Law Review*: 1021–1042.

24. Jones. *The European Miracle: Environments, Economies and Geopolitics in the History of Europe and Asia* (p. 245).

25. Fergusson. *The Square and the Tower* (p. 65).

26. Levathes. *When China Ruled the Seas: The Treasure Fleet of the Dragon Throne, 1405–1433.*

27. Ibid. (p. 20).

Chapter Eight

Sand or Grease

POWER CORRUPTS AND CORRUPTION EMPOWERS

Corruption sometimes acts as a catalyst for rebellion by people to demand an end to this pernicious practice by their rulers, as was the case in the Arab spring for example. One day before the octogenarian President of Egypt, Mubarak, was ousted from power during the events of the Arab Spring, *Foreign Policy* published a piece titled "Mubarak's $70 billion nest egg." The writer, Steven Cook, states in the article that[1]

> It's hard to see why Hosni Mubarak is so reticent to leave office—not least because he wouldn't exactly be retiring to a life of austerity. According to a report first published in Al Khabar, the family fortune that would await the departing president could amount to as much as $70 billion. How on earth did the Egyptian president get so rich? (For some perspective: Egypt's GDP is only slightly more than twice that amount, $188 billion.) The answer is a combination of corruption and business deals forged with foreign investors and businessmen in Egypt.

Cook also expresses his opinion on the causes of the rebellion on the banks of the Nile in another article where he writes that[2] "Certainly, there was a perception—and I think quite rightly—that corruption in the late-Mubarak period had run rampant and that people needed to be held accountable for what many Egyptians saw as absconding with national resources." Thus, corruption can incite fundamental changes in societies who have the misfortune to suffer from this practice. This chapter discusses the literature on the economic consequences of corruption as a component of the quality of institutions.

Corruption is the use of public office for private gain. Thus, it is a form of dishonesty by someone entrusted with a position of authority often to

99

acquire personal benefit. Corruption occurs when a public officer, or a government agent, acts in an official capacity fraudulently for pure self-interest. Corruption is a persistent feature of societies and takes various forms, such as bribery, fraud, extortion, malfeasance, profiteering, cronyism, favoritism, nepotism, and others. Corruption also occurs at various levels, as it can be committed by a clerk in a public office, by the leader of a country, or by anyone in between. Petty corruption occurs at the implementation end of public services, especially in registration offices, licensing boards, and permit stations. Grand corruption occurs at the highest levels of governance in a way that entails substantial subversion of the political, legal, and economic systems to satisfy specific interests. Bernard Shaw said that "Power does not corrupt men; fools, however, if they get into a position of power, corrupt power."

The common wisdom is that corruption, at any level, tarnishes the quality of institutions and accordingly distorts economic outcomes. However, some scholars beg to differ and argue that there could be a favorable effect of corruption that cannot be ignored. The former view argues that corruption sands the wheels of the administration by creating barriers and obstacles to transactions. The latter counterintuitive perspective posits that corruption can grease the wheels of an otherwise inefficient bureaucratic structure. This chapter is an exposition of the debate on whether corruption sands or greases the wheels of the administration.

Before delving into its economic consequences, it is worth exploring the sources of corruption especially its geographic origins. In this context, scholars observe that tropical countries suffer from a combination of intense corruption and abject poverty while temperate countries rank better in the list of least corrupt economies. Thus, some studies attempt to explore the connection between the tropical climate and corrupt practices. These studies point our attention to the fact that the intensity of ultraviolet radiation is highly correlated with latitude. This implies that tropical countries have a higher level of ultraviolet radiation which is associated with eye diseases, including cataracts, that can lead to impaired vision and blindness. This impacts the pattern of expected work-life for skilled workers since visual acuity is of paramount importance for skill-intensive occupations. In this context, skilled workers in tropical countries face a permanent threat of contracting eye diseases that shortens their work-life expectancy.

On the other hand, the incentives for engaging in corrupt practices critically depend on the duration of work-life. Specifically, officials are more likely to misappropriate public funds for private gain when their window of opportunity is short. In this context, Filipe Campante, Davin Chor, and Quoc-Anh Do argue that lucrative projects often take time to deliver rents unless the incumbent is dislodged from office.[3] The authors argue that an incumbent's security of tenure should, thus, be critical in determining his willingness and ability to extract these rents. An incumbent who is unstable finds it optimal to appropriate today instead of waiting into the uncertain future with the possibility of not being in power. The authors show that greater instability leads the incumbent to embezzle more during his short window of opportunity.

The threat of eye diseases, therefore, increases the frequency of corrupt behavior by shortening the official's horizon. Building on this intuition, Trung Vu explores the connection between the tropics and corruption.[4] The author finds support for the positive association between ultraviolet radiation and corruption. Using individual-level data from the World Values Survey, the author provides evidence that exposure to ultraviolet radiation is associated with higher surveyed respondents' tolerance toward corrupt activities.

Other studies argue that corrupt practices flourish with a high level of loyalty to one's group in a heterogeneous environment with diverse groups. For instance, some scholars posit that ethnolinguistic diversity is associated with worse corruption, as bureaucrats favor their ethnolinguistic group, officials provide more services to their co-ethnics, and the public recruitment is tilted toward selecting those from the same ethnolinguistic background. As will be discussed later in more detail, ethnolinguistic diversity has geographic origins. This is because mobility was curbed in the tropical zone due to the spread of diseases and the lack of domesticated animals for transportation. This caused isolation of societies, delineation of ethnic homelands, and emergence of ethnic identities. Thus, corruption has an indirect geographic origin through ethnolinguistic diversity.

Other studies argue that corruption tends to be higher in cultures that encourage individuals to prioritize loyalty toward one's social group, or collectivist societies versus individualistic ones. For instance, Nina Mazar and Pankaj Aggarwal examine the factors behind the differences in the propensity to bribe.[5] The study provides evidence that collectivism is associated with a higher propensity to offer bribes to international business partners. The authors argue that this is mediated by "collectivists' lower perceived responsibility for their own actions," and therefore feeling less guilty about offering a bribe. In another contribution that links corruption to collectivism, Jeanet Bentzen estimates the effect of corruption on economic development.[6] The author argues that corruption tends to be higher in cultures that encourage individuals to prioritize loyalty toward one's social group in addition to those with individuals who prefer large distances between themselves and people in power.[7] These societies end up being more hierarchical and highly corrupt. The author provides evidence that corruption, predicted by these cultural traits of collectivism and power distance, exerts an adverse effect on productivity.

Collectivism, on the other hand, is influenced by geographic factors. For instance, some studies argue that the need to collaborate within groups in farming communities facing the risk of rainfall fluctuations favored the emergence of a collectivist culture. These collectivist attitudes increased cohesiveness and facilitated the coordination of agricultural production. Thus, corruption has another indirect geographic origin through collectivist cultures.

SAND THE WHEELS

According to some, corruption creates rather than corrects inefficiencies. This is because corruption adversely affects the provision of public goods, the quality of public administration, the allocation of resources, the stability of the political scene, the distribution of income, the level of investment in physical capital and the accumulation of human capital.

For instance, corrupt officials have an incentive to cause administrative delays to be able to solicit bribes to speed up the bureaucratic procedures. This is particularly the case when the administration is made of a succession of decision centers. In this case, civil servants at each stage have some capacity to slow down the process of approval of a project, the conferral of a license, or the bestowal of a permit. This creates a situation where those in urgent need of a service will have to find alternative ways to sidestep the intentionally complicated procedures and to expedite the process through the payment of bribes.

Corrupt officials also have an incentive to create distortions in the economy to preserve the flow of their illegal source of income.[8] For instance, a civil servant has an incentive to control the provision of a public service and to decide to whom that service is allocated in exchange for a bribe. Thus, creating artificial bottlenecks by public officials can increase their ability to collect bribes.

In a corrupt environment, public officials are appointed based on nepotism, cronyism, favoritism, or blatant bribe payments. Thus, aspects of experience and qualification are discarded in the public recruitment process. This lowers the average quality and productivity of civil servants. Similarly, corrupt civil servants have the incentive to limit access to instrumental official positions to retain the rent from corruption for themselves.

Corruption may also affect skill acquisition and cause a misallocation of talents.[9] By distorting the tax administration, due to higher levels of tax evasion, corruption diminishes the funds available for the public provision of education and health.[10] In addition, corruption deflects public funds toward outlays that allow for the collection of undetected bribes, which typically do not include spending on education and health.[11] These factors limit the ability of the state to improve educational attainment and overall health conditions which proves detrimental to long run economic growth.[12] In addition, the pace of technological progress is predicated on the pool of talented individuals in the innovation sector. Corruption lures talents away from the innovation sector to the rent-seeking one by the supplementary illegal but lucrative source of income. On the other hand, innovators are also adversely affected by corruption as they have to secure licenses and permits to start, whereas established producers do not. All these factors prove so costly to innovation, allocation of talent and economic growth.[13]

Corruption can also affect the amount and the allocation of public expenditure. Corrupt officials seek to optimize their extraction potential to increase their rents either by underreporting available public funds or by channeling such funds into private bank accounts. This could potentially lower public expenditure on education and health.

Corruption also renders some officials incapable or unwilling to promote public welfare.[14] This is because those projects that promise large side-payments with lower detection are preferred by corrupt officials to those that benefit the public at large. In this case, corruption tilts the decision-making process in favor of projects that promise more for the pockets of the officials in charge, on the expense of those enterprises that enhance social welfare. An example would be the "White Elephant Projects" which are extremely expensive projects with little or no output or return.

A corrupt climate determines the type of firms to be awarded a project, and the quality of their product. In this environment, well-connected contractors and those willing to pay bribes are preferred to those providing the best quality product. Thus, a firm may be able to pay the highest bribe because it compromises on the quality of the items it will produce once it earns the license or the permit. Along the lines of this intuition, Da-Hsiang Donald Lien explores allocation inefficiencies associated with corrupt practices.[15] The author considers the case in which two firms compete to be awarded a project through bribery of a corrupt public official. The author shows that the possibility of inefficient allocation increases as the extent of corruption intensifies.

Corruption can also cause price inflation.[16] Corrupt activities can take the form of embezzlement of public funds which does not leave the government with sufficient liquidity to finance its expenditures. Accordingly, the government is forced to depend on other sources of income such as seigniorage which causes inflation. This acts as a tax on consumption and investment which, in turn, decreases capital accumulation and economic growth.

Corruption undermines the legitimacy of the political establishment as it fuels perceptions of impropriety in wealth accumulation. This can cause political instability when the perceived lack of distributive justice instigates the destitute to engage in defiant acts against those who accumulated wealth through corrupt means. Political instability, as can be seen in a later chapter, has serious economic repercussions. In this context, Pak Hung Mo finds that corruption hinders economic growth through the channel of political instability, which accounts for about 53 percent of the total effect, in addition to its adverse effect on the level of human capital and the share of private investment.[17]

Some studies argue that corruption can increase the level of income inequality. In this context, corruption can enrich those officials who practice it. The benefits of corruption are more likely to accrue to the well-connected, and wealth is likely to be accumulated by those in positions of power compared to others. Corruption also creates incentives for investment in capital-intensive projects and not in labor-intensive ones. Such a bias increases income inequality as it deprives workers of employment opportunities. Corruption can also lead to tax evasion, poor tax administration, and exemptions that disproportionately favor the well-connected and the wealthy. This can diminish the tax base and lower the funding available for the public provision of education and health which affects the poor disproportionately. In this context, Hamid Davoodi, Sanjeev Gupta, and Rosa Alonso-Terme provide evidence that corruption increases income inequality and poverty.[18] The authors find that an increase of one standard deviation in corruption increases the Gini Coefficient by about 11 points. Kwabena Gyimah-Brempong uses data from African countries to investigate the effects of corruption on economic growth and income distribution.[19] The author finds that corruption decreases economic growth but is positively correlated with income inequality. The author concludes that these combined effects suggest that corruption hurts the poor in African countries.

Finally, corruption can affect international trade and foreign investment. Barriers on trade, in the form of quotas or licenses, provide public officials substantial sources of additional income. This can create incentives for public officials to impose those barriers which can hinder trade flows and commercial exchange. Moreover, foreign entrants often lack familiarity with local customs and procedural intricacies needed to keep bribe expenses to a minimum. This may lower the amount of foreign investment that can be attracted by a country riddled with corruption. In this context, Shang-Jin Wei finds that a higher tax rate on multinational corporations, or a higher level of corruption in the host country, lowers foreign direct investment.[20] Andrzej Cieslik and Łukasz Goczek formulate a model that predicts that corruption adversely affects the stock of international investment in the host country.[21] The authors find that lack of corruption has a statistically significant positive effect on economic growth and the investment ratio.

Given these arguments, several studies examine empirically the effect of corruption on economic performance, identify the channels through which corruption affects the economy, and examine whether the effect of corruption differs in different countries. For instance, Paolo Mauro wrote a seminal paper that examines the effect of corruption on economic growth.[22] The author uses subjective indices of the level of corruption, the extent of red tape, the quality of bureaucracy, the efficiency of the judiciary, and political stability for a cross section of countries. The author argues that ethnolinguistic diversity is associated with worse corruption, as bureaucrats favor their ethnolinguistic group. The analysis shows that corruption, predicted by ethnolinguistic fractionalization, decreases investment and economic growth. In another contribution, Paolo Mauro examines whether predatory behavior by corrupt politicians distorts the composition of government expenditure.[23] The author shows that corrupt officials find it easier to collect bribes on certain expenditure items compared to others that do not promise as many lucrative opportunities, such as public education. Thus, corruption lowers government spending on educational attainment which is crucial for economic growth.

Andrew Hodge, Sriram Shankar, Dasari Prasada Rao, and Alan Duhs find that corruption hinders economic growth through its adverse effects on investment in physical capital, political stability, and accumulation of human capital, but enhances economic growth by decreasing government consumption and increasing trade openness.[24] Combining these channels, an overall negative effect of corruption on growth is estimated by the authors. Toke Aidt shows that there is no correlation between an index of firms' actual experience with corruption and economic growth.[25] Instead, the author finds a negative correlation between corruption and wealth per capita growth. Some scholars argue that it is not the extent of corruption as much as its predictability that matters for economic outcomes. For instance, Edgardo Campos, Donald Lien, and Sanjay Pradhan focus on the effect of predictability of corruption, which is the degree to which those seeking favors from public officials are confident that they will be able to obtain them if they pay bribes.[26] The authors find that corrupt practices that are more predictable have less of an adverse effect on investment.

Some studies also suggest that the effect of corruption on the economy is predicated on the quality of political institutions and democratic governance. In this context, centralized corruption lowers income less than decentralized corruption because of the "tragedy of the commons."[27] A corrupt official wants to extract the highest possible bribe without driving a firm out of business. If corruption is decentralized with numerous officials independently demanding bribes, these bureaucrats will set the total bribe amount too high which may drive firms out of business. Given that democracies feature less centralized concentration of power, combating corruption should have greater growth effects in democracies.

Given the view that the effect of corruption depends on the quality of institutions, Toke Aidt, Jayasri Dutta, and Vania Senac argue that the effect of corruption on economic growth depends on the quality of political institutions.[28] The authors find that corruption has a substantial adverse effect on economic growth only in countries with high quality political institutions. Andreas Assiotis and Kevin Sylwester explore whether the association between corruption and economic outcomes depends on the level of democracy.[29] The authors find that a decrease in corruption increases economic growth more in authoritarian countries. Fabio Mendez and Facundo Sepulveda examine whether the effect of corruption on economic growth depends on political freedom.[30] The authors find evidence of a non-linear relationship where corruption is conducive for economic growth at low levels of political freedom but is detrimental otherwise. Pierre-Guillaume Méon and Khalid Sekkat find a negative effect of corruption on investment and economic growth that tend to worsen when indicators of the quality of governance deteriorate, especially a weak rule of law and an inefficient government.[31] Pierre-Guillaume Méon and Laurent Weill observe that corruption is less detrimental to efficiency in countries where institutions are less effective, and to be even positively associated with efficiency in countries where institutions are extremely ineffective.[32]

GREASE THE WHEELS

On the other hand, there is an alternative view that argues that corruption is a necessary grease to lubricate the stiff wheels of public administration.[33] In this context, corruption facilitates beneficial transactions that would otherwise not have taken place. Thus, corruption allows private agents to circumvent existing bureaucratic encumbrances, failures, and deficiencies. Samuel Huntington states that[34] "in terms of economic growth, the only thing worse than a society with a rigid, over centralized, dishonest bureaucracy is one with a rigid, over centralized honest bureaucracy."

According to this view, there are various concerns in the bureaucratic system that can be evaded by engaging in corrupt activities. An inefficient bureaucracy, with slow procedures and pervasive red tape, constitutes an obstacle to entrepreneurial initiatives and productive activities. One way to avert these administrative delays is by paying "speed money" to public officials to accelerate bureaucratic procedures. This allows beneficial enterprises to be carried out at a faster pace, as bribes offer bureaucrats an incentive to expedite the process. Some studies also show how bribes cut the waiting cost associated with queuing in a sluggish public administration.[35] Thus, corruption acts as a trouble-saving device thereby enhancing investment and economic growth.

Some argue that corruption can affect the quality of public officials and the effort they commit to accomplish their tasks. On one hand, corruption can improve the quality of civil servants.[36] If wages in government agencies are inadequate, the existence of extra perks and perquisites in a corrupt environment may attract skilled applicants who would have otherwise opted for another line of work. This allows the government agencies to attract workers of better quality. In addition, public employees who collect bribes work harder, especially in cases where bribes act as a piece-rate. This enticement increases the productivity of public workers and the effort they put forthwith. Thus, corruption works like piece-rate pay for bureaucrats inducing a more efficient provision of government services and public goods.[37]

Corruption can also be a hedge against poor public policies, as bribes can help private agents eschew a bad policy. This may in turn limit the adverse consequences of these policies, allow for an improvement in the policy's outcome, or for an alteration of the policy in a way that is more propitious to economic outcomes.

Graft can also limit the adverse effects of inefficient government spending while creating incentives for private investment.[38] If corruption takes the form of tax evasion, the stream of income from tax collection diminishes. This limits the ability of the government to increase its spending which typically crowds out investment spending. Corruption can also act as a hedge against political hazards such as expropriation or confiscation by those in power. By paying bribes and illicit campaign contributions, investors are less likely to be targeted by powerful politicians. Thus, investment becomes less uncertain and may increase accordingly.

Enforcing laws that curtail the level of corruption may also hurt domestic firms by increasing the international competitiveness of foreign firms that are allowed to engage in corrupt practices in their own countries. This will have adverse effects on the profitability and the ability of domestic firms to compete in international markets.

Few studies find evidence for the "grease the wheels" hypothesis especially when we focus on areas in the world with rampant corruption and a growing economy. For instance, Michael Rock and Heidi Bonnett conduct a series of tests to examine the connection between corruption and economic performance.[39] The authors find that corruption hinders economic growth and lowers investment in most developing countries but increases growth in the economies of East Asia. The authors conclude that the latter finding provides possible explanation to the "East Asian paradox" or the combination of high levels of corruption and high economic growth in that part of the world.

NOTES

1. https://foreignpolicy.com/2011/02/10/mubaraks-70-billion-nest-egg/

2. Cook. "Corruption and the Arab Spring." *The Brown Journal of World Affairs*: 21–28.

3. Campante, Chor, and Do. "Instability and the Incentives for Corruption." *Economics and Politics*: 42–92.

4. Vu. "Climate, Diseases, and the Origins of Corruption." *Economics of Transition and Institutional Change*: 621–649.

5. Mazar and Aggarwal. "Greasing the Palm: Can Collectivism Promote Bribery?" *Psychological Science*: 843–84.

6. Bentzen. "How bad is Corruption? Cross Country Evidence of the Impact of Corruption on Economic Prosperity." *Review of Development Economics*: 167–184.

7. Hofstede. *Culture's Consequences: Comparing Values, Behaviors, Institutions and Organizations across Nations*.

8. Kurer. "Clientelism, Corruption, and the Allocation of Resources." *Public Choice*: 259–273.

9. Murphy, Shleifer, and Vishny. "The Allocation of Talent: Implications for Growth." *The Quarterly Journal of Economics*: 503–530.

10. Mauro. "Corruption and the Composition of Government Expenditure." *Journal of Public Economics*: 263–279.

11. Witvliet, Kunst, Arah, and Stronks. "Sick Regimes and Sick People." *Tropical Medicine and International Health*: 1240–1247.

12. Tanzi and Davoodi. "Corruption, Public Investment, and Growth." In *The Welfare State, Public Investment, and Growth*, edited by H. Shibata and T. Ihori. Tokyo: Springer.

13. Murphy, Shleifer, and Vishny. "Why Is Rent-Seeking So Costly to Growth?" *American Economic Review Papers and Proceedings*: 409–414.

14. Bardhan. "Corruption and Development: A Review of Issues." *Journal of Economic Literature*: 1320–1346. Lambsdorff. "Corruption and Rent-seeking." *Public Choice*: 97–125.

15. Lien. "Corruption and Allocation Efficiency." *Journal of Development Economics*: 153–164.

16. Blackburn and Powell. "Corruption, Inflation and Growth." *Economics Letters*: 225–227.

17. Mo. "Corruption and Economic Growth." *Journal of Comparative Economics*: 66–79.

18. Gupta, Davoodi, and Alonso-Terme. "Does Corruption Affect Income Inequality and Poverty?" *Economics of Governance*: 23–45.

19. Gyimah-Brempong. "Corruption, Economic Growth, and Income Inequality in Africa." *Economics of Governance*: 183–209.

20. Wei. "How Taxing is Corruption on International Investors?" *Review of Economics and Statistics*: 1–11.

21. Cieslik and Goczek. "Control of Corruption, International Investment, and Economic Growth." *World Development*: 323–335.

22. Mauro. "Corruption and Growth." *The Quarterly Journal of Economics*: 681–712.

23. Mauro. "Corruption and the Composition of Government Expenditure." *Journal of Public Economics*: 263–279.

24. Hodge, Shankar, Rao, and Duhs. "Exploring the Links between Corruption and Growth." *Review of Development Economics*: 474–490.

25. Aidt. "Corruption, Institutions and Economic Development." *Oxford Review of Economic Policy*: 271–291.

26. Campos, Lien, and Pradhan. "The Impact of Corruption on Investment: Predictability Matters." *World Development*: 1059–1067.

27. Murphy, Schleifer, and Vishny. "Why is Rent-seeking So Costly to Growth." *American Economic Review*: 409–14.

28. Aidt, Dutta, and Senac. "Governance Regimes, Corruption and Growth: Theory and Evidence." *Journal of Comparative Economics*: 195–220.

29. Assiotis and Sylwester. "Do the Effects of Corruption upon Growth Differ Between Democracies and Autocracies?" *Review of Development Economics*: 581–594.

30. Mendez and Sepulveda. "Corruption, Growth, and Political Regimes: Cross Country Evidence." *European Journal of Political Economy*: 82–98.

31. Meon, Pierre Guillaume, and Khalid Sekkat. "Does Corruption Grease or Sand the Wheels of Growth?" *Public Choice*: 69–97.

32. Meon and Weill. "Is Corruption an Efficient Grease?" *World Development*: 244–259.

33. Leff. "Economic Development through Bureaucratic Corruption." *American Behavioral Scientist*: 8–14.

34. Huntington. *Political Order in Changing Societies* (p. 386).

35. Lui. "An Equilibrium Queuing Model of Bribery." *Journal of Political Economy*: 760–781.

36. Bayley. "The Effects of Corruption in a Developing Nation." *The Western Political Quarterly*: 719–732.

37. Acemoglu and Verdier. "Property Rights, Corruption and the Allocation of Talent: A General Equilibrium Approach." *The Economic Journal*: 1381–1403.

38. Leff. "Economic Development through Bureaucratic Corruption." *American Behavioral Scientist*: 8–14.

39. Rock and Bonnett. "The Comparative Politics of Corruption." *World Development*: 999–1017.

Chapter Nine

Nature's Democratic Dividend

THE GENESIS OF DEMOCRACY

Our discussion of institutions cannot be complete without an overview of the economic effects of the quality of political institutions, in the form of political freedoms and the democratic system of governance. Democracy comes from the Greek, Demokratia, which combines demos or "people" and kratos or "rule." Thus, democracy literally means "rule by people." Democracy is a system of governance in which power is vested in the people and is exercised by them either directly or indirectly. In a direct democracy, citizens as a whole form a governing body and vote directly on each issue. In a representative system, people freely elect those who represent them to form a governing body, such as a legislature, to decide on each issue.

The historical origins of democracy are debatable. However, we can find clues in what Anthony Pagden wrote in his *Worlds at War: The 2500-Year Struggle between East and West* where he describes the genesis of democratic governance in the context of a protracted conflict between the East and the West[1]

Democracy was a very recent creation. After the expulsion from Athens in 510 B.C.E. of the tyrant Hippias (who would play an important role in the subsequent encounter between Athenians and Persians) and the collapse of an attempt to establish an oligarchy with Spartan aid, the Athenian politician Cleisthenes had reformed the Athenian constitution in such a way as to break the power of the rich families whose feuding had plagued the city for centuries. He divided the peoples of Attica into ten new tribes, organized along entirely artificial lines, thus substantially weakening the older tribal, familial allegiances. A body known as the Council of Five Hundred was then established; its function was to prepare business for the larger assembly and to manage financial and foreign affairs. Each year, each tribe appointed fifteen members, who were chosen by lot. Around 500 B.C.E. a meeting place for the assembly, the *ekklesia*, was carved out of the rock on a hill known as the Pnyx, overlooking the city. From then on, this body met regularly to frame the policies of the state. Its meetings were open to all free male citizens and were attended by upwards of six thousand people. Simple and still subject to corruption and manipulation though it was, the government that Cleisthenes created was the basis for all subsequent democratic constitutions.

These earlier democratic practices did not spread to many areas around the world until the reintroduction of these ideals later in history. Anthony Pagden also eloquently describes the more modern debut of democracy:[2]

> In the seventeenth century a radically different theory of the origin and sources of political power emerged. This claimed that political authority could derive only from those over whom it was exercised, that is, the people themselves. Furthermore, it could be exercised only with their consent and in their interests. This is known as the contract theory of government. Its most powerful original exponents were English, Thomas Hobbes and John Locke. But it was rapidly taken up in France, where it provided the ideological inspiration for what in 1789 became the greatest rebellion against the power of kings in the modern world: the French Revolution.

Over time, this system of governance mutated, metamorphosed, and transformed into various forms. The essence of each is that people impose their will directly or indirectly through representatives that they elect with their own free will. There were periods when this system of governance gained traction around the world. These periods were dubbed waves of democratization. Francis Fukuyama in *The Origins of Political Order: From Prehuman Time to the French Revolution* states that[3] "During the forty-year period from 1970 to 2010, there was an enormous upsurge in the number of democracies around the world. In 1973, only 45 of the world's 151 countries were counted as 'free' by Freedom House, a nongovernmental organization that produces quantitative measures of civil and political rights for countries around the world." He continues to state that[4] "By the late 1990s, some 120 countries around the world—more than 60 percent of the world's independent states—had become electoral democracies. This transformation was Samuel Huntington's third wave of democratization; liberal democracy as the default form of government became part of the accepted political landscape at the beginning of the twenty-first century."

The Arab Spring was the latest episode where people in some countries in that part of the world were calling for a transition from an authoritarian system to a more democratic one. The shared aspiration of the protestors was that democracy would eventually improve their lot. This sentiment was supported by an opinion that if people have their say in policymaking, they will choose policies that will ultimately benefit them. If policymakers do not take people's interests into consideration, the electorate can replace them with others who would. This implies that even though democracy does not guarantee the optimal choice of policymakers at all times, it allows people at least to change a suboptimal one if deemed necessary. This is also supported by what historian Niall Ferguson suggested that[5] "Apart from the inherent appeal of political freedom, more inclusive polities seem to be associated with more sustained economic development. They are also better able to cope with complexity as populations grow and technologies advance."

There were also periods where the democratic systems receded before an autocratic tide. It is insightful what Francis Fukuyama wrote about the state of governance in the twenty-first century:[6] "The third wave crested after the late 1990s, however, and a 'democratic recession' emerged in the first decade of the twenty-first century. Approximately one in five countries that had been part of the third wave either reverted to authoritarianism or saw a significant erosion of democratic institutions." He also states that[7] "The problem in today's world isn't just that authoritarian powers are on the move but that many existing democracies aren't doing well either."

In these times, people get frustrated with the sluggishness and the gridlocks in democratic institutions. This paralysis in the political system tempts people to aspire to replace endless democratic wrangling with swift action by a benevolent autocrat. Another concern was the failure of some democracies to deliver, which cast a shadow on the legitimacy of such political systems. The very legitimacy of democracy is also sometimes corroded because influential groups buy politicians with campaign contributions and excessive lobbying. In addition, democracies may collapse if one group feels that the only way they can capture political power is to overturn the entire democratic experience if it does not usually work in its favor. In some cases, these desperate groups may call the armed forces to interfere on their behalf to overthrow a democratically elected government.

It was John Adams who wrote in one of his letters to John Taylor[8] on December 17, 1814, "Remember Democracy never lasts long. It soon wastes, exhausts, and murders itself. There never was a Democracy Yet, that did not commit suicide. It is in vain to say that Democracy is less vain, less proud, less selfish, less ambitious or less avaricious than Aristocracy or Monarchy." It was also Winston Churchill who said in one of his speeches to the House of Commons on November 11, 1947, that[9] "Many forms of Government have been tried, and will be tried in this world of sin and woe. No one pretends that democracy is perfect or all-wise. Indeed, it has been said that democracy is the worst form of Government except all those other forms that have been tried from time to time."

Scholars dispute the merits of a democratic system, and debate on whether it delivers on its promises. The idea that democracy leads to economic prosperity is controversial, and subject to intense debate. Some argue that democracy is essential for favorable economic outcomes since most developed countries are democratic in nature. Others argue that economic prosperity is not predicated on any political system especially as we see some economic success stories of countries without a democratic system of governance.

In this chapter, we focus on the economic effect of the quality of political institutions in the form of a democratic system of governance. In this context, some studies provide evidence for the prominent effect of political institutions compared to other types of institutional structures. For instance, James Butkiewicz and Halit Yanikkaya compare the effects of the maintenance of the rule of law versus the adoption of democratic practices on economic growth.[10] The authors find that both institutions enhance economic growth, but democratic governance appears to be particularly critical for developing countries. In a similar vein, Jon Jellema and Gerard Roland find that broadly defined political institutions of checks and balances, as well as a political participatory culture, are the most robust institutional determinants of economic growth.[11]

GEOGRAPHIC ORIGINS

Climatic fluctuations and weather shocks can influence the system of governance or political regime. This is because the opportunity cost of contesting an incumbent may change due to variations in climatic conditions that may affect incomes. According to some arguments, adverse precipitation shocks can induce a democratic transition particularly in an economy dependent on rainfall farming. Transitory income shocks caused by these climatic disturbances permit a window of opportunity for citizens to contest power. This is because the opportunity cost of challenging the entrenched authorities is low when income is shrinking due to a weather shock. Autocratic rulers may also have to offer concrete concessions when the citizens' opportunity cost of contesting power is temporarily low, thus opening a window of opportunity for democratic change. To test this hypothesis, Markus Brückner and Antonio Ciccone examine the connection between economic downturns, driven by rainfall fluctuations, and democratic transitions in sub-Saharan Africa.[12] The authors find that precipitation shocks are followed by improvements in democratic institutions captured by higher executive constraints, greater political competition, and more open recruitment for executive positions.

In a similar vein, some scholars argue that irrigation agriculture allows landed elites in arid areas to monopolize water and arable land. Agriculture depends on irrigation if climatic conditions do not allow for any reliance on rainfall. Irrigation agriculture depends on dams, canals, and other costly infrastructure. In ancient times, only the monarch or the elite could command sufficient funds to invest in such large-scale irrigation projects. By controlling the infrastructure, the elites had a monopoly over water resources in arid areas with limited amount of rain. Thus, those who controlled the irrigation systems were more able to impose their will on the entire populace. To provide evidence for this intuition, Jeanet Bentzen, Nicolai Kaarsen and Asger Wingender show that countries whose agriculture depends on irrigation are less democratic than countries where farming is reliant on rainfall.[13]

Some scholars also observe that stable democracies are located where climate favors highly storable crops, such as the temperate zone.[14] The ability to store and accumulate surpluses creates incentives for trade, specialization, protection of property, and investment in human capital. Democracy is more likely to consolidate with a high level of human capital because well-educated citizens are better able to monitor politicians and to hold them accountable. Conversely, what could be cultivated in the tropics tends to have very low degree of storability. This meant that it was difficult to accumulate a surplus and, thus, the incentives to create institutions designed to protect that surplus were weaker. In this context, democratization was less likely to consolidate.

The topographic features of a country can also affect its democratic prospects. For instance, a rugged terrain is a natural barrier that allows for protection from the heavy handedness of a central government. Societies protected by these landscapes usually have an insubordinate character as they feel comfortable being isolated from the clutch of an autocrat. It is common to see insurgencies in countries where the terrain allows the combatants to strike and escape from the authorities. For instance, guerrilla warfare depends on such schemes such as ambushes, raids, sabotage, espionage, assassinations, and others. These hit-and-run tactics are more feasible where the landscape is suitable for such pursuits without suffering heavy losses.

Natural disasters can also induce a democratic transition if citizens hold the incumbent authority accountable for the lack of preparedness or for the failure to react competently to such a calamity. This could lead to demands for change and political reform. The opportunity cost to challenge the incumbent is also lower when incomes are diminished after a disaster that curtails economic activities. On the other hand, disasters can slow the transition into democratic governance because of the increase in incomes from humanitarian aid and the recovery efforts. This increases the opportunity cost of contesting the incumbent authorities.

The resource curse can also take the form of increased authoritarian tendencies of the rulers. In economies well-endowed with natural resources, governments do not need to tax their citizens because they have a guaranteed source of income from resource extraction and exports. Thus, they feel less obligated to satisfy their citizens' demands. As the country's citizens are less taxed in these countries, they also have less incentive to be watchful of how their government spends. In addition, the ruling elite who control resources may also take serious steps against any effort to share the political arena with anyone who may threaten this lucrative source of income.

FREEDOM OR BREAD

Democracy and its effect on economic outcomes have always been a source of concern for social scientists. Some argue that democracy enhances economic performance, while others claim that democracy is not essential for economic success. In either case, these studies argue that democracy influences factors that are critical for economic performance such as political stability, policy quality, institutional quality, government size, income inequality, trade openness, human capital, physical capital, and social capital. In this section, we discuss the effect of democracy on these factors in detail.

Political Stability

In a democratic system, there are transparent provisions for the succession of political forces in power. These stipulations are stated clearly and explicitly in constitutions and electoral laws. The political brokers and the electorate are aware of the timing and the procedures that lead to a potential change in political office. The electorate gets invited at specific times and locations to cast their vote to determine the politicians and political forces that will be in power for an established period. Therefore, democracy allows for a peaceful and predictable transfer of political power. Furthermore, democracies encourage a free discourse over policies and policymakers. This eliminates the need for a takeover of government by illegitimate means and ensures political stability. Political stability, in turn, fosters investment and economic growth. Based on this intuition, Yi Feng examines the interactions between democracy, political stability, and economic growth.[15] The author shows that democracy has a positive indirect effect on economic growth through its impact on the probabilities of both regime change and constitutional government change from one ruling party to another. Paul Collier and Dominic Rohner address the effect of democracy on political repression, rebellion and other forms of political violence.[16] The authors find that democracy increases the likelihood of political violence in countries below a certain income threshold but not in high income countries. William Easterly, Roberta Gatti and Sergio Kurlat examine the relationship between the occurrence of episodes of mass killing and the levels of development and democracy in the period from 1820 C.E. to 1998 C.E.[17] The authors find that mass killings appear less likely at very high levels of democracy.

Policy Quality

Democratic governance can influence the quality of policymaking. This is because democracy constrains the abuses of politicians by submitting them to incessant public scrutiny. Democratic institutions also limit the potential of public officials to implement unpopular policies or to spend on nonproductive projects. Given the frequent voting in a democracy, public officials feel the imperative of proposing and implementing policies that are popular and beneficial to their electorate to ensure their reelection. Democracies also allow for viable policy alternatives proposed by the opposition parties. On the other hand, policymakers in an autocratic system tend to implement policies that benefit a small set of insiders, or their cronies, on the expense of the public. Given the lack of accountability in an autocratic system, public officials do not feel the obligation to satisfy the demands of their subjects.

Alternatively, democracies tend to be trapped in a gridlock that can hinder the adoption of policies that may be beneficial to economic performance. This is because law makers and policy makers may have insurmountable opposing points of view with a limited scope for compromise or reconciliation. Autocracies, on the other hand, have a smoother process of decision making given the fact that there are only few influential decision nodes. In the case of a benevolent autocrat, advantageous projects can be adopted and executed at a faster pace to the benefit of the entire economy.

Institutional Quality

Democracy can enhance the quality of institutions, especially protection of property rights and constraints against expropriation. The ruling elite may want to expropriate the property of others, but democracy is characterized by checks against such transgression. There is also more power dispersion in democracies, which limits the ability of a single powerful actor to infringe on others. On the other hand, confiscation of property and distributing it to political backers can be a survival tactic in a dictatorship to expand the coalition supporting an autocrat. This can lower the quality of institutions in an authoritarian system. In this context, Uwe Sunde and Rainer Kotschy explore whether the favorable effect of democracy on the quality of economic institutions is eroded by excessive income inequality and distributional conflict.[18] The authors provide evidence that excessively high levels of income inequality diminish institutional quality even in democracies.

Government Size

In a democratic system, the electorate may exercise their political rights in support of state interference in the economy financed by higher taxes. This may discourage private economic activities and can hinder economic growth. On the other hand, bureaucrats attempt to increase the scope of their bureau since their power derives directly from the pool of resources under their command. Thus, autocrats have an incentive to expand the spectrum of government activities to increase their leverage over the economy. The increase in government size in an autocracy, in this case, can also deter economic growth.

Income Inequality

The extent of income inequality is determined by societal choices expressed through the political system. The enfranchised poor may use the political process to exert pressure on policy makers to carry out income redistribution. Thus, the tendency of democracies to implement taxation and transfer policies can deter private investment and economic growth. On the other hand, these policies can decrease the level of income inequality eventually which can have a favorable effect on economic outcomes.

Trade Openness

The degree of trade openness can also be influenced by the climate of political freedoms. Protectionist policies tend to be imposed to benefit and protect a few producers who cannot handle competition in a free trade environment. These trade barriers come at the expense of consumers who stand to gain from better prices under free trade. Democracies may weigh the preferences of the consumers more heavily and support less protectionism. On the other hand, if trade liberalization hurts the employment prospects of the workers due to the competitive pressures that firms face, voters may support protectionist policies to save their jobs. As will be discussed in a later chapter, trade liberalization has serious economic consequences.

Human Capital

A substantial portion of education expenditure is publicly financed. A large fraction of people depends more on public education than the costly private alternative. If decision makers in democracies are eager to satisfy the needs and demands of the voters, they will channel funds toward the promotion of educational attainment and human capital accumulation. In this context, Matthew Baum and David Lake find that the effect of democracy on economic growth is positive but largely indirect through increased life expectancy in poor countries and increased secondary education in wealthy countries.[19]

On the other hand, democracies should not be expected to outperform autocracies in the quality of education. This is because education quality is less visible to voters than expanding school enrollment or the construction of educational facilities. This makes policies to promote the quality of instruction a less attractive option for politicians seeking office in a democracy. Sirianne Dahlum and Carl Henrik Knutsen examine whether democracy enhances the quality of education and accordingly economic growth.[20] The authors find that while democracies typically provide more education than autocracies, measured by average years of schooling, there is no systematic evidence that democracies offer better education, captured by international student achievement test scores.

Physical Capital

Democracies can increase the incentive for investment in physical capital by securing property, ensuring contract enforcement, increasing sociopolitical stability, and decreasing economic uncertainty. On the other hand, policymakers in democracies may be more partial to labor by giving a greater voice to unions and workers' interests. Ceteris paribus, higher wages that aim to satisfy union demands decrease the return to capital which creates disincentives for capital accumulation and private investment.

Social Capital

Democracy can also foster trust and encourage associational activities. Both are components of social capital which is essential for economic success as will be seen in a later chapter. In a democratic system, it is more likely that people trust the government that they choose freely in a fair election compared to an autocratic system where rulers are imposed upon them through other means. The people are also more likely to trust the politicians, the political parties, and the political institutions in a democratic system as transparency allows people to oversee their behavior and to hold them accountable. Transparency allows the citizens to scrutinize the behavior of public officials, while accountability ensures that these officials are aware that they cannot act with impunity. Both can ensure the citizenry that they can trust the system of governance and trust the behavior of their elected officials.

In addition, a democratic environment allows differences in opinion to be tolerated, conflicts of interest to be settled in a peaceful manner, state surveillance and disappearances to be diminished, and a variety of civil liberties to be expanded. These features create a climate that allows sentiments of trust to blossom. Associational activities are also encouraged in a democratic system compared to an autocratic one that attempts to constrain any engagement or activity by civil society. In this context, Martin Ljunge finds evidence that democratic political institutions foster trust.[21] Comparing individuals born and residing in the same country, those whose father was born in a more democratic country express higher trust than those whose father was born in a less democratic country.

Technological Progress

Some scholars suggest that democracy promotes technological progress compared to autocracies. This conclusion is derived from the assumption that there is a higher probability of accepting novel ideas and innovations when the decision-making authority is distributed horizontally than in a hierarchical manner. As democracies exhibit greater dispersion of power, we should expect a democratic technological advantage. Democracies also guarantee a free environment for debate, which is instrumental for eliminating unfounded knowledge and for embracing new emerging ideas. Freedom of speech may also spur an intensive and inclusive discourse on the most efficient and proper solutions to a specific problem. This can lead to the spread of economically productive ideas and technologies. Historian Niall Ferguson offers us an example of how the networks of enlightenment were possible through the exchange of ideas between the great thinkers of the time:[22]

> Perhaps paradoxically, the Enlightenment owed as much, if not more, to the old-fashioned written word. To be sure, the *philosophes* published, many of them prolifically. Yet some of their most important exchanges of ideas were by private letter. Indeed, it is the survival of so much of this correspondence— tens of thousands of letters exchanged between more than 6,000 authors—that enables modern scholars to reconstruct the Enlightenment network.

SUFFRAGE AND GROWTH

Several studies examine the effect of democratic governance on economic outcomes, the effect of different forms of democratic governance, the effect of democratic capital on economic outcomes, and compare between the effect of democracy and democratization. This section is an exposition of these scholarly contributions and their main findings.

Democracy

The first set of studies finds a weak association between democracy and economic outcomes. This is usually attributed to the possibility that the favorable effects of democracy are often offset by the detrimental ones. In a seminal paper, Robert Barro finds a weak negative effect of democracy on economic growth.[23] The author also finds that there is a nonlinear relationship in which democracy enhances growth at low levels of political freedom but hinders growth when a high level of political freedom has been attained.

Romain Wacziarg and Jose Tavares examine the channels through which democracy affects economic growth.[24] Their analysis suggests that democracy fosters economic growth by increasing the accumulation of human capital and decreasing income inequality, but hinders growth by decreasing investment in physical capital and increasing government consumption. Once all these indirect effects are accounted for, the authors find the overall effect of democracy on economic growth moderately negative. Romain Wacziarg and Fabrice Murtin explore the economic factors behind the transitions to democracy from 1870 C.E. to 2000 C.E.[25] The authors find that primary schooling and income per capita are critical determinants of the quality of political institutions but find little evidence of causality from democracy to income or education. John Helliwell finds that democracy has an insignificant effect on economic growth, but a significant positive effect on education and investment in physical capital.[26] The author concludes that the insignificant direct effect of democracy on economic growth is counterbalanced by its positive indirect effect via education and investment in physical capital.

Recent studies, however, find a favorable effect of democracy on economic outcomes using more reliable data and advanced empirical techniques. For instance, Daron Acemoglu, Suresh Naidu, Pascual Restrepo, and James Robinson provide evidence that democracy has a significant positive effect on Gross Domestic Product, and that democratization increases income per capita by about 20 percent in the long run.[27] Their analysis also suggests that democracy increases future Gross Domestic Product by encouraging investment, increasing schooling, promoting economic reforms, improving public good provision, and reducing social unrest. In a historical study, Jakob Madsen, Paul Raschky and Ahmed Skali examine the effect of democracy on income and growth during the period from 1500 C.E.–2000 C.E. The authors find that democracy has a significant positive effect on income and economic growth such that approximately 8 percent of the average increase in income since 1500 C.E. has been driven by democratization.[28]

Democratization

Some studies argue that it is not the democratic governance per se that can bring about economic growth, but rather it is the process of democratization or the democratic transition that can be conducive to economic outcomes. This implies that improvements in the quality of democratic governance are less important for economic performance compared to a complete transition from an authoritarian political system to a democratic one. In this context, Elias Papaioannou and Gregorios Siourounis examine the effect of democratization using a dataset of political transitions during the third wave of democratization.[29] Their estimates suggest that democratization is associated with an increase in economic growth in the medium and long run. Jacob Hariri attempts to explain the paradox that democratization, not democracy, is generally associated with higher economic growth.[30] The author shows that a substantial instantaneous influx of foreign aid into new democracies accounts for the favorable growth effect of democratization, while the political system's democratic characteristics do not seem to bring about economic growth.

Other studies examine the effect of democratization on violence, and the economic effect of violent democratic transitions. For instance, Uwe Sunde and Matteo Cervellati investigate the effect of democratization on the likelihood of civil conflict and coups d'état.[31] The analysis of the third wave of democratization suggests that this political transition has an adverse effect on the incidence and the onset of conflict. The authors also find that peaceful democratic transitions are more likely to decrease the occurrence of conflict and coups, while countries with a violent transition experience a shorter spell of peace. In another contribution, Uwe Sunde and Matteo Cervellati examine the interaction between violent conflicts, democratization, and economic growth in the third wave of democratization.[32] Their analysis shows that the economic effect of democratization depends on the transition scenario. The authors show that peaceful transitions to democracy have a significant positive effect on economic growth, whereas violent ones have no effect or even negative growth effects. Finally, Uwe Sunde, Matteo Cervellati, and Piergiuseppe Fortunato investigate the effect of violence during democratization on the institutional quality of the emerging democracies.[33] The evidence from the third wave of democratization suggests that violent democratic transitions have persistent adverse effects on the institutional quality of the nascent democracies.

Form of Democracy

Some studies compare between different forms of democratic governance. This is because the form of the political system determines the process of adopting policies that may promote economic performance, and the ease with which such policies are implemented. In this context, Torsten Persson finds that parliamentary, proportional, and permanent democracies appear to produce the most growth-enhancing outcomes compared to other systems.[34]

Democratic Capital

Some studies argue that it is the accumulation of the democratic experience over time, rather than how democratic the system is at a certain point in time, that influences economic performance. This is referred to as the "democratic capital" which is a nation's historic experience with democracy. The consolidation of democracy as a valuable form of government necessitates a period during which citizens can learn to cherish democracy, to be familiar with the democratic environment, to be able to organize for political participation, to be prepared for active civic engagement, and to be able formulate opinions on how to vote in a democratic environment. Thus, democratic capital enhances the stability of the democratic system which can stimulate economic growth. Building on this intuition, Torsten Persson and Guido Tabellini examine the economic effects of democratic capital.[35] Their analysis suggests a virtuous cycle, where democratic capital leads to stability of the democratic system, which promotes physical capital accumulation and economic development. This helps further consolidate democracy, which leads to the accumulation of more democratic capital with additional favorable effects on investment and income.

NOTES

1. Pagden. *Worlds at War: The 2500-Year Struggle between East and West* (p. 23).
2. Ibid. (p. 318).
3. Fukuyama. *The Origins of Political Order: From Prehuman Times to the French Revolution* (p. 18).
4. Ibid. (pp.18–19).
5. Ferguson. *The Square and the Tower* (p. 22).
6. Ibid. (p. 19).
7. Fukuyama. "At the 'End of History' Still Stands Democracy." *The Wall Street Journal*, June 6, 2014.
8. https://founders.archives.gov/documents/Adams/99-02-02-6371
9. *Winston Churchill: His Complete Speeches, 1897–1963*, edited by Robert Rhodes James, 7, 1974 (p. 7566).
10. Butkiewicz and Yanikkaya. "Institutional Quality and Economic Growth: Maintenance of the Rule of Law or Democratic Institutions, or Both?" *Economic Modelling*: 648–661.

11. Jellema and Roland. "Institutional Clusters and Economic Performance." *Journal of Economic Behavior & Organization*: 108–132.

12. Brückner and Ciccone. "Rain and the Democratic Window of Opportunity." *Econometrica*: 923–947.

13. Bentzen, Kaarsen, and Wingender. "Irrigation and Autocracy." *Journal of the European Economic Association*: 1–53.

14. Haber and Menaldo. "Rainfall, Human Capital, and Democracy." Manuscript.

15. Feng. "Democracy, Political Stability and Economic Growth." *British Journal of Political Science*: 391–418.

16. Collier and Rohner. "Democracy, Development, and Conflict." *Journal of the European Economic Association*: 531–540.

17. Easterly, Gatti, and Kurlat. "Development, Democracy, and Mass Killings." *Journal of Economic Growth*: 129–156.

18. Kotschy and Sunde. "Democracy, Inequality, and Institutional Quality." *European Economic Review*: 209–228.

19. Baum and Lake. "The Political Economy of Growth: Democracy and Human Capital." *American Journal of Political Science*: 333–347.

20. Dahlum and Knutsen. "Do Democracies Provide Better Education? Revisiting the Democracy-Human Capital Link." *World Development*: 186–199.

21. Ljunge. "Social Capital and Political Institutions: Evidence that Democracy Fosters Trust." *Economics Letters*: 44–49.

22. Ferguson. *The Square and the Tower* (p. 101).

23. Barro. "Democracy and Growth." *Journal of Economic Growth*: 1–27.

24. Wacziarg and Tavares. "How Democracy Affects Growth." *European Economic Review*: 1341–1378.

25. Wacziarg and Murtin. "The Democratic Transition." *Journal of Economic Growth*: 141–181.

26. Helliwell. "Empirical Linkages between Democracy and Economic Growth." *British Journal of Political Science*: 225–248.

27. Acemoglu, Naidu, Restrepo, and Robinson. "Democracy Does Cause Growth." *Journal of Political Economy*: 47–100.

28. Madsen, Raschky and Skali. "Does Democracy Drive Income in the World, 1500–2000?" *European Economic Review*: 175–195.

29. Papaioannou and Siourounis. "Democratisation and Growth." *The Economic Journal*: 1520–1551.

30. Hariri. "Foreign Aided: Why Democratization Brings Growth when Democracy Does Not." *British Journal of Political Science*: 53 – 71.

31. Sunde and Cervellati. "Democratizing for Peace? The Effect of Democratization on Civil Conflicts." *Oxford Economic Papers*: 774–797.

32. Sunde and Cervellati. "Civil Conflict, Democratization, and Growth: Violent Democratization as Critical Juncture." *The Scandinavian Journal of Economics*: 482–505.

33. Cervellati, Fortunato, and Sunde. "Violence during Democratization and the Quality of Democratic Institutions." *European Economic Review*: 226–247.

34. Persson. "Forms of Democracy, Policy and Economic Development." National Bureau of Economic Research Working Paper 11171.

35. Persson and Tabellini. "Democratic Capital: The Nexus of Political and Economic Change." *American Economic Journal: Macroeconomics*: 88–126.

Chapter Ten

Elixir or People's Opium

After our detailed discussion of the economic consequences of institutions, it is time to shift our attention to the effects of culture on economic performance. In particular, we start by focusing on one cultural aspect, our faith and our adherence to its tenets, that are known to influence our daily actions and accordingly economic outcomes. Thus, this chapter is an exploration into whether religious affiliation, beliefs and practice influence economic performance. This can be seen as a debate between Karl Marx's postulation that "Religion is the sigh of the oppressed creature, the heart of a heartless world, and the soul of soulless conditions. Religion is the people's opium," and Max Weber's insistence that the "Fulfillment of duties in worldly affairs is the highest form which the moral activity of the individual could assume."

THE TERRESTRIAL GARDEN OF EDEN

Economic performance is the outcome of the actions of many individuals. The behavior and decisions of these economic agents are influenced, to a large extent, by their culture that can shape the personal traits which can promote economic performance. In this context, religion is a crucial component of a society's culture. Faith determines what behavior is encouraged and what is frowned upon and condemned. Religion dictates which actions are prescribed and which ones are proscribed. Religiosity also provides incentives to behave in a certain way to seek salvation, and determines the constraints that people have to abide by.

From a society's point of view, religion may influence the legal, political, and economic systems. Religion can provide a frame of reference for our laws, legal traditions, jurisprudence, and the flavor of constitutions. Faith can also provide an incentive for political participation and civic engagement, a justification for acts of defiance against tyranny, an excuse for submissiveness to tyrants, a direction for voting trends, and a pretext for the extent of separation between church and state. Religion can also determine our economic attitudes toward profit motives, commercial competition, wealth accumulation, material wellbeing, interest rates, usury, thrift, insurance, distributive justice, charitable donations, payment of taxes versus tithe, engagement in credit and banking, and the spread of corruption. Religion also shapes our outlook on labor participation, the role of women in society, gender standards, fertility decisions, educational attainment, dietary choices, and other critical decisions.

From an individual point of view, religion brings with it a spiritual elevation, an aspiration for self-improvement, a way for self-forgiveness through redemption and atonement, a disinclination for criminal and sinful actions, a sense of belonging to a community or a congregation, a connection with others who are from a different background, a way of handling and overcoming hardships, a pathway to finding an objective in life, a strive for purity and perfection, a sense of charity and compassion, a tendency for forgiveness, a trust in wisdom beyond our comprehension, and a way of making sense of things that might otherwise seem senseless. All these factors can produce a strong well-adjusted individual who is capable of being a productive member of the community.

On the other hand, religion is also associated with such attitudes that have bad connotations. These include a literalist interpretation of scriptures, a misguided comprehension of divine commands, an uncompromising and strict adherence to religious decrees irrespective of circumstances or admissible excuses, a tendency for submission to the doctrine rather than rational reasoning, a clerical determination of fate through remission of sins, a resignation to fatalism, a disinclination for science and knowledge, an overemphasis on liturgy and observance compared to productive work, a focus more on rituals and worship practices than on the spirit of faith, an adoption of a simplistic view of the world as a battle between the evil and the benevolent or a duality between the secular and the ecclesiastical, a diversion of resources toward religious but otherwise not so productive causes, a substitution of success in life with absolution in the afterlife, an antagonism toward others who do not share similar beliefs, a narrow minded approach toward the role of women, a tendency for self-sacrifice for the sake of martyrdom, a propensity to proselytizing and spreading the word by force or by taking advantage of those in desperate conditions, an ability to mobilize masses to commit atrocities, a propensity to manipulate some toward acts of discrimination, and an ability to brain wash some toward voting consistently with cherished values that are, nonetheless, at odds with their material interests.

The pogroms, the crusades, the wars of religion, the inquisitions, forced conversions, the persecution of heretics, holy wars waged against the infidels, and acts of terrorism have all been committed in the name of some god or another throughout human history. As Anthony Pagden clarifies in his *Worlds at War: The 2,500 Years Struggle between East and West,*[1] "Henceforth Catholics would slaughter Protestants; Protestants would slaughter Catholics; and both would slaughter Jews and Muslims, not to regain territory, not to avenge injustice, not even from simple dynastic greed. They would do so because they believed, or claimed to believe, that God wished them to do so, because they were, as the Crusaders so often said, acting on God's behalf."

The clergy also attempted at different points in time to be the arbiter between God and the worshippers to ensure their power over the followers. This ranged from a monopoly over the interpretation of scripture, to installing themselves as an intermediary between God and his creations, to asserting that the path to absolution only goes through them, and to allowing the people to pay their way to paradise. As an example, Anthony Pagden describes the church indulgences in the wake of the reformation:[2]

> The papacy, in the person of Julius II, patron of Michelangelo, a man said to be better on horseback than at prayer, was enlarging Saint Peter's Basilica into the magnificent building it is today. To do this he needed money, and so, he had—or so it seemed to Luther—put Christianity up for sale, in the form of something called an indulgence. To put it simply—and simply was how Luther saw it— indulgences were documents issued by the Church that promised to eliminate the burden of human sin and thus reduce, by millions of years, the suffering the penitent invariably faced, however virtuous he or she might have been, in purgatory. The more you paid, the more speedily you would gain admittance to paradise.

The misconstrued commands or the intentionally misinterpreted ones were also used as justifications for atrocities at different points in time. There are examples in the Abrahamic traditions of Judaism, Christianity, and Islam. As an example from Judaism, calls for the eradication of the other or for forced conversions of the gentiles are found in the Jewish tradition. Some verses in the Old Testament offer explicit instructions to the followers: "Go in and clean house, and don't leave anything breathing! Don't leave a donkey, child, woman, old man, or old woman breathing." William Horbury also writes in *The Cambridge History of Judaism* that the annihilation of the other was sometimes substituted with forcing that other into the tight embrace of faith:[3] "The evidence is best explained by postulating that an existing small Jewish population in Lower Galilee was massively expanded by the forced conver- sion in c. 104 BCE of their Gentile neighbours in the north."

As an example from Christianity, the historian and crusades expert Christopher Tyerman describes how the clergy distorted the doctrine to vali- date their exploits:[4]

The beatitudes had to be reconciled with human civilization, specifically the Graeco-Roman world, or, to put it crudely, ways found around the Sermon on the Mount. Being extravagantly well versed in the highest traditions of classical learning, the Church Fathers did this rather well. Beside these majestic exercises of the intellect, which extended even to manipulating the wording of some inconvenient biblical texts, Scripture attracted apocryphal additions and spawned a massive literature of imitative hagiography often supported by legends surrounding relics of biblical characters or events. The experience of the church over the centuries provided its own corpus of law, tradition, history, legend and saints that reflected neither the idealism nor experience of the first century AD.

He also describes the work of Augustine of Hippo who combined the classical and biblical doctrines of just war:[5]

Nonetheless, Augustine had moved the justification of violence from law books to liturgies, from the secular to the religious. His lack of definition in merging holy and just war, extended in a number of later pseudo-Augustinian texts and commentaries, produce a convenient conceptual plasticity that characterized Christian attitudes to war. The language of the *bellum justum* often described what came closer to *bellum sacrum*. This fusion of ideas might conveniently be called religious wars, waged for and by the church, sharing features of holy and just war, allowing war to become valid as an expression of Christian vocation second only to monasticism itself.

Another example comes from the use of Christianity as an excuse for some actions of the conquerors of the new world. For instance, Bernal Díaz del Castillo was a Spanish conquistador who participated as a soldier in the conquest of Mexico under Hernán Cortés. He later wrote an account of the events in his memoirs *The True History of the Conquest of New Spain* where he states that

We were the persons who made this good beginning, and it was not until two years later, when we had made the conquest, and introduced good morals and better manners among the inhabitants, that the pious Franciscan brothers arrived, and three or four years after the virtuous monks of the Dominican order, who further continued the good work, and spread Christianity through the country. The first part of the work, however, next to the Almighty, was done by us, the true Conquistadores, who subdued the country, and by the Brothers of Charity, who accompanied.

It was also President George W. Bush who proclaimed in the wake of the 9/11 terrorist attacks that[6] "the American people are beginning to understand. This crusade, this war on terrorism is going to take a while. And the American people must be patient." This rhetoric was an obvious attempt to cajole his zealous evangelical supporters to huddle behind his wretched decisions to wage wars that claimed the lives of thousands.[7]

As an example from Islam, Steven Cook explores the roots of Islamism through a discussion of Sayyed Qutb's insights in *Milestones Along the Way*. This text is considered by some as one of the core references of Political Islam. Cook states that[8] "Qutb's answer was straightforward: the Muslim community must marshal its resources to confront the jahili system with which there could be no compromise. Islam was at fundamental odds with societies organized around man's sovereignty over man, which was the sources of mankind's travails." Qutb also adds that[9]

> This movement uses the methods of preaching and persuasion for reforming ideas and beliefs; and it uses physical power and jihad for abolishing the organizations and authorities of the jahili system which prevents people from reforming their ideas and beliefs but forces them to obey their aberrant ways and makes them serve human lords instead of the Almighty Lord. This movement does not confine itself to mere preaching to confront physical power, as it also does not use compulsion for changing the ideas of people. The two principles are equally important in the method of this religion. Its purpose is to free people who wish to be freed from enslavement so that they may serve God alone.

These words resonate with the call to arms addressed to Muslims by the leader of the self-proclaimed "Islamic State" when he declared,[10]

> So rush O Muslims and gather around your khalīfah [caliphate], so that you may return as you once were for ages, kings of the earth and knights of war. Come so that you may be honored and esteemed, living as masters with dignity. Know that we fight over a religion that Allah promised to support. We fight for an ummah [global Muslim community] to which Allah has given honor, esteem, and leadership, promising it with empowerment and strength on the earth.

Given these contradictory effects of religion, social scientists and economists are particularly interested in the effect of religious beliefs, religious practices, religious participation, and religious affiliation on economic outcomes.[11] This chapter is an exposition of the arguments and the findings of the scholarly work on the association between religion and the economy.

HOW GOD IS GOOD (FOR GROWTH)?

Cast into Hell

One fundamental aspect common to all faiths is that they prescribe codes of conduct and behavior that constrain followers with varying degrees of strictness. Thus, religiosity can affect economic outcomes by fostering individual traits such as honesty, integrity, rectitude, decency, work ethics, thrift, compassion, trust, tolerance, and others. Beliefs in heaven and hell can also affect productivity by creating perceived rewards and punishments in the afterlife that depend on lifetime behavior.

Thou Shalt Not Eat

A secular identity can be accompanied by higher levels of satisfaction derived from consumption and more pleasure from material possessions. This can lead secular individuals to work harder and to save more to be able to experience and enjoy higher future felicity from consumption.[12] This behavior can be conducive to economic growth. On the other hand, religiosity can be accompanied by austerity and asceticism which can inhibit productivity and economic growth. Religious practices can also affect productivity by imposing dietary food stipulations, the practice of fasting, abstinence, or avoiding overindulgence altogether. These factors may adversely affect consumption spending, demand for goods and services, and the ability of followers to work under certain conditions.

Thou Shalt Make Thy Prayer unto Him

Religious practice entails that time, money and effort be dedicated for the fulfillment of the articles of faith. These resources, however, will not be available for productive activities. Thus, there is a tradeoff in the allocation of scarce resources between the religious sector and the production sectors of the economy. To clarify this idea, beliefs can be viewed as the output of the religion sector where attendance in services can serve as an input. This implies that the more attendance in services performed in places of worship, the more likely the congregants will apply their beliefs in their daily lives. On the other hand, if we assume beliefs to be constant, an increase in attendance in places of worship signifies that the sector is less productive. That is because more resources are allocated for the same amount of output. Thus, higher levels of attendance may depress economic growth.

Gathered in My Name

Adam Smith argues that membership in religious communities and sects could potentially convey economic advantages to the adherents.[13] These sects pave the way to promoting trust and sanctioning miscreants in transactions, thus diminishing uncertainty especially where secular enforcement of contracts is weak. Adam Smith states that[14]

> [The man of low condition] never emerges so effectually from this obscurity, his conduct never excites so much the attention of any respectable society, as by his becoming the member of a small religious sect. He from that moment acquires a degree of consideration which he never had before. All his brother sectaries are, for the credit of the sect, interested to observe his conduct, and if he gives occasion to any scandal, if he deviates very much from those austere morals which they almost always require of one another, to punish him by what is always a very severe punishment, even where no civil effects attend it, expulsion or excommunication from the sect. In little religious sects, accordingly, the morals of the common people have been almost always remarkably regular and orderly; generally much more so than in the established church.

On the other hand, a religious outlook on life can be accompanied by anti-materialistic sentiments. This could manifest itself in hostile attitudes toward formal institutions whose mundane purpose is to protect material property and wealth. There is also belief in reward and punishment in the afterlife among some religious people. This could cause the faithful to regard worldly punishment as less important, since justice is expected to be administered posthumously. Organized religion can also influence laws,[15] rules and regulations that affect the institutional framework which ultimately determines economic incentives.[16]

Some studies explore the effect of religion on the quality of institutions and social capital. For instance, Niclas Bergrren and Christian Bjornskov examine the effect of religiosity, captured by the share of population for which religion is important in daily life, on protection of property rights and the rule of law.[17] The authors find that religiosity is negatively related to the institutional quality indicators only in democracies, which implies that religiosity affects the way institutions work through the political process.

Obey Your Leaders and Submit to Them

Some studies show a strong association between religiosity and political participation. These studies find that those who attend service in places of worship more frequently are much more likely to vote and exercise their electoral rights.[18] This is because those who attend and participate have opportunities to interact and work with other members of the community in planning meetings, organizing events, giving speeches, and making decisions on congregation affairs. These activities help develop general civic attitudes that can induce political involvement outside the sphere of the place of worship.

In addition, institutions of faith are conduits of political information and recruitment. In their sacrosanct places of worship, members are exposed to information about community affairs and political petitions that are consistent with their beliefs. The members may also be used for political mobilization, as they are expected to be receptive to appeals by the clergy, faith leaders or the preachers to participate in political causes that are of concern to the entire congregation.

Do Not Spare them

Religion shapes the way people behave, their view on life, and their conceptions of right and wrong. When religions come in contact with each other, the possibility of misunderstanding and the potential for a clash increase. Within countries, the degree of heterogeneity along religious lines can increase the likelihood of internal conflict. This problem also occurs between countries whose borders act as a fault line between followers of different faiths. Some scholars observe that most of the areas in the world that experience chronic armed conflicts, such as the Middle East, the Balkans, the Caucasus, Central Asia, and South Asia, are also fault lines where Judaism, Christianity, Islam, Buddhism, and Hinduism intersect.

And All the Tithe of the Land is the Lord's

Religious institutions provide services to their members and the public in the form of soup kitchens, medical assistance, homeless shelters, and others. The government also provides these services through welfare programs that offer protection against income loss in the form of food stamps, social security, unemployment insurance and subsidized medical care. Thus, church and state appear to be substitutes in providing social insurance. Accordingly, a decline in religiosity is expected to strengthen support for government welfare programs. On the other hand, those with strong religious sentiments tend not to favor formal transfer payments since they have access to services through their religious institutions. Faith also induces individuals to engage in charitable giving, which causes the followers to prefer making their contributions privately and voluntarily rather than through the compulsory state venues. To the extent that people's preferences are reflected in policy outcomes, religiosity leads to lower levels of taxation and hence lower provision of public goods and redistribution.[19] Thus, higher levels of religiosity are observed to be associated with greater income inequality as well.

In this context, Ceyhun Elgin, Turkmen Goksel, Mehmet Gurdal, and Cuneyt Orman find that religiosity, captured by the share of people who believe in afterlife, increases income inequality.[20] Religiosity is also found to lower both total government spending and government spending excluding welfare payments. This suggests that the religious have a preference to make their contributions privately and voluntarily rather than through the state channels.

Read in the Name of thy Lord

Faith creates incentives for literacy to be able to read the holy books and scriptures. Most religious testaments are available in written form to be preserved for all eternity. This puts pressure on the faithful to learn how to recite and to comprehend the commands that they are obligated to follow. This can increase the level of educational attainment which is beneficial to productivity and economic outcomes. On the other hand, the focus on theological studies by the faithful can take some talent away from other fields of study that are essential for productive activities.

In addition, some religious communities and sects advocate the view that women's appropriate place is within their domestic sphere. On one hand, this decreases the incentives for female education and thus lowers overall educational attainment. On the other hand, females' accumulated human capital will be lost if not utilized in the workplace after graduation. In both cases, the level of human capital used in the production process diminishes to the detriment of the entire economy.

Thou Shalt Not Be to Him as an Usurer

Accumulation of physical capital sometimes requires access to credit to finance this sort of investment through the financial system and the banking institutions. However, borrowing a loan implies repayment of principal and interest at some point in time. Some religions consider interest rate payments as a form of usury and exploitation. This is because interest is considered as an unjustified increment, above the amount of the loan, as a condition imposed by the creditor. In this context, the Bible states that "If you lend money to any of my people with you who is poor, you shall not be like a moneylender to him, and you shall not exact interest from him." Similarly, the Quran states that "Those who swallow usury cannot rise up save as he ariseth whom the devil hath prostrated by (his) touch. That is because they say: Trade is just like usury; whereas Allah permitteth trading and forbiddeth usury.

He unto whom an admonition from his Lord cometh, and (he) refraineth (in obedience thereto), he shall keep (the profits of) that which is past, and his affair (henceforth) is with Allah. As for him who returneth (to usury)—Such are rightful owners of the Fire. They will abide therein." Thus, the religious may be reluctant to participate in financial transactions that entail payments of interest. This can hinder the ability of some economic agents to secure sufficient funds to finance their investment to the detriment of economic activities. On the other hand, steep interest rates can impede the ability to borrow to finance investment. By inhibiting high interest rates, religiosity may promote economic activities.

We Were All Baptized into One Body

Religion could directly affect productivity by limiting social interactions with nonbelievers or those following other faiths. Some religious people restrict their communication to those of the same creed or persuasion, to those who adopt the same doctrine, or even to the members of the same place of worship. This lowers the level of trust, tolerance, cooperation, and solidarity in a society. Religion may also create a divide in society if the followers see others as morally inferior, or if they are more prone to condemn what they consider as sinful behavior. Thus, stricter behavioral codes can increase distrust between believers and others.

On the other hand, organized religion can be a source of creation and accumulation of social capital which is considered an essential determinant of political and economic outcomes. Robert Putnam[21] and other scholars argue that houses of worship are civic organizations.[22] According to this view, the interactions emanating from these places of worship are essential elements for the accumulation of social capital. Thus, engagement in religious organizations creates networks of communication that fosters trust, cooperation, and reciprocity. Collective religious rituals can also cement social cohesion.

Religions also urge their followers to adhere to a code of reciprocity toward others in the sense of "Do unto others as you would have them do unto you." Religion may, in this way, stimulate selfless, philanthropic, and altruistic preferences. Religions also prohibit socially destructive behavior, such as cheating or stealing. To the extent that people believe that followers adhere to these teachings, such persons are perceived as more trustworthy which may in turn induce a higher level of social trust.

In this context, Niclas Bergrren and Christian Bjornskov examine the effect of the importance of religiosity, measured by the share of population for which religion is important in their daily life, on the share of population who think that people in general can be trusted.[23] The authors find a negative relationship between religiosity and trust, both internationally and within the United States.

THE SCALE OF FAITH

Given the ambiguity of the effect of religion on economic outcomes, an empirical analysis becomes imperative. The dilemma is how to quantify the extent of religiosity to assess its effect on economic performance. Scholars were creative in compiling indicators that can capture some aspect of religiosity to focus on. In this context, surveys serve as an essential source of information on whether the respondents consider themselves to be religious, whether religion plays an important role in their life, whether the respondents are affiliated to a particular religion, how frequently they practice their faith, and whether they cherish certain beliefs.

In this context, we need to distinguish between affiliation, beliefs, and practices. Affiliation refers to adherence to one of the world religions. This can be measured by the proportion of people in a country who follow that religion. Another way is to consider some beliefs embraced by those who belong to a particular faith. The common ones are beliefs in God, in the afterlife, and in heaven and hell. This can be measured by the proportion of people who believe in God, in the afterlife, and in heaven and hell. Religious practice reflects whether those affiliated with a religion practice the tenets of their faith. These include attendance in places of worship, participating in prayers, observing fasting, paying tithe, alms giving, performing pilgrimage and others. The common indicator in the literature is the share of people who attend a place of worship, and the frequency of that participation.

Besides affiliation, beliefs and practices, scholars also consider other indicators that capture the level of religious pluralism, the degree of religious tolerance, the extent of state sponsorship of religion, and the presence of a regulated market in which the government approves or appoints religious leaders. There is a plethora of studies that use statistical analyses to examine the effect of religious beliefs, practice, and affiliation on economic outcomes. This section is an exposition of some of their principal findings.

Before delving into these studies, we need to consider some studies that argue that geography affects certain cultural attributes such as religiosity which has a significant effect on the economy.[24] Affiliation to religious communities often offers the only source of social support beyond the family. These communities provide solace in the spirit of charity and a sense of belonging that protects from the sorrow of loneliness. This support is a sort of mutual insurance especially valuable in agricultural societies that usually face lots of uncertainty. Thus, a larger proportion of people is observed to organize in religious communities in economies that depend on rain-fed farming where output is prey to rainfall fluctuations. Based on this intuition, Antonio Ciccone and Phillipe Ager conduct an analysis on the effect of rainfall fluctuations at the county-level in the nineteenth-century United States.[25] The authors find that a larger share of the population participated in religious communities in counties with greater agricultural risk of rainfall fluctuations, that the effect is stronger in those agricultural counties exposed to climate shocks during the growing season, and that these effects persisted until the twenty-first century.

Natural disasters can also have an influence on some cultural traits such as religiosity. We observe that individuals hit by various adverse life events usually become more religious. Religion provides individuals with a higher power to turn to in times of hardship. Individuals also draw on religious beliefs and practices to deal with and to withstand unbearable situations. As disasters are adverse experiences, some observe that religiosity increases in afflicted areas. In this context, Jeanet Bentzen shows that individuals living in districts frequently hit by earthquakes, volcanic eruptions and tsunamis are more religious.[26] This finding applies to individuals belonging to all major denominations and those living in every continent.

In their seminal paper, Robert Barro and Rachel McCleary examine the effects of beliefs and church attendance on economic growth.[27] The authors argue that since the secularization hypothesis states that religion loses its authority in all aspects of life as societies develop, economic conditions can affect the degree of religiosity. Thus, there is a need to isolate the direction of causation from religiosity to economic development. Dealing with this issue, the authors show that economic growth is positively associated with beliefs in hell and heaven, but negatively related to church attendance. The authors conclude that these findings accord with a model in which beliefs are an output of the religion sector where church attendance is an input. Hence, for the same set of beliefs higher church attendance signifies wasted resources which hinder economic growth. In a response to this study, Steven Durlauf, Andros Kourtellos, and Chih Ming Tan attempt to assess the strength of the evidence provided by Robert Barro and Rachel McCleary.[28] The authors find that while the analysis is replicable, it is not statistically robust. The authors find no evidence that beliefs in hell or heaven have a significant effect on economic growth, and that there may be weak evidence for an adverse effect of church attendance on economic growth.

After the seminal work by Robert Barro and Rachel McCleary, other scholars pursued this line of research on the effect of religiosity on income. For instance, Dierk Herzer and Holger Strulik show a negative relationship between church attendance and income per capita, and that causality goes in both directions such that secularization appears to be both cause and consequence of economic development.[29] Jean-Francois Carpantier and Anastasia Litina show that church attendance, church membership, and feeling close to God are associated with higher income.[30] However, when controlling for trust and attitudes toward hard work and helping others, the effect of church attendance and membership on economic outcomes disappears. Leon Bettendorf and Elbert Dijkgraaf find that whereas church membership is found to have a positive effect on income for high-income countries, the effect is negative for low-income countries.[31]

Other studies opt to explore the effect of religiosity on attitudes that are critical for better economic outcomes. For instance, Luigi Guiso, Paola Sapienza, and Luigi Zingales attempt to identify the association between religiosity and economic attitudes.[32] The authors consider the share of people who are raised religiously, who attend services regularly, who believe in God, and who adhere to a particular religion. Their analysis suggests that religiosity is associated with attitudes conducive to higher income per capita and economic growth, but that religious people also tend to be more intolerant and less favorable to working women.

Some studies examine the effect of religion on attitudes toward science and innovation. For instance, Roland Bénabou, Davide Ticchi, and Andrea Vindigni analyze the joint dynamics of religiosity and scientific progress.[33] The authors find that there is a negative association between religiosity and patents per capita, which reflects the recurrent tension between science and organized religion from time immemorial. In another contribution, Roland Bénabou, Davide Ticchi, and Andrea Vindigni examine the relationship between religion and individual openness to innovation.[34] The authors find that greater religiosity is uniformly associated with less favorable views of innovation captured by attitudes toward science and technology, new versus old ideas, importance of risk taking, whether people change their own fate, and importance of imagination and independence in children.

Several studies also focus on the effect of religious practices, such as fasting and pilgrimage, on economic outcomes. For instance, Filipe Campante and David Yanagizawa-Drott study the economic effects of fasting in Ramadan, one of the central tenets of Islam.[35] The authors find that longer Ramadan fasting has a negative effect on output growth, but a positive effect on subjective well-being among Muslims. David Clingingsmith, Asim Ijaz Khwaja and Michael Kremer estimate the impact on Muslim pilgrims of performing the pilgrimage to Mecca.[36] The authors find that participation in the pilgrimage, Hajj, increases observance of other practices such as prayer and fasting, increases beliefs in harmony among ethnicities and sects, leads to more favorable attitudes toward female education and employment, and increases beliefs in peace among adherents of different faiths. The evidence suggests that these attitudes are likely due to the exposure to and interaction with other Hajjis from around the world.

NOTES

1. Pagden. *Worlds at War: The 2,500 Year Struggle between East and West* (p. 226).

2. Ibid. (p. 298).

3. Horbury, William. *The Cambridge History of Judaism: Volume 3, The Early Roman Period* (p. 599).

4. Tyerman. *God's War* (p. 29).

5. Ibid. (pp. 34–35).

6. https://georgewbush-whitehouse.archives.gov/news/releases/2001/09/20010916-2.html

7. https://www.washingtonpost.com/news/wonk/wp/2013/04/24/george-w-bushs-presidency-in-24-charts/

8. Cook. *The Struggle for Egypt: From Nasser to Tahrir Square* (p. 117).

9. Ibid. (p. 117).

10. Vick. "ISIS Militants Declare Islamist 'Caliphate.'" *Time*, June 29, 2014.

11. Iannacone. "Introduction to the Economics of Religion." *Journal of Economic Literature*: 1465–1495.

12. Strulik. "Secularization and Long-Run Economic Growth." *Economic Inquiry*: 177–200.

13. Anderson. "Mr. Smith and the Preachers: The Economics of Religion in the Wealth of Nations." *Journal of Political Economy*: 1066–1088.

14. Smith. *An Inquiry into the Nature and Causes of the Wealth of Nations*, edited by Roy H. Campbell, Andrew S. Skinner, and W. B. Todd. Oxford: Clarendon. (pp. 795–796).

15. Rubin. "Institutions, the Rise of Commerce and the Persistence of Laws: Interest Restrictions in Islam and Christianity." *The Economic Journal*: 1310–1339. Rubin. "Bills of Exchange, Interest Bans, and Impersonal Exchange in Islam and Christianity." *Explorations in Economic History*: 213–227.

16. Lydon. "A Paper Economy of Faith without Faith in Paper: A Reflection on Islamic Institutional History." *Journal of Economic Behavior & Organization*: 647–659. Kuran. "Why the Middle East is Economically Underdeveloped: Historical Mechanisms of Institutional Stagnation." *Journal of Economic Perspectives*: 71–90. Kuran. "The Islamic Commercial Crisis: Institutional Roots of Economic Underdevelopment in the Middle East." *The Journal of Economic History*: 414–446. Greif. "Contract Enforceability and Economic Institutions in Early Trade: The Maghribi Traders' Coalition." *American Economic Review*: 525–48. Greif. "Cultural Beliefs and the Organization of Society: A Historical and Theoretical Reflection on Collectivist and Individualist Societies." *Journal of Political Economy*: 912–50.

17. Berggren and Bjørnskov. "Does Religiosity Promote Property Rights and the Rule of Law?" *Journal of Institutional Economics*: 161–185.

18. Driskell, Embry, and Lyon. "Faith and Politics: The Influence of Religious Beliefs on Political Participation." *Social Science Quarterly*: 294–314.

19. Dills and Hernández-Julián. "Religiosity and State Welfare." *Journal of Economic Behavior & Organization*: 37–51.

20. Elgin, Goksel, Gurdal, and Orman. "Religion, Income Inequality, and the Size of the Government." *Economic Modelling*: 225–234.

21. Putnam. *Bowling Alone: The Collapse and Revival of American Community*.

22. Sacerdote and Glaeser. "Education and Religion." *Journal of Human Capital*: 188–215.

23. Bergrren and Bjornskov. "Is the Importance of Religion in Daily Life Related to Social Trust?" *Journal of Economic Behavior & Organization*: 459–480.

24. Barro and McCleary. "Religion and Economic Growth across Countries." *American Sociological Review*: 760–781. Barro and McCleary. "Religion and Political Economy in an International Panel." *Journal for the Scientific Study of Religion*: 149–175.

25. Ager and Ciccone. "Agricultural Risk and the Spread of Religious Communities." *Journal of the European Economic Association*: 1021–1068.

26. Bentzen. "Acts of God? Religiosity and Natural Disasters across Subnational World Districts." *Economic Journal*: 2295–2321.

27. Barro and McCleary. "Religion and Economic Growth across Countries." *American Sociological Review*: 760–781.

28. Durlauf, Kortellos, and Tan. "Is God in the Details? A Reexamination of the Role of Religion in Economic Growth." *Journal of Applied Econometrics*: 1059–1075.

29. Herzer and Strulik. "Religiosity and Income: a Panel Cointegration and Causality Analysis." *Applied Economics*: 2922–2938.

30. Carpantier and Litina. "Dissecting the Act of God: An Exploration of the Effect of Religiosity on Economic Activity." *The B.E. Journal of Macroeconomics*.

31. Bettendorf and Dijkgraaf. "Religion and Income: Heterogeneity between Countries." *Journal of Economic Behavior & Organization*: 12–29.

32. Guiso, Sapienza, and Zingales. "People's Opium? Religion and Economic Attitudes." *Journal of Monetary Economics*: 225–282.

33. Bénabou, Ticchi, and Vindigni. "Forbidden Fruits: The Political Economy of Science, Religion, and Growth." National Bureau of Economic Research Working Paper 21105.

34. Bénabou, Ticchi, and Vindigni. "Religion and Innovation." *American Economic Review: Papers and Proceedings*: 346–351.

35. Campante and Yanagizawa-Drott. "Does Religion Affect Economic Growth and Happiness? Evidence from Ramadan." *The Quarterly Journal of Economics*: 615–658.

36. Clingingsmith, Khwaja, and Kremer. "Estimating the Impact of the Hajj: Religion and Tolerance in Islam's Global Gathering." *The Quarterly Journal of Economics*: 1133–1170.

Chapter Eleven

In (Trust) We Trust

BEYOND BELIEF

As much as faith is a critical component of a nation's culture, there are other cultural attributes whose impact on economic performance is also worth exploring. Culture refers to the set of society's beliefs, convictions, ethics, customs, norms, habits, traditions, taboos, and codes of conduct. Some scholars argue that there are cultural traits that promote economic performance. These traits include individualism, thrift, hard work, trust, tolerance, cooperation, independence, respect, responsibility, and others. Scholars argue that these espoused cultural attributes are of economic significance due to their effect on saving behavior, work ethics, entrepreneurial spirit, civic engagement, communal interactions, associational activities, and others. This chapter discusses the effects of some of these cultural traits on economic outcomes.

In this context, culture is said to be influenced by climate. The idea that climate influences a nation's culture dates back to Ibn Khaldun's opus magnum[1] "*Al Muqaddimah.*" Historian Arnold Toynbee regarded this seminal contribution as[2] "undoubtedly the greatest work of its kind that has ever yet been created by any mind in any time or place." The Arab philosopher, historian, and the true father of sociology, Ibn Khaldun, who lived during the period between 1332 C.E. and 1406 C.E. was the first to study the influence of the physical settings of a location on the non-physical characteristics of the society who inhabits it. Ibn Khaldun attempted to explain the difference between societies, including their customs, in terms of their habitat, climate, and soil. Thus, he studied how the geography of an area can shape the culture of its inhabitants.

His philosophy of history made him a predecessor of the Baron de Montesquieu in his controversial theory of climate.[3] The latter argues that "there are countries where the excess of heat enervates the body and renders men so slothful and dispirited that nothing but the fear of chastisement can oblige them to perform any laborious duty." He also states that "You will find in the climates of the north, peoples with few vices, many virtues, sincerity and truthfulness. Approach the south, you will think you are leaving morality itself, the passions become more vivacious and multiply crimes. . . . The heat can be so excessive that the body is totally without force. The resignation passes to the spirit and leads people to be without curiosity, nor the desire for noble enterprise." Whether you agree with his conjectures or not, Montesquieu believed that climate affects the temperament of a society.

There are other contemporary studies which argue that climate stability ensures the persistence of some cultural traits. In a very stable environment, the customs of one's ancestors are beneficial in ascertaining which actions are suitable in the current circumstances. Given that those customs evolved and survived over generations, they continue to be valuable in dealing with current conditions. Thus, there are potential benefits to following and cherishing the traditions of the previous generations. Conversely, the customs of previous generations are not likely to be germane for those living in a very unstable environment. Such a society places less value on preserving tradition and is more willing to adopt new practices and to embrace new beliefs. In this context, Paula Guiliana and Nathan Nunn examine the effect of the variability of average temperature across generations from 500 C.E. to 1900 C.E. on gender norms, polygamy, and consanguineous marriage.[4] Looking across countries, ethnic groups, and the descendants of immigrants, the authors find that populations with ancestors who lived in stable environments place importance in maintaining traditions today and exhibit more persistence in their traditions over time than those with unstable climates.

In addition, the difficulty in estimating a causal effect of culture is that it is endogenous to economic development. As stressed by some scholars, economic development has predictable effects on our culture and social life. For instance, industrialization produces pervasive social and cultural consequences that lead to the decline of traditional values and their substitution with modern ideals. Along the lines of this intuition, Ronald Ingelhart and Wayne Baker find that economic development is associated with shifts toward values that are increasingly rational, tolerant, trusting, and participatory.[5] This implies that it is important to determine the direction of causality from culture to economic development in this literature.

SOCIAL CAPITAL

One of the cultural traits that attracts lots of attention is trust. Trust is confidence in the integrity, strength, and capability of someone or something.

James Coleman in his *Foundations of Social Theory* offers a definition that indicates that[6] "an individual trusts if he or she voluntary places resources at the disposal of another party without any legal commitment from the latter, but with the expectation that the act of trust will pay off." Scholarly work on the association between trust and economic performance focuses essentially on generalized trust. This type of trust emphasizes sentiments among individuals who are not bound by personal ties. One of the advantages of this approach is to define trust as a behavior that can be directly quantified.[7]

Trust is also tied to the concept of social capital. Robert Putnam in his *Making Democracy work: Civic Traditions in Modern Italy* explains that[8] "Social capital refers to features of social organization, such as trust, norms, and networks that can improve the efficiency of society by facilitating coordinated actions." Luigi Guiso, Paola Sapienza, and Luigi Zingales define social capital as the ensemble of[9] "those persistent and shared beliefs and values that help a group overcome the free rider problem in the pursuit of socially valuable activities." Accordingly, social capital is essential for effectively functioning groups in which transactions are marked by reciprocity, trust, cooperation, interpersonal relationships, and a shared sense of identity and common values. Thus, trust is undeniably an indispensable component of social capital.

There is also a growing literature that argues that trust is one of the critical determinants of economic outcomes. According to these studies, a prerequisite for the success of market economies is to expand transactions to anonymous others. In this context, trust favors cooperative behavior, facilitates the extension of anonymous exchange, and allows mutually advantageous trade in the presence of incomplete contracts and imperfect information. Thus, social trust expands the boundaries of economic transactions beyond groups who are bound by family, tribal, ethnic, or other forms of preexisting ties. As Nobel laureate Kenneth Arrow suggests,[10] "trust acts as a lubricant to economic exchange."

On the other hand, lack of trust is associated with suspicion and fear of fraud. This increases the cost of transactions due to the need for enforcement of contracts by third parties. On the other hand, trust enhances the functioning of institutions as it limits the need for external enforcement of contractual agreements. In this context, Thomas Hobbes states in *Leviathan* that

> If a covenant be made wherein neither of the parties perform presently but trust one another, in the condition of mere nature, which is a condition of war of every man against every man, upon any reasonable suspicion, it is void; but, if there be a common power set over them both with right and force sufficient to compel performance, it is not void. For he that performeth first has no assurance the other will perform after, because the bonds of words are too weak to bridle

men's ambition, avarice, anger, and other passions, without the fear of some
coercive power, which in the condition of mere nature, where all men are equal
and judges of the vastness of their own fears, cannot possibly be supposed.

There is a burgeoning literature which examines the effect of trust on economic performance. The extent of trust can be quantified by using surveys
that identify the share of people who generally trust others, who trust in
people from a different background, who trust in neighbors, who trust in
people they know, who trust in people they meet for the first time, and so on
and so forth.

Before delving into the economic effects of trust, we will first discuss some
studies that investigate the effect of climate variability on the evolution of
trust and social cooperation. For instance, the rise of the sentiments of trust
could be attributed to the desire of subsistence farmers to cope with weather
disturbances. In the absence of properly functioning capital and insurance
markets, farmers had to depend on various strategies to shield their consumption from weather shocks. These include expanding ties to individuals living
in other communities, which could have favored the emergence of a culture
of trust that persisted until the present time. Johannes Buggle and Ruben
Durante test this prediction using historical data from Europe.[11] Their study
indicates that provinces with higher climate variability during the growing
season in pre-industrial times display higher levels of interpersonal trust
today. The authors also show that these regions were more closely connected
to the medieval trade networks, were more likely to adopt early participatory political institutions, and are characterized by a higher quality of local
governments today.

Other studies argue that the topographic features of the land can influence
the level of trust. Elevation and terrain ruggedness are natural barriers that
prevent different groups from communicating and interacting with each other.
These inconsistent landscapes can preclude the sentiments of trust toward
others who are kept at a distance by the uneven features of the land. Rugged
terrain also hinders trade and commercial exchange between communities.
This does not allow these communities the opportunity for interactions that
allow trust sentiments to blossom. To examine these ideas, Sherif Khalifa
estimates the effect of trust, predicted by mean elevation and terrain ruggedness, on economic development.[12] The author focuses on trust in people from
another nationality, trust in people from another religion, trust in people you
know personally, trust in people you meet for the first time, trust in your family, and trust in your neighborhood. The evidence shows that trust, predicted
by these topographic features, has a statistically significant positive association with economic development.

Other studies argue that ethnolinguistic diversity is associated with lower levels of trust. In this context, individuals in diverse settings compete for scarce resources along group lines, thereby increasing the salience of existing ethnic differences with lower levels of trust between groups. As discussed later in more detail, the extent of ethnolinguistic diversity is higher in the tropics because the disease environment curbed mobility and increased the cost of transportation due to the lack of domesticated animals. This caused isolation of societies with a strong emphasis on ethnic affiliation. In this context, Amanda Lea Robinson evaluates the association between ethnic diversity and the degree to which coethnics are trusted more than non-coethnics.[13] Using public opinion data from some African countries, the study finds that those from ethnically diverse states express, on average, more ethnocentric trust. Roland Hodler, Sorawoot Srisuma, Alberto Vesperoni, and Noémie Zurlinden also show that ethnic stratification is associated with low levels of trust in other people and institutions at the local level in Africa.[14]

TRUST (IN) GROWTH

There is a stream of literature that examines the effect of trust on economic outcomes. For instance, Stephen Knack and Paul Zac present a theoretical framework in which agents may trust those with whom they transact, but they can also allocate resources to verify the truthfulness of claims made by the other parties to the transaction.[15] The model predicts that a low trust environment hurts investment and economic growth, which is supported by evidence from a cross section of countries. In another contribution, Stephen Knack and Paul Zac examine the ability of policy makers to influence trust and economic performance.[16] The authors find that policies that increase trust, by increasing educational attainment and decreasing income inequality through transfer payments, efficiently stimulate economic activity. Stephen Knack and Phillip Keefer examine whether interpersonal trust, associational activity, and civic cooperation matter for economic performance.[17] The authors find that only trust and civic cooperation are associated with better economic performance, and that both are stronger in nations with lower income inequality, with formal institutions that protect property and enforce contracts, and with less polarization along class or ethnic dimensions.

Yann Algan and Pierre Cahuc show that the inherited trust of the descendants of immigrants in the United States is significantly influenced by the country of origin and the timing of arrival of their forebears.[18] The authors use the inherited trust of the descendants of the United States immigrants as a measure of inherited trust in their country of origin. The authors find that inherited trust explain a significant share of the economic backwardness of developing countries, and of the economic differences between developed countries over the twentieth century.

Some studies focus on the effect of trust on economic outcomes at the regional level. In this context, Sjoerd Beugelsdijk and Anton van Schaik investigate whether variations in economic growth between European provinces can be explained by differences in social capital, in the form of generalized trust and associational activity.[19] The authors provide evidence that economic growth is positively associated with active associational activity, but not with trust or passive group membership. In another contribution, Sjoerd Beugelsdijk and Anton van Schaik introduce a new index of social capital, based on trust and social networks, at the regional level in Europe.[20] The authors find a positive association between this index of social capital and regional economic development.

In a similar vein, Jesús Peiró-Palomino, Emili Tortosa-Ausina and Anabel Forte examine the effect of social trust, associational activities and social norms, on economic growth for a sample of European regions.[21] Their analysis suggests that higher levels of trust and active associational activities lead to higher economic growth, while social norms are not a pertinent growth predictor. In a related contribution, Jesús Peiró-Palomina and Emili Tortosa-Ausina examine the effect of social trust on economic performance at different stages of economic development.[22] The authors find that trust is one of the drivers of economic development, that trust is not pertinent for the poorest economies, and that the effect of trust on income decreases as an economy becomes wealthier. Guido Tabellini examines whether cultural values, such as trust and confidence in self-determination, have a causal effect on economic development in European regions.[23] The analysis suggests that the exogenous component of culture, predicted by the literacy rate at the end of the nineteenth century and the political institutions in place over the past few centuries, is strongly correlated with current regional economic development.

Some studies focus on whether the effect of trust on economic outcomes depends on the quality of institutions. For instance, Roman Horváth shows that trust exerts a positive effect on economic growth especially in countries with a weak rule of law.[24] Ola Olsson, Pelle Ahlerup and David Yanagizawa explore whether interpersonal trust is a substitute or a complement to formal institutions in achieving economic growth.[25] The authors show that social capital has the greatest economic effect at lower levels of institutional strength while the effect vanishes when institutions are strong.

INVESTMENT AND INNOVATION

Trust can influence the accumulation of human capital and physical capital. Human capital is expected to be higher in communities with high levels of trust. This is because firms hire workers with high levels of human capital to perform complex tasks. The cost of monitoring workers is higher with the complexity of tasks but lower in an environment with high levels of trust. Furthermore, workers with high levels of human capital may be better able to cooperate and share information with other workers in an environment with high levels of trust. Thus, trust increases the firm's demand for workers with higher levels of human capital.

Similarly, trust can increase the level of investment in physical capital. Higher levels of trust are accompanied by an increase in information dissemination about a larger variety of investment opportunities. Higher levels of trust also diminish the need for extensive contracts and lower the probability of costly litigation. Thus, investment spending can take place in an environment of trust easier than in an atmosphere fraught with suspicion and distrust.

Along the lines of this intuition, some studies focus on the effect of trust on investment, which is critical for economic growth. For instance, Jacob Dearmon and Kevin Grier show that trust is a significant determinant of economic development, and that the positive effect of investment on economic performance is enhanced in a high trust environment.[26] Jacob Dearmon and Robin Grier show that trust has a significant positive effect on human capital and a non-linear effect on physical capital.[27] Accordingly, an increase in trust in a low-trust country has a greater effect on the accumulation of physical capital than an identical increase in a high-trust country.

Some scholars also argue that there is a positive association between trust and innovation. Innovators need venture capitalists to finance their innovative ideas even when the outcome is uncertain. Thus, the risky enterprise benefits if the venture capitalist and the innovator trust each other. Based on this intuition, some studies explore the effect of trust on innovation. For instance, Semih Akçomak and Bas ter Weel investigate the connection between trust, innovation, and economic growth in regions of the European Union.[28] The authors show that social capital fosters innovation, captured by patent applications, which is conducive to economic growth. Semih Akçomak and Hanna Müller-Zick compare the effect of various trust indicators on inventive activities in European regions.[29] Their findings indicate that only generalized trust and non-egoistic fairness have a robust impact on inventive activities. Their analysis shows that a one standard deviation increase in generalized trust increases patents per million by 2 percent on average.

GOVERNMENT INTERVENTION

Some studies argue that trust affects the extent of government involvement in the economy due to its effect on the demand for government regulations and the support for government-funded welfare programs. The intuition is that a high level of trust may increase the support for the welfare state as it bolsters the belief that others will not use the welfare system inappropriately. In addition, a low level of trust in public officials and private agents increases the demand for government regulations that impose restrictions on their actions. These government interventions have a significant effect on aggregate economic outcomes.

Some scholars focus on the association between trust and government regulations. For instance, Yann Algan, Pierre Cahuc, Phillippe Aghion, and Andrei Shleifer argue that the lack of trust creates public demand for regulation, whereas regulation in turn discourages the formation of trust.[30] The authors provide evidence that government regulation is negatively correlated with trust in others, in the government, in banks, and in foreign companies. Their results also imply that the lack of trust fuels demand for regulation even when people realize that the government is corrupt and ineffective.

Other studies attempt to understand the association between an environment of trust and the support for the welfare state. For instance, Yann Algan, Pierre Cahuc and Marc Sangnier propose a theoretical framework that predicts the existence of a twin-peaks relationship between trust and the size of the welfare state.[31] This implies that individuals who evade taxes, but extract social benefits, support large welfare states because they expect to benefit from them without bearing the brunt of the cost. On the other hand, civic individuals support welfare programs only when they are surrounded by trustworthy individuals. The authors provide evidence for their predictions where individuals who declare that it is excusable to claim benefits to which they are not entitled, besides individuals who think that they are surrounded by trustworthy people, are found to support the welfare state.

Christian Bjørnskov and Gert Tinggaard Svendsen find that trust determines the size of welfare states and three features that are essential for their sustainability: high levels of political confidence, strong institutions protecting property rights, and low levels of bureaucratic corruption.[32] Christian Bjørnskov and Andreas Bergh find that populations with higher levels of trust are more inclined to create and maintain welfare states with high levels of taxation and publicly financed social insurance schemes.[33] In another contribution, Christian Bjørnskov and Andreas Bergh examine the direction of causality between social trust and income inequality.[34] The authors argue that trust explains support for the welfare state which can lead to a decrease in income equality, and find that trust "has a positive effect on pre-tax pre-transfer market equality as well as for post-redistribution net equality." Finally, Gianmarco Daniele and Benny Geys argue that trust in fellow compatriots can play a critical role for welfare state support because it bolsters the belief that others will not use the welfare system inappropriately.[35] The authors find a strong positive association between interpersonal trust and welfare state support, and that trusting people are more likely to support higher taxes to fund social programs.

INTERNATIONAL FLOWS

Some studies argue that trust has implications for international trade and capital flows. In an engaging contribution, Luigi Guiso, Paola Sapienza, and Luigi Zingales examine how cultural biases affect economic exchange.[36] The authors use data on bilateral trust between European countries and show that trust is affected by the cultural affinity between the trusting country and the trusted one in terms of their history of conflicts and their religious, genetic, and somatic similarities. The authors find that lower bilateral trust leads to less trade, less foreign portfolio investment, and less foreign direct investment between two countries. Sjoerd Beugelsdijk, ShuYu, and Jakob de Haan show that the effect of trust on trade is conditional on the maintenance of the rule of law.[37] The argument is that the effect of trust on trade flows depends on whether the importing country's judicial and legal system is amply reassuring for the exporting country. Otherwise, there is uncertainty concerning potential expropriation, which causes traders to rely on trust to assess future payoffs. Thus, as the rule of law improves in the importing country the effect of trust on trade dwindles.

CENTRAL BANKS

Some scholars argue that social trust is expected to affect the extent of central bank independence. In countries with high levels of trust, the ability to implement central bank reforms is high. Trust entails lower transaction costs of political agreement and makes it easier for politicians to trust and delegate power to independent central bankers. In countries with low levels of trust, the need for independence provides a strong incentive to change the standing of the central bank. This is because the time-inconsistency problem is worse, and the credibility of political decision-making is weaker. Countries with an intermediate level of trust have neither the need nor the ability to implement far-reaching reforms.

Some studies examine these predictions. For instance, Niclas Bergrren, Sven-Olov Daunfelt, and Jorgen Hellstrom provide evidence that countries with low and high social trust implemented central bank independence earlier than countries with intermediate levels.[38] The authors also find that the political process comes to agreement on central bank standing faster in the presence of central actors trusting each other. In a related contribution, Niclas Bergrren, Sven-Olov Daunfelt, and Jorgen Hellstrom argue that central banks have become more independent in many countries due to the existence of a credibility problem.[39] The authors find that at low trust, the need for central bank independence is sufficiently strong to bring it about. At high trust, the ability to implement reforms is strong despite a low need for it. At intermediate trust levels, neither need nor ability is strong enough to generate independent central banks.

INSTITUTIONAL QUALITY

Trust can be essential for both the transition to a democratic system and for democracy to consolidate. An environment with a high level of trust can provide a safe venue for antigovernment discourse and for individuals to indicate their intent to oppose the state, thus propelling the critical mass essential for defiant collective action that may lead to a democratic transition. For a democratic system to succeed, citizens must trust in elected officials to act on their behalf, in policy makers to enact policies to their benefit, in politicians and political parties to represent their interests, in other people's willingness and ability to support policies that are likely to improve their lot, and in each other to abide by democratically established laws. Trust also makes it easier and less risky to participate in political affairs and to increase civic engagement, which helps create the civil society structures upon which a stable and functioning democracy depends.

On the other hand, democratic institutions are founded on the lack of trust in the powerful clique for fear they may act to promote their own interests on the expense of the entire populace. This lack of trust is what instigates the support for a transition to a democratic system in which ordinary people's demands are more likely to be fulfilled. Therefore, it is also possible that the lack of trust can create conducive conditions for democratic governance.

Based on this intuition, some studies examine the effect of trust on democracy. For instance, Pamela Paxton shows that trust and associational activity are positively associated with democracy which in turn affects social capital.[40] Christian Bjornskov examines the transmission channel between trust and the political system. The author finds that the trust-governance association reflects politicians in high-trust democracies being conscious of voters' demands for good governance.[41] Other studies in the literature not only examine the effect of trust on the quality of institutions, but also whether trust allows institutions to be efficient in curbing corruption. For instance, Christian Bjornskov finds that the efforts of combating corruption by formal institutions are more effective in countries with high levels of social trust.[42]

NOTES

1. Ibn Khaldun. *Al Muqqadimah: Prolegomena.*

2. Toynbee. *A Study of History.*

3. Gates. "The Spread of Ibn Khaldun's Ideas on Climate and Culture." *Journal of the History of Ideas*: 415–422.

4. Guiliano and Nunn. "Understanding Cultural Persistence and Change." *Review of Economic Studies*: 1541–1581.

5. Ingelhart and Baker. "Modernization, Cultural Change, and the Persistence of Traditional Values." *American Sociological Review*: 19–51.

6. Coleman. *Foundations of Social Theory.*

7. Fehr. "On the Economics and Biology of Trust." *Journal of the European Economic Association*: 235–266.

8. Putnam. *Making Democracy Work: Civic Traditions in Modern Italy* (p. 167).

9. Guiso, Sapienza, and Zingales. "Civic Capital as the Missing Link." National Bureau of Economic Research Working Paper 15845.

10. Aghion, and Durlauf. *Handbook of Economic Growth* (p. 52).

11. Buggle and Durante. "Climate Risk, Cooperation, and the Co-Evolution of Culture and Institutions." *The Economic Journal*: 1947–1987.

12. Khalifa. "Trust, Landscape, and Economic Development." *Journal of Economic Development*: 19–32.

13. Robinson. "Ethnic Diversity, Segregation and Ethnocentric Trust in Africa." *British Journal of Political Science*: 217–239.

14. Hodler, Srisuma, Vesperoni, and Zurlinde. "Measuring Ethnic Stratification and its Effect on Trust in Africa." *Journal of Development Economics*: 102–475.

15. Zac and Knack. "Trust and Growth." *The Economic Journal*: 295–321.

16. Knack and Zak. "Building Trust: Public Policy, Interpersonal Trust, and Economic Development." *Supreme Court Economic Review*: 91–107.

17. Knack and Keefer. "Does Social Capital Have an Economic Payoff? A Cross Country Investigation." *The Quarterly Journal of Economics*: 1251–1288.

18. Algan and Cahuc. "Inherited Trust and Growth." *The American Economic Review*: 2060–2092.

19. Beugelsdijk, and van Schaik. "Social Capital and Growth in European Regions." *European Journal of Political Economy*: 301–324.

20. Beugelsdijk and van Schaik. "Differences in Social Capital between 54 Western European Regions." *Regional Studies*: 1053–1064.

21. Peiró-Palomino, Tortosa-Ausina, and Forte. "Does Social Capital Matter for European Regional Growth?" *European Economic Review*: 47–64.

22. Peiró-Palomino and Tortosa-Ausina. "Can Trust Effects on Development be Generalized?" *European Journal of Political Economy*: 377–390.

23. Tabellini. "Culture and Institutions: Economic Development in the Regions of Europe." *Journal of the European Economic Association*: 677–716.

24. Horváth. "Does Trust Promote Growth?" *Journal of Comparative Economics*: 777–788.

25. Ahlerup, Olsson, and Yanagizawa. "Social Capital vs Institutions in the Growth Process." *European Journal of Political Economy*: 1–14.

26. Dearmon and Grier. "Trust and Development." *Journal of Economic Behavior & Organization*: 210–220.

27. Dearmon and Grier. "Trust and the Accumulation of Physical and Human Capital." *European Journal of Political Economy*: 507–519.

28. Akçomak and ter Weel. "Social Capital, Innovation and Growth: Evidence from Europe." *European Economic Review*: 544–567.

29. Akçomak and Müller-Zick. "Trust and Inventive Activity in Europe." *The Annals of Regional Science*: 529–568.

30. Aghion, Algan, Cahuc, and Shleifer. "Regulation and Distrust." *The Quarterly Journal of Economics*: 1015–1049.

31. Algan, Cahuc, and Sangnier. "Trust and the Welfare State: The Twin Peaks Curve." *The Economic Journal*: 861–883.

32. Bjørnskov and Svendsen. "Does Social Trust Determine the Size of the Welfare State?" *Public Choice*: 269–286.

33. Bjørnskov and Bergh. "Historical Trust Levels Predict the Current Size of the Welfare State." *Kyklos*: 1–19.

34. Bjørnskov and Bergh. "Trust, Welfare States and Income Equality." *European Journal of Political Economy*: 183–199.

35. Daniele and Geys. "Interpersonal Trust and Welfare State Support." *European Journal of Political Economy*: 1–12.

36. Guiso, Sapienza, and Zingales. "Cultural Biases and Economic Exchange." *The Quarterly Journal of Economics*: 1095–1131.

37. Yu, Beugelsdijk, and de Haan. "Trade, Trust and the Rule of Law." *European Journal of Political Economy*: 102–115.

38. Bergrren, Daunfelt, and Hellstrom. "Does Social Trust Speed up Reforms? The Case of Central-Bank Independence." *Journal of Institutional Economics*: 395–415.

39. Bergrren, Daunfelt, and Hellstrom. "Social Trust and Central-Bank Independence." *European Journal of Political Economy*: 425–439.

40. Paxton. "Social Capital and Democracy: An Interdependent Relationship." *American Sociological Review*: 254–277.

41. Bjornskov. "How Does Social Trust lead to Better Governance?" *Public Choice*: 323–346.

42. Bjornskov. "Combating Corruption: On the Interplay between Institutional Quality and Social Trust." *The Journal of Law & Economics*: 135–159.

Chapter Twelve

Me, Myself, and Society

We discussed in detail the economic consequences of social trust in the previous chapter. In this chapter, we continue our account of the economic consequences of other cultural traits such as individualism, social solidarity, tolerance, and others. The debate focuses on whether we need to stress the individual worth on the expense of the collective or otherwise underscore the significance of solidarity between individuals in a society, for better economic outcomes.

Individualism and collectivism are cultural traits that are also influenced by geographic factors. For instance, some studies argue that pathogen prevalence can predict the variability in individualism and collectivism across countries. The argument is that certain collectivist attitudes such as obedience and conformity can contain pathogen transmission. In other words, collectivist behaviors create a societal defense against the spread of diseases. In this context, collectivists are usually more circumspect of contact with outsiders and enforce within group conformity. These attitudes decrease exposure to pathogens which are spread in lots of cases due to climatic factors as discussed earlier. Thus, collectivism is expected to be a cultural characteristic in areas that have historically had higher prevalence of pathogens that evoke the priority of protecting one's group.

In this context, Corey Fincher, Randy Thornhill, Damian Murray, and Mark Schaller use epidemiological data and worldwide surveys on cultural values to show that the prevalence of pathogens has a strong positive correlation with cultural indicators of collectivism and a strong negative correlation with individualism.[1] Serge Morand and Bruno Walther explore if the lifestyles of collectivist countries serve as a social defense against pathogen transmission.[2] The authors show that individualism has a negative association with historical pathogen burden and a significant positive correlation with the number of infectious and zoonotic disease outbreaks.

Other studies argue that the need to collaborate within groups in agricultural communities favored the emergence of a collectivist culture. These collectivist attitudes increased cohesiveness and facilitated the coordination of agricultural production. For instance, farming communities adopted several alternatives to cope with climatic risks latent in agricultural production. These include food storage and water administration technologies, which needed significant levels of cooperation and collective action to implement and maintain. Along these lines, Johannes Buggle examines the effect of the adoption of irrigation agriculture on cultural attitudes of contemporary populations.[3] The author finds that societies whose ancestors practiced irrigation agriculture have stronger collectivist cultural norms today. Lewis Davis argues that collectivism was common in agricultural communities that faced the risk of rainfall fluctuations.[4] The author finds that individual responsibility, predicted by rainfall fluctuations, has a large positive effect on economic development.

Some studies also argue that natural disasters can pose a societal threat, which triggers collectivist sentiments or the priority of protecting one's group. Societies that face these events have to work together to be able to withstand the calamity and to deal with its consequences. In this context, Sigihiro Oishi and Asuka Komiya show that nations with higher levels of exposure to natural disasters were more collectivistic in nature than those with lower risk.[5]

THE (I) IN INDIVIDUALISM

Individualism is a cultural aspect that attracts lots of attention. Individualism is the social stance that emphasizes the independence and autonomy of the individual, that encourages the endeavor to chase one's dreams and objectives, that advocates that the interests of the individual should take precedence over those of a social group, that favors individual freedom over collective action, and that reflects the belief that individuals are supposed to stand for themselves and their views as opposed to being integrated into and loyal to a cohesive group.

Individualism is argued to have a significant influence on human behavior, actions, decisions, and choices that can ultimately determine economic outcomes. For instance, an individualist culture attaches social status rewards to personal accomplishments. This creates incentives for innovation, creativity and taking individual initiatives. In individualistic societies, the attention afforded to personal achievements and individual worth also contributes to a more meritocratic system where those who perform better are compensated accordingly. Alternatively, a collectivist culture encourages favoritism, prizes loyalty, cherishes cohesion and enforces mutual obligations toward other members of the group. This is likely to engender corruption, nepotism, and favoritism. Thus, some argue that an individualist culture can be more conducive to economic outcomes.

On the other hand, individualism can hinder the ability of a society to deal with an adversity that necessitates the concerted effort of the entire community to overcome it. In this context, those in collectivist cultures are more likely to sacrifice their personal freedom to follow the instructions imposed for the common good and to work selflessly to the benefit of the community. Alternatively, those in individualistic cultures value more their individual freedoms and personal rights even in the face of a calamity that requires the collective involvement of every individual to be able to deal with it. This is particularly the case in societies facing events such as natural disasters or health epidemics. In cases of epidemics for instance, authorities interfere to contain an outbreak before it strains or overwhelms the health care system. Examples of such interventions include stay-at-home orders, shelter-in-place decrees, restrictions imposed on in-person transactions, lockdowns, and social distancing. Some studies find that the higher the level of individualism, the higher the cases and the fatalities from the infectious disease and the higher the chances that people would not adhere to epidemic advisories.[6] This delays the containment of the disease and the resumption of economic activities. In cases of exposure to a natural disaster, a society needs to work together to deal with the immediate aftermath of a calamity until the authorities can reach the stricken area with their resources.

Several studies compare the effect of individualism versus collectivism on economic outcomes. For instance, Yuriy Gorodnichenko and Gerard Roland compare the economic effects of individualism versus a large set of other cultural traits.[7] The authors find that individualism is the central cultural attribute that matters for economic growth, while the other cultural traits do not appear to robustly impact economic outcomes. In a follow up paper, Yuriy Gorodnichenko and Gerard Roland show that an individualist culture induces innovation, captured by patents per capita, and economic development.[8] In a subsequent contribution, the same authors show a strong association between individualism, the level of democratic governance and the duration of democracy. The authors also provide evidence that individualist countries are more likely to transition into democracy.[9]

Some studies focus on the effect of individualism on institutions. For instance, Lewis Davis and Farangis Abdurazokzoda construct a new linguistic dataset based on the World Atlas of Language Structures.[10] The authors argue that some linguistic expressions can echo an innate sense of individual worth. The authors find that individualism, predicted by the new linguistic variables, has a positive effect on the quality of institutions. Lewis Davis and Claudia Williamson investigate whether individualism affects the regulation of entry for new firms.[11] The authors find that countries with an individualistic culture regulate entry lightly, especially those with democratic institutions or a common law tradition. This finding is consistent with the idea that culture influences social preferences for regulation, while institutions determine the degree to which those preferences are expressed as policy outcomes. Claudia Williamson and Brandon Cline examine the influence of individualism on the efficiency of contract enforcement.[12] The authors find that individualism has a significant positive association with efficient contract enforcement, especially in democracies.

Mariko Klasing assesses the role of culture in determining the quality of institutions, captured by protection of property rights and the quality of bureaucracy.[13] The author finds that differences in the degree of individualism, and the extent of tolerance of inequality in the distribution of power, are statistically significant predictors of the observed differences in institutional quality. Andreas Kyriacou argues that individualism can influence economic development through its effect on the quality of government.[14] This is because individualist societies appreciate personal achievement and worth which contribute toward a more meritocratic system. The evidence provided by the author suggests that individualism has a positive effect on economic development through its advancement of good governance.

SENSE OF ASABIYA

As we have seen in our previous discussion, some studies stress the importance of self-interest and the value of individual worth versus social cooperation to achieve collective goals. Other scholars, however, argue that cooperation, cohesiveness, collective effort, and social solidarity are critical for human progress. This is referred to as "Asabiya" by the social scientist and historian Ibn Khaldun.

Ibn Khaldun introduces the concept of cooperation in his *Al Muqaddimah*. Asabiya is the ability of members of a society to cooperate and enjoy a high level of solidarity. In this context, Ibn Khaldun uses this idea to formulate a theory of the expansion and the subsequent decline of states. In this context, when a state in the civilization zone falls into internal strife it becomes susceptible to conquest from the desert. A coalition of tribes with high asabiya conquers the civilization zone and establishes a new state there. The conquering generation and their offspring preserve their desert ways, maintain their military prowess, and safeguard their group solidarity. As generations succeed generations, the conditions of indulgent life begin to erode the asabiya due to the corrosive effect of luxury on solidarity. At this point, the dynasty goes into decline, and sooner or later another coalition arises and the cycle repeats itself.

Historian Peter Turchin also offers an insight on the formation and fall of empires that emphasizes that cooperation is crucial in these historical processes.[15] Turchin argues in *War and Peace and War: The Rise and Fall of Empires* that emperiogenisis or the formation of empires[16] "is made possible only because groups are integrated at the micro level by cooperation among their members" and that[17] "the ability of an empire to expand territory and to defend itself against external and internal enemies is determined largely by the characteristics of the imperial nation, especially its asabiya or solidarity because only groups possessing high levels of asabiya can construct large empires." Turchin also underscores that[18] "In the pressure cooker of a metaethnic frontier, poorly integrated groups crumble and disappear, whereas groups based on strong cooperation thrive and expand." He offers an example to support his proposition:[19]

> It would not be an exaggeration to say that they built the three (Muscovites, Mongols, Americans) most powerful empires in world history. Less obviously, each of these three societies, although in its own culturally unique way, had a high capacity for concerted collective action. In fact, such a capacity seems to be a necessary condition for successful empire building. The society-level capacity for concerted action was, in turn, based on the ability of individuals to cooperate.

Turchin also provides another example from the history of the Arab conquests of the seventh century:[20] "The spectacular Arab conquests of the seventh century continue to cause wonder. Many explanations have been offered, but most of them do not make sense. The Arabs did not have a numeric or technological advantage over their adversaries; in fact, quite the reverse." Then he offers an explanation:[21] "The single advantage that the Arabs had was their fighting spirit and willingness to fight to the death. The Arabs defeated the Byzantines and the Persians because the Arab asabiya was much greater than the asabiya of their opponents. Centuries of life squeezed between two imperial frontiers changed the Arab society in ways that made it possible for Muhammad to forge them into a unified powerful entity."

Asabiya also contributed to the traditions of administrative cohesiveness that allowed some Muslim states to build on the work of predecessors and to improve how justice was applied to the people of the realm. To examine these ideas, Linda Darling conducts a historical study of the late medieval Muslim world and finds a positive correlation between a regime's social cohesion and its ability to provide a justice system.[22] The author concludes that

> The high level of administrative continuity and growth in the high asabiyya regimes must therefore have been due not only to the presence of the secretaries and their traditions, but also to their ability to operate their administrative

systems and preserve their literatures more or less intact, without being too much undercut by fighting among the princes and great men of state or too often falling victim to violence within the regime. The stronger group cohesion of the initial conquerors may have created a governing culture with a lower level of internal competition, one that allowed civilian bureaucrats to participate more fully in governance, exert a greater influence on its direction, and survive to hand their traditions down to their successors.

In the context of social cohesion, some studies also attempt to explore the economic consequences of tolerance. Tolerance is the ability or willingness to tolerate someone or something. In specific, it is the ability to tolerate someone from a different background, or to tolerate some behavior that is not familiar to us, or to tolerate a practice that we do not approve of, or to tolerate opinions that one does not concur with. Richard Florida defines tolerance as[23] "openness, inclusiveness, and diversity to all ethnicities, races, and walks of life." Tolerance apparently enhances social solidarity especially if each member feels accepted as part of society.

Tolerance boosts economic performance as it enhances social cohesion, diminishes the likelihood of conflict, allows for a more politically open climate, and fosters the ability to work and cooperate with those from a different background. Tolerance leads to inclusion which implies that work is performed, and decisions are taken, by the most qualified irrespective of their background. In societies that commit, or experience discrimination, talents and qualifications are overlooked due to bias, bigotry, prejudice, and favoritism. This adversely affects the average quality of the workforce and hurts productivity. Intolerance can also be associated with persecution, massacres, slaughter, ethnic cleansing, genocide, and mass murder.

Few studies examine the effect of tolerance on the economy. For instance, Niclas Berggren and Mikael Elinder examine how tolerance, measured by attitudes toward different types of neighbors, affects economic growth in a sample of countries.[24] The authors argue that tolerance toward homosexuals is negatively related to economic growth. In a response, Eduard Bomhoff and Grace Lee reexamine the results of Niclas Berggren and Mikael Elinder.[25] The authors properly account for conditional convergence in their analysis and find no statistical pattern that associates bias against homosexuals with economic growth.[26]

Given the significance of both individualism and social solidarity, we can conclude that societies need to walk a tight rope, or maintain a delicate balance, between honoring individual achievements without breaking the ties with society and promoting social cohesion without sacrificing the individual on the altar of societal priorities.

SPEAK ONE'S MIND

There is a new burgeoning literature that explores the effect of certain linguistic characteristics on economic outcomes. Language is what we use to articulate our ideas, to express our emotions, to communicate our opinions, to declare our intentions, to disclose our feelings, and to enunciate our preferences. Language is, thus, an indispensable way of unveiling our cultural traits and attributes. Thus, language can be considered as a vehicle that our thoughts drive to their destination. On the other hand, our language also defines the limitations of our expressions. It was the philosopher Ludwig Wittgenstein who stated in his *Tractatus Logico Philosophicus* that "The limits of my language mean the limits of my world." This implies that sometimes we can go as far as our language permits.

Alternatively, language can influence our culture by shaping the form and content of cultural information that is delivered from one generation to another. This implies that as much as our language allows us to communicate our thoughts, the structure of our language can also influence our thinking and accordingly our actions. In the context of this chapter, language is the tool that allows us to voice how we are conscious of our self-worth and in what way we connect with our society. As discussed earlier, certain linguistic characteristics can also predict the degree of individualism or collectivism in a society.

Given the significance of language, it is worth mentioning that there is a new discipline of study called language geography which is a branch that studies the geographic distribution of languages or its constituent elements. In this context, proximity can determine how likely it is that we are able to comprehend our neighbors. For instance, broad areas with flat terrain are considered linguistic spread zones where diverse speaker groups overlap with each other. On the other hand, there are topographical features such as mountains, large bodies of water, deserts, or untamed forests that separate communities and limit contact between them. This geographic isolation limits the amount of mutual intelligibility and cause languages to diverge as to be barely recognizable to one another.

Altitude can also influence the types of sounds humans produce when speaking their language. For instance, Caleb Everett examines whether the geographic context in which a language is spoken directly affects its phonological form with a focus on the association between elevation and whether a language employs ejective phonemes.[27] The author provides evidence that languages with phonemic ejective consonants occur closer to inhabitable areas of high elevation, compared to languages without such class of sounds. In another study, Carol Ember and Elvin Ember argue that people in warmer climates communicate at a distance more often than in colder ones. In these communities, it is adaptive to use syllables and sounds that can be easily heard and discerned at a distance.[28] The authors find that languages in warm climates are characterized by a higher proportion of consonant-vowel syllables and sonorous or more audible sounds.

As much as geography influences the characteristics of language, it is also argued that these linguistic features can have economic consequences. There is a growing body of literature that studies the connection between linguistic structures and socioeconomic outcomes. Since each language has its unique structure and spirit, its effect is expected to be different. Some of the studies in the pertinent literature focus specifically on the differences between languages in terms of their use of future tense, gender marking, and pronoun drop.[29]

There is a stream of literature that associates the pronoun drop with economic outcomes. The pronoun drop is a linguistic characteristic which indicates whether a language allows speakers to drop a personal pronoun when it is used as the subject of a sentence. Some studies argue that non-pronoun drop languages are expected to be associated with individualism which is known to promote economic performance. In this context, Emiko Kashima and Yoshihisa Kashima were the first to address this question in two of the seminal contributions of the literature. The authors find that cultures with pronoun drop languages tend to be less individualistic than those with non-pronoun drop languages.[30] Lewis Davis and Farangis Abdurazokzoda use a new linguistic dataset based on the World Atlas of Language Structures and show a statistically significant negative effect of the pronoun drop on individualism.[31]

There is another stream of literature that focuses on the linguistic characteristic of future time reference which is argued to influence speaker's intertemporal choices, long term orientation, patience, economic performance, and corporate decisions. The argument is that languages that grammatically separate the future and the present lead speakers to feel that the future is more distant. On the other hand, languages which equate the future and the present lead speakers to be more willing to prepare for a future which seems less remote. Studies in this stream of literature use an indicator that linguists refer to as "future time reference" which captures how languages mark the timing of events. In this context, there are two categories of languages: weak future time reference languages which associate the present and the future, and strong future time reference languages which separate the present from the future.

Some studies explore the effect of future time reference on economic outcomes. For instance, Keith Chen investigates whether speaking in a specific way about the future affect speakers' intertemporal choices.[32] The author finds that speakers of weak future time reference languages save more, retire with more wealth, and adopt healthier lifestyles. Malte Hubner and Gonzague Vannoorenberghe examine whether patience, captured by indicators of time discounting and long-term orientation, is a determinant of economic outcomes.[33] The authors provide evidence for a positive association between patience, predicted by future time reference, and output per worker, total factor productivity, innovation, and capital stock. Oasis Kodila-Tedika and Sherif Khalifa explore the economic effects of whether a country's policymakers have a long-term strategic vision and whether they can induce public and private agents to act according to that vision.[34] The authors find that the adoption of a long-term vision, predicted by future time reference, has a statistically significant positive association with economic development. David Figlio, Paola Giuliano, Umut Özek, and Paola Sapienza study the effect of long-term orientation, using future time reference as one measure, on the educational attainment of immigrants.[35] The authors find that students from long-term oriented cultures perform better, have fewer absences and less disciplinary incidents, are less likely to repeat a school year, are more likely to enroll in advanced courses, and are more likely to graduate from high school in four years.

Languages also differ in the way they mark gender which is argued to influence personal opinions and public policies toward gender roles. In this context, several studies examine the economic consequences of gender marking. For instance, Lewis Davis and Megan Reynolds show that languages that emphasize gender distinction are associated with a larger gender gap in educational attainment.[36] Victor Gay, Daniel Hicks, Estefania Santacreu-Vasut and Amir Shoham show that females who speak a language with sex-based grammatical structure have lower labor force participation and fewer hours of work.[37] Victor Gay, Estefania Santacreu-Vasut, and Amir Shoham find that grammatical gender distinction is a significant determinant of gender political quota and female political participation.[38] Astghik Maviskalyan shows that countries whose language is gender-intensive have lower female participation in the labor force and higher discriminatory attitudes against women.[39] Yehonatan Givati and Ugo Troiano find that countries whose language had more gender-based pronouns offer a shorter maternity leave.[40]

NOTES

1. Fincher, Thornhill, Murray, and Schaller. "Pathogen Prevalence Predicts Human Cross-cultural Variability in Individualism/Collectivism." *Proceedings of the Royal Society*: 1279–85.

2. Morand and Walther. "Individualistic Values are related to an Increase in the Outbreaks of Infectious Diseases and Zoonotic Diseases." *Nature*. https://doi.org/10.1038/s41598-018-22014-4

3. Buggle. "Growing Collectivism: Irrigation, Group Conformity and Technological Divergence." *Journal of Economic Growth*: 147–193.

4. Davis. "Individual Responsibility and Economic Development." *Kyklos*: 426–470.

5. Oishi and Komiya. "Natural Disaster Risk and Collectivism." *Journal of Cross-Cultural Psychology*: 1263–1270.

6. Maaravi, Levy, Gur, Confino, and Segal. "The Tragedy of the Commons: How Individualism and Collectivism Affected the Spread of the COVID-19 Pandemic." *Front Public Health*: 1–6.

7. Gorodnichenko and Roland. "Which Dimensions of Culture Matter for Long Run Growth." *The American Economic Review: Papers and Proceedings*: 492–498.

8. Gorodnichenko and Gerard Roland. "Culture, Institutions, and the Wealth of Nations." *Review of Economics and Statistics*: 402–416.

9. Gorodnichenko and Roland. "Culture, Institutions, and Democratization." National Bureau of Economic Research Working Paper 21117.

10. Davis and Abdurazokzoda. "Language, Culture and Institutions." *Journal of Comparative Economics*: 541–561.

11. Davis and Williamson. "Culture and the Regulation of Entry." *Journal of Comparative Economics*: 1055–1083.

12. Cline and Williamson. "Individualism, Democracy, and Contract Enforcement." *Journal of Corporate Finance*: 284–306.

13. Klasing. "Cultural Dimensions, Collective Values and their Importance for Institutions." *Journal of Comparative Economics*: 447–467.

14. Kyriacou. "Individualism–Collectivism, Governance and Economic Development." *European Journal of Political Economy*: 91–104.

15. Turchin. *War and Peace and War: The Rise and Fall of Empires*. Turchin. *Historical Dynamics: Why States Rise and Fall*. Turchin. *Ultrasociety: How 10,000 Years of War Made Humans the Greatest Cooperators on Earth*. Turchin. *Secular Cycles*.

16. Turchin. *War and Peace and War: The Rise and Fall of Empires* (p. 5).

17. Ibid. (p. 6).

18. Ibid. (p. 6).

19. Ibid. (p. 53).

20. Ibid. (p. 102).

21. Ibid. (p. 103).

22. Darling. "Social Cohesion ('Asabiyya') and Justice in the Late Medieval Middle East." *Comparative Studies in Society and History*: 329–357.

23. Florida. "Cities and the Creative Class." *City and Community*: 3–19.

24. Bergrren and Elinder. "Is Tolerance Good or Bad for Growth?" *Public Choice*: 283–308.

25. Bomhoff and Lee. "Tolerance and Economic Growth Revisited." *Public Choice*: 487–494.

26. Other things being equal, a country grows faster if it starts from a poorer initial condition.

27. Everett. "Evidence for Direct Geographic Influences on Linguistic Sounds." *PLOS One*. https://doi.org/10.1371/journal.pone.0065275

28. Ember and Ember. "Climate, Econiche, and Sexuality." *American Anthropologist*: 180–185.

29. Mavisakalyan and Weber. "Linguistic Structures and Economic Outcomes." *The Journal of Economic Surveys*: 916–939.

30. Kashima and Kashima. "Culture and Language: The Case of Cultural Dimensions and Personal Pronoun Use." *Journal of Cross-Cultural Psychology*: 461–486. Kashima and Kashima. "Erratum to Kashima and Kashima (1998)." *Journal of Cross-Cultural Psychology*: 396–400.

31. Davis and Abdurazokzoda. "Language, Culture and Institutions." *Journal of Comparative Economics*: 541–561.

32. Chen. "The Effect of Language on Economic Behavior." *American Economic Review*: 690–731.

33. Hubner and Vannoorenberghe. "Patience and Long-run Growth." *Economics Letters*: 163–167.

34. Kodila-Tedika and Khalifa. "Long-term Vision and Economic Development." *The World Economy*: 3088–3102.

35. Figlio, Giuliano, Özek, and Sapienza. "Long-Term Orientation and Educational Performance." *American Economic Journal: Economic Policy*: 272–309.

36. Davis and Reynolds. "Gendered Language and the Educational Gender Gap." *Economics Letters*: 46–48.

37. Gay, Hicks, Santacreu-Vasut, and Shoham. "Decomposing Culture: An Analysis of Gender, Language, and Labor Supply in the Household." *Review of Economics of the Household*: 879–909.

38. Gay, Santacreu-Vasut, and Shoham. "Do Female/Male Distinctions in Language Matter?" *Applied Economics Letters*: 495–498.

39. Maviskalyan. "Gender in Language and Gender in Employment." *Oxford Development Studies*: 403–424.

40. Givati and Troiano. "Law, Economics, and Culture." *The Journal of Law & Economics*: 339–364.

Chapter Thirteen

The Wrath and Wealth of Nations

Conflict is a fundamental component of the narrative of human history. The story of humanity is saturated with incidents of conflict, warfare, and strife. Humans have been engaged in a tug of war from time immemorial. Conflict can be associated with the best and the worst of humanity. On one hand, it can be coupled with casualties, death, destruction, savagery, genocide, and senseless killings. On the other hand, conflict can be identified with a heightened sense of patriotism, a desire for self-sacrifice for a cause or a country, an embrace of martyrdom, acts of bravery and valor, deeds of humanitarianism and chivalry, and endurance under duress. Winston Churchill once declared: "Never in the field of human conflict was so much owed by so many to so few." It is not uncommon in conflicts that there are those few who sacrifice themselves for the sake of the many in the best expression of human selflessness. In a similar vein, historian and archaeologist Ian Morris offers a bold argument that war actually made humanity safer as he posits that[1]

> beginning about ten thousand years ago in some parts of the world, then spreading across the planet, the winners of wars incorporated the losers into larger societies. The only way to make these larger societies work was for their rulers to develop strong governments, and one of the first things these governments had to do, if they wanted to stay in power, was suppress violence within the society. The Men who ran these governments hardly ever pursued policies of peacemaking purely out of the goodness of their hearts. They cracked down on killing because well-behaved subjects were easier to govern and tax than angry, murderous ones. The unintended consequence, though, was that rates of violent death fell by 90 percent between Stone Age times and the twentieth century.

Conflicts can be instigated by grievances, greed, anger, or other factors. Wars can also be prolonged because of humans' inability to admit their folly. It is eye opening what Scott Andersen wrote about the inertia of the Great War that can be applied to other conflicts:[2]

167

It is a question that has faced peoples and nations at war since the beginning of time, and usually produced a terrible answer: in contemplating all the lives already lost, the treasure squandered, how to ever admit it was for nothing? Since such an admission is unthinkable, and the status quo untenable, the only option left is to escalate. Thus among the warring states in Europe at the end of 1915 it was no longer a matter of satisfying what had brought them into the conflict in the first place—and in many cases, those reasons had been shockingly trivial—but to expand beyond them, the acceptable terms for peace are not lowered, but raised. This conflict was no longer about playing for small advantage against one's imperial rivals, but about hobbling them forever, ensuring that they might never again have the capability to wage such a devastating and pointless war.

Thus, conflicts usually start and continue for no purpose that is worth the sacrifices that societies submit in the altar of war. When it comes to the human urge to engage in conflict, there are no better than the words of John Steinbeck that "all war is a symptom of man's failure as a thinking animal." When it comes to the human desire to continue in a state of war, there is no better than the warning of Mahatma Gandhi that "an eye for an eye will only make the whole world blind."

There are three types of conflicts that we will focus on in this chapter and the following ones. The first is conflict between people and authority, the second is conflict between different groups of people, and the third is distributional conflict. The first creates political instability. The second leads to armed conflict, internal strife, and bloody warfare. The third is caused by income inequality that is not justified in the eyes of those who suffer its consequences.

CLIMATE, RESOURCES, AND CONFLICT

Climate, and climatic variability, can create conducive conditions for conflict.[3] Warfare adversely affects economic outcomes due to the death toll; the casualties that need medical attention; the destruction of property, infrastructure, and productive facilities; the diversion of supplies for the war effort rather than for productive purposes; and the use of scarce resources for reconstruction after the ceasefire.

In this context, weather shocks can affect economies that are reliant on rain-fed farming.[4] In these cases, weather disturbances are considered income shocks. This is because the abrupt fall in precipitation leads to lower production and income. Dwindled income leads to crumbling infrastructure, worse provision of public goods and weaker militaries. This complicates the ability of the authorities to provide services to the entire population and to suppress insurgencies. Adverse weather shocks and the ensuing deterioration in economic conditions also make it easier for armed militias to recruit combatants from an expanding pool of frustrated unemployed young people who find themselves without a source of income. Detrimental weather shocks can also produce wider poverty and income inequality, which could increase resentment and exasperation toward the state or create tensions across social classes.

There are several studies that attempt to examine the effect of climate on conflict. For instance, Marshall Burke, Solomon Hsiang, and Edward Miguel conduct a meta-analysis to synthesize various studies on the effect of climate change on conflict.[5] The authors find that deviations from temperature and precipitation patterns systematically increase the likelihood of different types of conflict including crimes, demonstrations and civil war. In another contribution, Marshall Burke, Solomon Hsiang, and Edward Miguel also carry out a comprehensive synthesis of the growing literature on climate and conflict in an article in *Science*.[6] The authors show that deviations from typical precipitation and temperature systematically increase the perilous prospect of conflicts including violent crime, intergroup conflict, political instability, institutional breakdown, and the collapse of civilizations. Solomon Hsiang, Kyle Meng, and Mark Cane argue, in an article in *Nature*, that planetary-scale climate changes, estimated by El Niño/Southern Oscillation, are associated with conflict.[7] The authors also show that the probability of conflict throughout the tropics doubles during El Niño years compared to La Niña years. Edward Miguel, Shanker Satyanath and Ernest Sergenti find that lower economic growth, driven by falling rainfall, is strongly associated with higher likelihood of conflict.[8] In a subsequent article, Edward Miguel and Shanker Satyanath reconfirm their original findings that adverse economic shocks, driven by declining rainfall, increases the likelihood of conflict in sub-Saharan Africa.[9]

There are some historical studies as well on the association between climate and conflict. In an engaging paper, Murat Iyigun, Nathan Nunn, and Nancy Qian examine the effects of cooling on conflict in Europe, North Africa, and the Near East during the period of the "Little Ice Age" from 1400 C.E. to 1900 C.E.[10] The authors show that cooling is associated with increased conflict especially in areas that are suitable for the production of agricultural staples. The authors conclude that this is consistent with the hypothesis that climate change influences conflict by lowering agricultural productivity.

On the other hand, there are other studies that find no clear association between climate change and conflict. For instance, Mathieu Couttenier and Raphael Soubeyran examine the effect of some climate components on civil war in sub-Saharan Africa.[11] The authors find that precipitation, temperature, and a drought severity index do not have a significant effect on conflict. However, the study finds that ethnically fractionalized and less democratic countries are more prone to conflict when hit by a drought. Antonio Ciccone argues that rainfall shocks are likely to be followed by a reversal to average values.[12] Contrary to other studies that examine the effect of rainfall annual growth rates on conflict, the author explores the effect of lagged and current rainfall levels. The analysis shows that negative rainfall shocks do not increase the onset and incidence of conflict in sub-Saharan Africa. In another study, Antonio Ciccone investigates the effect of weather and weather-driven transitory income changes on the onset and incidence of conflict.[13] The author finds that adverse transitory income shocks, driven by rainfall fluctuations, lower the risk of conflict.

Resource earnings are also both a source of funding for insurgency and an instigator of grievances as discussed earlier in more detail. These proceeds provide the initial funding to launch a civil war, increase grievances due to the activities of resource extraction companies that adversely affect local communities, and relieve governments from the need to levy taxes and thus become less responsive to their people. Natural wealth can also prolong a conflict as it enables the rebels to continue funding the rebellion instead of being defeated or forced to the negotiating table.

PEOPLE DEMAND THE END OF THE REGIME

It was an inspiring moment when hundreds of thousands of protestors poured into the streets of the Arab world in 2011 in what came to be known as the Arab Spring. The protestors shared similar sentiments of simmering anger and broiling rage against the entrenched tyrants. Endless waves of protests erupted and swept through the Arab world in Tunisia, Egypt, Libya, Yemen, Syria, and others with the stunning spectacle of crowds surging into the streets and chanting angry slogans toward the regime. The one that stood out was "The People demand the end of the regime." As the Arab poet Abul Qasim Al Shabi wrote, "If, one day, a people desire to live, then fate will answer their call. And their night will then begin to fade, and their chains break and fall." Fate answered the call and some of these dictatorships that seemed once invincible fell like a house of cards.

In this context, the source of state tenacity and the cause of its fragility is an issue that attracts lots of attention. State strength depends on appeal, loyalty, or coercion. The first refers to the ability of the state to convince the people of its vision through a social contract that will ensure people's willing participation. The second is about buying loyalty or patronage in a way that ensures the support of backers. The third is about the threat of coercion to keep the population in check. The deceivingly strong Arab states gave the appearance of stability until they were faced with defiant demonstrators who did not believe in their appeal, who were not bought into their circle of loyalty, and who broke the barrier of fear from their power of coercion ensured by a ruthless police apparatus and brutal armed forces.

The unfortunate failures to accomplish the aspirations of the Arab spring, notwithstanding, humans have occasionally stood up to their autocratic rulers and the corrupt clique in other instances of human history. This is usually accomplished through a wide variety of actions in the form of peaceful protests, civil disobedience, labor strikes, revolutions, and armed rebellions. These activities lead to political instability which causes policy uncertainty, disruptions to productive activities, destruction to infrastructure, increases in casualties, and has adverse effects on the quality of institutions, the quality of policymaking, and the accumulation of human capital and physical capital.

In this context, scholars face the challenge of quantifying political instability, but some were able to define it in a way that facilitates the estimation of its effect. Political instability can be defined as the propensity of change in the executive power, either by peaceful means or otherwise. Political instability can also be captured by the frequency of certain actions such as protests, labor strikes, assassinations, revolutions, armed rebellions, coups d'état and others. The following sections elaborate on the intuition behind the economic consequences of political instability.

IN THE TUG OF CONFLICT

Building on the intuition presented in the previous section, several studies attempt to examine the economic consequences of political instability. This section surveys these studies and discusses their main findings.

In their seminal paper, Alberto Alesina, Sule Olzer, Nouriel Roubini, and Philip Swagel examine the effect of political instability, captured by the propensity of a government collapse, on economic growth.[14] The authors distinguish between peaceful transfer of executive power, that is typical of democracies, and coups. The authors find that a high propensity of political instability hinders economic growth, and that this effect is stronger in the case of unconstitutional executive changes through coups in addition to the ones that significantly change the ideological composition of the executive.

Ari Aisen and Francisco José Veiga attempt to determine the channels of transmission between political instability and economic growth.[15] The authors capture political instability by the number of times in a year in which a new premier is named and/or half or more of the cabinet posts are occupied by new ministers. The authors find that higher degrees of political instability are associated with lower economic growth by discouraging the accumulation of physical capital and human capital. Richard Jong-A-Pin examines the economic effect of political instability within the political regime, and that of political instability of the political regime.[16] The author finds that only instability of the political regime has a negative effect on economic growth, while instability within the political regime is conducive to economic growth.

Yi Feng examines the interaction between democracy, political stability, and economic growth.[17] The author provides evidence that democracy enhances economic growth indirectly through its positive effect on major regular government change that has a favorable effect on growth, and its negative effect on irregular regime change that has a detrimental effect on growth. In another contribution, Yi Feng examines whether political freedom and political instability, captured by the variability of political freedom, have any consequences for private investment.[18] The author finds that political freedom promotes private investment, while political instability has an adverse effect. Yi Feng and Baizhu Chen formulate a model that proposes that political instability, political polarization, and political repression have an adverse effect on economic outcomes.[19] The authors conduct an empirical analysis that provides evidence for the model prediction that political instability and assassinations have a negative effect on economic growth.

On the other hand, some studies find either an inconclusive or even favorable effect of political instability on economic performance. For instance, Nauro Campos and Jeffrey Nugent find no evidence for a causal negative association between political instability and economic growth.[20] In another paper, Nauro Campos and Jeffrey Nugent examine the direction of causality between political instability and the level of investment.[21] Their analysis suggests a positive causal effect from political instability to investment particularly in low-income countries. The authors conclude that this could be because political instability prompts a replacement of the destroyed capital stock.

Policy Uncertainty

Political instability adversely affects economic performance because it increases policy uncertainty. A higher likelihood of change in the executive branch implies uncertain future policies by the successors. This affects the incentives to invest since investors need some sort of constancy of policies at least in the foreseeable future. Otherwise, risk-averse domestic investors may delay productive initiatives or even invest somewhere else. Similarly, foreign investors are not likely to commit their capital into an unstable political environment. Incumbent politicians who expect a short term in office may also increase their rent by taxing productive capital inducing capital flight. Thus, political instability undermines the domestic accumulation of physical capital and the inflow of foreign capital to the detriment of the economy.

On the other hand, political instability, captured by a high probability of government change, might be viewed favorably if the current government is incompetent or corrupt and its possible successor is seen as a likely improvement. However, this increase in probability might lead to an increase in policy uncertainty if both the characteristics and the identity of the successor are unknown.

Monetary Policy

Political instability can shorten the incumbent policymakers' horizons, since they are not certain that they will keep their position. This leads to short-sighted and myopic economic policies as greater weight is placed on short term goals. Political instability also leads to frequent changes in policies leading to volatility, which adversely affects economic performance.[22]

An unstable political climate can also create inflation. This is because instability causes the administration of tax collection to be costly. Governments increase their dependence on seignorage when tax collection is not adequate. This causes an increase in the supply of printed money into the economy causing prices to soar. Therefore, it is difficult to maintain low inflation in this political climate. Some studies examine the effect of political instability on inflation. For instance, Guido Tabellini, Sebastian Edwards and Alex Cukierman present a framework that shows that the more unstable the political system the costlier the administration of tax collection.[23] If tax collection is inadequate, the government depends on seigniorage. The authors test the prediction of their model and find that political instability explains the share of government revenue derived from seigniorage, which causes inflation.

Ari Aisen and Francisco José Veiga attempt to determine the causes of inflationary experiences worldwide that have adverse effects on welfare and economic growth.[24] The authors show that political instability is associated with higher inflation, especially for developing countries. In another contribution, Ari Aisen and Francisco José Veiga analyze the determinants of inflation volatility, or the standard deviation of inflation.[25] The authors find that higher political instability, higher social polarization, lower democracy, and de facto central bank independence are associated with higher inflation volatility. The study also shows that political instability has greater effect on inflation volatility in developing countries with lower degrees of central bank independence and economic freedom. In another paper, Ari Aisen and Francisco José Veiga find that higher political instability and ethnic heterogeneity lead to higher seigniorage.[26] This effect is stronger in countries that are developing, socially polarized, have high inflation, have high domestic debt, have lower central bank independence, have lower levels of economic freedom, have lower levels of political freedom, have poorer credit rating, and have lower trade openness.

Fiscal Policy

Political instability can also lead governments who are uncertain about the time left in power to engage in excessive spending to increase their chances of reelection in a democratic system, or to decrease the likelihood of their ouster from office in an autocratic one. Policy makers also tend to ramp up spending to bolster the police apparatus to be able to suppress the opposition whose actions are contributing to political instability.

Policy makers may also resort to borrowing excessively to cover the budget deficit caused by lower tax collection and excessive spending. Some scholars argue that political instability can partially explain the observed accumulation of sovereign debt. This is because frequent political turnover creates an incentive for executives with short horizons to borrow heavily and encumber future governments with the burden of debt repayment.[27] In this context, Michael Devereux and Jean-François Wen argue that political instability causes governments who are uncertain about the time left in power to engage in excessive spending, compared to an economy with certainty of government tenure.[28] Thus, the incumbent government spends more to increase its chances of being re-elected in a democratic system, or to decrease the chances of being overthrown from office in an authoritarian one. The authors provide evidence that political instability causes higher government spending and lower economic growth.

Institutional Quality

An atmosphere of political instability does not allow the authorities to protect property, and thus have an adverse effect on the quality of institutions that are essential to create incentives for investment and innovation. Political instability can also increase acts of rent seeking and corruption. A weak executive, constantly under threat of losing office, can be particularly prone to pleasing lobbyists, special interests, and pressure groups. This type of executive exhibits a type of corruption that is more deleterious to economic outcomes than that of strong governments. Andrei Shleifer and Robert Vishny argue that corrupt governments allow various agencies to collect bribes from private agents that is not excessive, but economies with weak governments that do not have control over these agencies experience very high levels of corruption.[29]

Productive Activities

Political instability is a situation that exposes the weakness of rulers who cannot ensure some semblance of stability. In countries where rulers are weak, or easily overthrown, citizens have larger incentives to engage in acts of defiance rather than in productive activities. In periods of political instability, workers participate more in protests and labor strikes than in fulfilling their tasks in an assembly line. Based on this intuition, Herschel Grossman examines the allocation of labor time between insurrection, soldiering, and production.[30] The author finds that the more propitious the technology for a successful insurrection, the smaller the fraction of time devoted to production. The author concludes that the equilibria with low political stability suffer from low production and low expected income.

Acts of defiance, that cause political instability, can lead to retaliation by authorities. Demonstrations can be contained, and sit-ins can be dispersed, using brutal force by the police or the armed forces. This causes loss of life and scores of casualties, which can affect labor supply.

Capital Accumulation

Political instability may disrupt the educational process due to security concerns and may possibly lead to the destruction of some educational facilities. This unstable political climate also often leads to the emigration of the most qualified in the labor force, or what is referred to as the brain drain. Skilled workers are the ones who can find employment opportunities in more prosperous and stable destinations when their countries experience some sort of political instability. Unskilled workers do not usually have the same good fortune. In this context, Abubakar Lawan Ngoma and Normaz Wana Ismail find that domestic political instability is one of the determinants of the brain drain.[31]

Political instability can also lead to the destruction of infrastructure and other facilities essential for production and trade. On the other hand, if the destruction caused by political instability is followed by efforts to replace and restore the old infrastructure and capital with better ones, then instability can eventually improve productivity and economic outcomes.

Informal Sector

In an atmosphere of political instability, there are fewer employment opportunities in the formal sector of the economy, which encourages workers to seek employment in the informal sector. The value of economic activity conducted in the informal sector of the economy is not counted in the typical indicators of national income. Thus, political instability may lower the estimates of national income by expanding the informal sector. This led some studies to explore the effect of political instability on the informal sector. For instance, Nasr El Bahnasawy, Michael Ellis, and Assandé Désiré Adom attempt to address whether the political climate leads to policies that allow the informal sector to swell.[32] The authors show that political instability, social polarization along ethnic and religious lines, and an autocratic authority are associated with a larger informal economy.

Instability Spillovers

Some studies show that instability in one country may spill over to others as well. This is because some of the warring factions can use the territory of neighboring countries to escape from the authorities in their country, or because the conflict can disrupt the supply of goods and services to these neighbors, or because the neighbors attempt to hedge against a likely spillover by increasing their defense spending. In this context, Alberto Ades and Hak Chua show that political instability in neighboring countries has a strong negative effect on a country's economic performance as it disrupts trade flows and causes an increase in defense spending.[33] The authors conclude that the policies directed at settling current territorial disputes can have large favorable effects for parties not directly involved in the conflict.

NOTES

1. Morris. *War! What Is It Good For?: Conflict and the Progress of Civilization from Primates to Robots* (p. 8).

2. Anderson. *Lawrence in Arabia: War, Deceit, Imperial Folly and the Making of the Modern Middle East* (p. 151).

3. Burke, Hsiang, and Miguel. "Climate and Conflict." *Annual Review of Economics*: 577–617.

4. Miguel, Satyanath, and Sergenti. "Economic Shocks and Civil Conflict." *Journal of Political Economy*: 725–753.

5. Burke, Hsiang, and Miguel. "Climate and Conflict." *Annual Review of Economics*: 577–617.

6. Burke, Hsiang, and Miguel. "Quantifying the Influence of Climate on Human Conflict." *Science*.

7. Hsiang, Meng, and Cane. "Civil Conflicts are Associated with the Global Climate." *Nature*: 438–441.

8. Miguel, Satyanath, and Sergenti. "Economic Shocks and Civil Conflict." *Journal of Political Economy*: 725–753.

9. Miguel and Satyanath. "Re-examining Economic Shocks and Civil Conflict." *American Economic Journal: Applied Economics*: 228–232.

10. Iyigun, Nunn, and Qian. "Winter is Coming: The Long Run Effects of Climate Change on Conflict: 1400–1900." National Bureau of Economic Research Working Paper 23033.

11. Couttenier, and Soubeyran. "Drought and Civil War in sub-Saharan Africa." *Economic Journal*: 201–244.

12. Ciccone. "Economic Shocks and Civil Conflict." *American Economic Journal*: Applied Economics: 215–227.

13. Ciccone. "Estimating the Effect of Transitory Economic Shocks on Civil Conflict." *Review of Economics and Institutions*: 1–14.

14. Alesina, Ozler, Roubini, and Swagel. "Political Instability and Economic Growth." *Journal of Economic Growth*: 189–211.

15. Aisen and José Veiga. "How Does Political Instability Affect Economic Growth?" *European Journal of Political Economy*: 151–167.

16. Jong-A-Pin. "On the Measurement of Political Instability and its Impact on Economic Growth." *European Journal of Political Economy*: 15–29.

17. Feng. "Democracy, Political Stability and Economic Growth." *British Journal of Political Science*: 391–418.

18. Feng. "Political Freedom, Political Instability, and Policy Uncertainty." *Institutional Studies Quarterly*: 271–294.

19. Chen and Feng. "Some Political Determinants of Economic Growth." *European Journal of Political Economy*: 609–627.

20. Campos and Nugent. "Who is Afraid of Political Instability?" *Journal of Development Economics*: 157–172.

21. Campos and Nugent. "Aggregate Investment and Political Instability." *Economica*: 533–549.

22. Glazer. "Politics and the Choice of Durability." *The American Economic Review*: 1207–1213. Persson and Svensson. "Why a Stubborn Conservative Would Run a Deficit." *The Quarterly Journal of Economics*: 325–345. Alesina and Tabellini. "A Positive Theory of Fiscal Deficits and Government Debt." *The Review of Economic Studies*: 403–414. Besley and Coate. "An Economic Model of Representative Democracy." *The Quarterly Journal of Economics*: 85–114. Besley and Coate. "Sources of Inefficiency in a Representative Democracy: A Dynamic Analysis." *The American Economic Review*: 139–156.

23. Cukierman, Edwards, and Tabellini. "Seigniorage and Political Instability." *The American Economic Review*: 537–55.

24. Aisen and José Veiga. "Does Political Instability Lead to Higher Inflation?" *Journal of Money, Credit, and Banking*: 1379–1389.

25. Aisen and José Veiga. "Political Instability and Inflation Volatility." *Public Choice*: 207–223.

26. Aisen and José Veiga. "The Political Economy of Seigniorage." *Journal of Development Economics*: 29–50.

27. Alesina and Tabellini. "External Debt, Capital Flight and Political Risk." *Journal of International Economics*: 199–220.

28. Devereux and Wen. "Political Instability, Capital Taxation, and Growth." *European Economic Review*: 1635–1651.

29. Shleifer and Vishny. "Corruption." *The Quarterly Journal of Economics*: 599–618.

30. Grossman. "A General Equilibrium Model of Insurrections." *The American Economic Review*: 912–921.

31. Ngoma and Ismail. "The Determinants of Brain Drain in Developing Countries." *International Journal of Social Sciences*: 744–754.

32. El Bahnasawy, Ellis, and Adom. "Political Instability and the Informal Economy." *World Development*: 31–42.

33. Ades and Chua. "The Neighbor's Curse: Regional Instability and Economic Growth." *Journal of Economic Growth*: 279–304.

Chapter Fourteen

Heterogeneous We Stand

CLEAVAGES AS AMMUNITIONS FOR THE FRAY

And you people who live . . . near Rugunga . . . go out. You will see the cockroaches' straw huts in the marsh . . . . I think that those who have guns should immediately go to these cockroaches . . . encircle them and kill them.[1]

This was the infamous radio broadcast that attracted a faithful audience of the Rwandans who became the main perpetrators of the genocide that claimed the lives of more than a million. The station preyed upon the deep animosities and prejudices of many Hutus against the Tutsis whom they referred to frequently as cockroaches. This was a manifestation of Bertolt Brecht's famous poem that says[2] "Then a hundred were butchered. But when a thousand were butchered and there was no end to the butchery, a blanket of silence spread. When evildoing comes like falling rain, nobody calls out 'stop!'"

This chapter focuses on conflict between groups of people. Conflict between people is more likely to occur when groups are heterogeneous along ethnic, linguistic, or religious lines. Scholars also consider diversity an essential determinant of the political economy of many nations and polities. In this context, ethnolinguistic diversity may lead to conflict, secession, political instability, political partisanship along ethnolinguistic lines, poor quality of institutions, pervasive corruption, high income inequality, incompetent economic policy, inadequate provision of public goods, inefficient public finance, and ultimately disappointing economic outcomes. This chapter is a discussion of these issues.

Before delving into the consequences of diversity, it is essential to discuss its geographic origins. Some studies argue that climatic factors had an influence on the degree of ethnolinguistic diversity within a country. As discussed earlier, mobility was curbed in the tropics due to the spread of diseases and the lack of domesticated animals for transportation. The presence of high pathogen loads in the tropics was also an isolating force especially when local communities have adapted to them. This disease environment limits the mobility of these people out of their territory and curbs other populations' movement into their land. This caused isolation of societies, delineation of ethnic homelands, and emergence of ethnic identities.

Some scholars also observe that language diversity is influenced by climatic fluctuations. Where climate is stable and allows for continuous food production throughout the year, small groups of people can be self-sufficient. Thus, populations fragment into small language groups. Where climate variability is greater, the scope of the network deemed necessary for subsistence is larger. Thus, languages tend to be more widespread. This decreases the degree of linguistic heterogeneity. Based on this intuition, Daniel Nettle examines the effect of climate variability on linguistic diversity and finds that countries characterized by low rainfall and short growing seasons sustain fewer languages.[3] Elizabeth Cashdan shows that areas with low ethnic diversity have unpredictable fluctuating climates and low pathogen loads.[4] There is indeed a plethora of other anthropological studies that show the association between climate and language diversity.[5]

Other studies find a connection between the distinct features of the land and ethnolinguistic diversity. First, geographic heterogeneity contributes to the separation and isolation of communities leading to the formation of distinct linguistic groups with different cultural traits. Second, in a stage of development when land is essential for production, people working on different types of land acquire location-specific skills that are not easily transferable to a different natural environment. Therefore, geographic diversity impeded the mobility of people from one area to another increasing isolation and leading to the formation of distinct languages. On the other hand, a homogeneous land endowment leads those inhabiting it to form a common ethnic identity to defend it against intruders. In this context, Stelios Michalopolous investigates the geographic determinants of ethnolinguistic diversity and finds that variation in land quality and elevation is a fundamental determinant of contemporary linguistic diversity.[6] The author concludes that these findings are consistent with the hypothesis that differences in land endowments generate location-specific human capital, leading to the formation of localized ethnicities.

After this discussion on the geographic origins of ethnolinguistic diversity, now we turn our attention to the consequences of heterogeneity along ethnic and linguistic lines.

CONFLICT

Ethnolinguistic diversity can be a catalyst for conflict, and even genocide and ethnic cleansing, between groups that do not share the same background. These disturbing incidents occur because one group has grievances as they feel underrepresented politically or marginalized economically. This could also be caused by one ethnolinguistic group trying to end the political hegemony and economic domination of another, or by one group trying to be liberated from the persecution and the oppression they suffer at the hands of the other. Conflict could also be instigated by a group feeling that their cultural heritage or identity is suppressed, or threatened, by another group. In these cases, the vulnerable group feels that there is no other way to protect one's existence than by engaging in a struggle for survival. The hostilities can lead to the death of scores of people and the destruction of infrastructure, property, and productive facilities.

An ethnic minority may also prefer to form its own country and break away from the multi-ethnic polity to which they belong. The threat of secession becomes more ominous if this group is segregated and lives close to the border of the country. Central governments can react to separatist threats by either suppression with force or by some form of compensation to buy back their loyalty. Both put additional stress on the coffers of the state and divert scarce resources away from the provision of public goods, which in turn lead to further deterioration in the quality of governance.

Some studies examine the association between ethnolinguistic diversity and civil wars. For instance, Paul Collier and Anke Hoeffler find that ethnolinguistic fractionalization is one of the critical determinants of the likelihood and duration of civil wars.[7] The authors also find that the association between civil wars and ethnic diversity is non-monotonic such that highly heterogeneous societies are no more prone to war than highly homogeneous ones. In another contribution, Paul Collier and Anke Hoeffler find that ethnic fractionalization is weekly significant, while religious fractionalization is insignificant, in predicting the outbreak of civil war.[8] James Fearon and David Laitin examine whether ethnic and religious antagonism were the root causes of the conflicts that proliferated by the end of the cold war.[9] The authors find that countries with high ethnic and religious fractionalization have been no more likely to experience civil violence during this period.

CORRUPTION

Ethnolinguistic diversity can lead to pervasive corruption because of the existence of strong ties and loyalties to one's group that are not extended to others.
For instance, diversity can lead to acts of nepotism in the recruitment process
for public office or for occupations in the private sector. This can adversely
affect the quality of the workforce as those in charge of the hiring process
prefer to employ those applicants from a similar ethnolinguistic background
irrespective of qualifications. Diversity can also lead to favoritism in the
provision of public goods, which implies that certain groups may be denied
access to services by government agencies even if they are entitled to them.

INEQUALITY

Ethnolinguistic diversity has serious implications on income inequality
through its effect on the provision of public goods and the support for redistribution. In diverse societies, individuals may have stronger sentiments of
compassion toward their own group but not to others. These individuals will
not be in favor of redistribution to those other groups. This implies that countries with higher degrees of diversity exhibit lower levels of redistribution and
higher levels of income inequality.

In countries with ethnolinguistic diversity, there are political parties whose
basis is mostly or exclusively ethnic. Segregation between different groups
may facilitate the creation of ethnically based parties because it makes policies that target a particular ethnolinguistic group and excludes others easier
to implement. These ethnically based parties are typically interested in the
promotion of the interests of their ethnic base rather than in the provision of
public goods to everyone. This also leads to an increase in the level of income
inequality along ethnolinguistic lines.

Some studies explore the effect of ethnolinguistic diversity on income
inequality. Alberto Alesina, Reza Baqir and William Easterly show that the
share of spending on public goods, education, roads, sewers, and trash pickup
in cities of the United States are inversely related to the city's ethnic fragmentation.[10] This is because individuals in diverse communities are less willing to
contribute to the public good which increases income inequality. Jan-Egbert
Sturm and Jakob De Haan find that countries with a high degree of ethnic
fractionalization redistribute less, while capitalist countries with a low degree
of fractionalization have a substantial degree of redistribution.[11]

DISTRUST

In countries where ethnolinguistic groups are segregated, there is less contact and communication between these groups who live separately in their enclaves. In these societies, sentiments of distrust may spread, and stereotypes may be reinforced, because segregated groups have less accurate information about each other.[12] In addition, the views of one group about another can be easily manipulated by politicians playing the ethnic card. This diminishes the desire by members of these societies to engage in any form of communal activities that may enhance the level of social trust. Alberto Alesina and Eliana La Ferrara study how the degree of heterogeneity in a community influences participation in social activities.[13] The authors find that participation is significantly lower in more unequal and in more ethnically fragmented localities.

EXCLUSION

Ethnic inclusion promotes the quality of policymaking, while ethnic exclusion has the opposite effect. If more ethnolinguistic groups are included in decision making, a larger portion of the population finds its preferences reflected in the process and will, thus, lend their support to the implementation of these policies. Policy quality also improves with greater variety in feedback from various groups who may bring different perspectives to the discussion. Finally, a greater number of ethnolinguistic groups included in policymaking increases the number of actors in the policy process. This ensures political stability as no group will feel shunned from participation.

Ethnolinguistic diversity could also affect the ability of societies to coordinate to influence politicians and policymakers. In an insightful example of how diversity may inhibit societies from coordination, Alberto Alesina, Caterina Gennaioli, and Stefania Lovo show that the level of deforestation is positively associated with the degree of ethnic fractionalization at the district level.[14] At the local level, some may be interested in preserving the forest if they use it for hunting, sheltering, and gathering. Others may want to exploit it for energy or for the earnings from cutting trees and logging. Corruption of politicians leads to over exploitation of forests compared to the preferences of the local populations. Ethnic diversity, however, lowers the ability of the locals to coordinate to lobby politicians against deforestation.

DIVERSITY UNDER THE SCALPEL

Ethnic Fractionalization

One challenge that scholars encounter in this field of study is how to capture the extent of diversity in an economy. Some studies use a fractionalization index, which reflects the probability that two randomly selected individuals from a population belong to different groups. The indicator increases in score with an increase in the number of different ethnolinguistic groups in a country. Lots of studies use this index to assess the effect of ethnolinguistic diversity on economic outcomes.

In a seminal paper, William Easterly and Ross Levine examine the relationship between Africa's ethnic fractionalization and school attainment, political stability, financial development, black market premiums, and infrastructure.[15] Their analysis indicates that high levels of ethnic divisions are strongly associated with distorted foreign exchange markets, low financial development, and low provision of infrastructure and education. In one of the most referenced papers in the literature, William Easterly, Alberto Alesina, Arnaud Devleeschauwer, Sergio Kurlat, and Romain Wacziarg introduce indices of ethnic, linguistic, and religious fractionalization to examine the effect of diversity on the quality of institutions and economic growth.[16] The authors conclude that ethnic and linguistic fractionalization have an adverse effect on economic growth and the quality of government in terms of the extent of corruption, bureaucratic quality, and the provision of health and education. Sefa Churchill and Russell Smyth examine the association between ethnic diversity and poverty for a sample of developing countries.[17] The authors find that ethnic and linguistic fractionalization contributes to the extent of poverty captured by the multidimensional poverty index, the multidimensional poverty headcount, the intensity of deprivation, the poverty gap, and the poverty headcount ratio.

Some studies find that the economic effect of diversity depends on institutional quality. For instance, William Easterly finds that ethnic diversity has a more adverse effect on economic growth when institutions are of poor quality, that poor institutions have an even more unfavorable effect on economic growth when ethnic diversity is high, and that better institutions decrease the likelihood of wars and genocides that are sometimes attributed to ethnic cleavages.[18] Paul Collier finds that ethnic diversity is detrimental to economic growth, particularly in countries with limited political rights.[19] The author argues that this is because in dictatorships, ethnic diversity tends to direct the government toward redistribution to a smaller group which can hinder economic growth. Chih Ming Tan finds that sufficiently high-quality institutions are essential to temper the adverse effects of ethnic fractionalization on economic development.[20]

Nauro Campos, Vitaliy Kuzeyev and Ahmad Saleh examine the effects of ethnic fractionalization on economic growth across countries.[21] The authors introduce a time varying index for diversity and address the issue of causality. The authors find that the dynamic endogenous ethnic fractionalization has a significant negative effect on economic growth. In another paper, Nauro Campos and Vitaliy Kuzeyev examine the effect of ethnic, linguistic, and religious fractionalization on economic performance in several former communist countries.[22] The authors find that the dynamic endogenous ethnic diversity index is negatively related to economic growth, which is not the case for linguistic and religious diversity.

Klaus Desmet, Ignacio Ortuño-Ortín, and Romain Wacziarg compare the effects of cultural and ethnic fractionalization on the incidence of civil conflict and the provision of public goods.[23] Cultural diversity is defined as the probability that two randomly chosen individuals respond differently to a question from the World Values Survey on a vector of cultural traits, values, and attitudes. The authors find that cultural fractionalization serves to decrease conflict and increase public goods provision, while ethnic divisions matter for conflict and public goods only when they are associated with cultural differences across ethnic groups.

Ethnic Polarization

Other scholars argue that the fractionalization index is not the appropriate indicator to capture the effect of heterogeneity on economic outcomes. Instead, some propose polarization as an alternative index. While the fractionalization index increases with the number of groups, the polarization index attains a maximum if there are two large groups. The argument is that there are more conflicts in societies where a large ethnic minority faces a majority from a different ethnicity. Thus, frictions that lead to conflict are more likely to occur where there are two large groups that are different along ethnolinguistic dimensions. In this case, the index of fractionalization is not adequate to capture the factors that can increase the likelihood of conflict.

In this context, several studies examine the effect of polarization on economic outcomes. For instance, Jose Montalvo and Marta Reynal-Querol find that ethnic polarization has a significant adverse effect on economic development as it decreases private investment, increases public consumption, and increases the incidence of civil war.[24] In another contribution, Jose Montalvo and Marta Reynal-Querol examine the effect of ethnic polarization on the duration of civil wars.[25] The authors show that ethnically polarized countries must endure longer civil wars. In yet another study, Marta Reynal-Querol and Jose Montalvo examine the effect of ethnic diversity on the incidence of genocides.[26] The authors find that ethnic fractionalization has no effect while ethnic polarization has a significant positive effect on the incidence of genocides. Marta Reynal-Querol shows that religious polarization is more important as a social cleavage that can lead to civil war than linguistic ones.[27] Marta Reynal-Querol and Jose Montalvo compare the effect of religious polarization and religious fractionalization, on economic outcomes.[28] The authors find that religious polarization, not fractionalization, has a negative effect on long-term economic growth through its effect on investment spending, government expenditure, and the probability of civil war.

Debraj Ray, Joan-Maria Esteban, and Laura Mayoral examine the effect of ethnic divisions on conflict using alternative indicators.[29] The authors argue that the effect of each indicator of ethnic division depends on whether the conflict is over public or private goods, and the extent of cohesion within the groups that are engaged in conflict. Their evidence shows that ethnic polarization influences conflict if the prize is public and group cohesion is high, while ethnic fractionalization influences conflict if the prize is private with a high level of cohesion within the groups in conflict.

Ethnic Inequality

Other scholars argue that it is the unequal concentration of wealth across ethnic lines that correlates with economic development rather than ethnic diversity per se. Therefore, income inequality across ethnicities matters more than the extent of diversity in a country. According to these arguments, it is ethnic inequality that would create tensions between ethnic groups who may disagree on the degree of distributional justice.

In this context, Alberto Alesina, Stelios Michalopoulos, and Elias Papaioannou argue that what matters for comparative development are economic differences between ethnic groups.[30] The authors construct an indicator of ethnic inequality combining information on the spatial distribution of ethnolinguistic groups with satellite images of light intensity at night that proxy for income differences across subnational groups. The authors find that ethnic inequality is negatively related to economic development. Kate Baldwin and John Huber examine the effect of between-group inequality on public goods provision.[31] Between-group inequality is defined as the expected difference in the mean income of the ethnic groups of any two randomly selected individuals. The evidence suggests that between-group income inequality leads to lower public goods provision, particularly in the less established democracies.

Ethnic Favoritism

Some scholars argue that the exclusion of some ethnolinguistic groups from policymaking has an adverse effect on the quality of policy and economic performance. These deleterious effects are caused by ethnic exclusion and not just the extent of ethnic diversity per se. In this context, ethnic favoritism can be considered as a sort of political inequality between ethnic groups, while the concept of ethnic inequality focuses on economic inequality across ethnicities. To estimate the extent of ethnic favoritism is challenging. Some scholars examine the effect of the ethnicity of the country's leader on different ethnic groups, introduce indicators of the extent of political engagement of different ethnic groups, or use measures of perceptions of policy impartiality.

The first group of studies focuses on the ethnic affiliation of the country's leader. For instance, Ilia Rainer and Raphael Franck examine the effect of the ethnicity of the countries' leadership on the educational attainment and health conditions of different ethnic groups in sub-Saharan Africa.[32] Their evidence indicates that the longer the term of the leader the higher the primary education and the lower the infant mortality in the group that the leader belongs to. Andrew Dickens explores the effect of ethnic favoritism in a panel of ethnolinguistic groups in African countries.[33] The author constructs an indicator of linguistic similarity between each ethnic group and the national leader as a proxy for ethnic proximity. The author finds that an increase in this indicator yields an increase in luminosity, which corresponds to an increase in group-level economic development. Remi Jedwab, Robin Burgess, Edward Miguel, Ameet Morjaria, and Gerard Padró i Miquel examine the effect of ethnic favoritism on the provision of public goods and economic development in Kenya.[34] The authors show that districts that share the ethnicity of the president obtain twice the expenditure on roads and have five times the length of paved roads compared to others. James Fearon, David Laitin and Kimuli Kasara examine whether countries face a higher likelihood of conflict when the state is controlled by a leader from an ethnic minority.[35] The authors find that there is a weak tendency for states with ethnic minority leaders to have a higher likelihood of civil war.

Other studies explore the economic impact of the perceptions of ethnic impartiality in policy making. For instance, Pelle Ahlerup, Thushyanthan Baskaran and Arne Bigsten examine whether the perceptions of impartiality in public policies, irrespective of the actual content of policies, is associated with economic growth in sub-Saharan Africa.[36] The authors show that countries whose governments are perceived as ethnically impartial are more likely to experience sustained economic growth.

Ethnic Segregation

Some scholars argue that segregation within countries, where different groups live separately, matters for economic outcomes more than the extent of diversity. According to these arguments, ethnic segregation may lead to a lack of common ground between ethnic groups literally and metaphorically. In this context, Alberto Alesina and Ekaterina Zhuravskaya explore the effect of segregation of ethnic, linguistic, and religious groups within a country on the quality of government.[37] The authors find that more ethnically and linguistically segregated countries have a lower quality of institutions, measured by the rule of law, political stability, government effectiveness, regulatory quality, and control of corruption.

Amanda Lea Robinson, Simon Ejdemyr and Eric Kramon test the hypothesis that politicians engage in ethnic favoritism in the provision of public goods when ethnic groups are segregated.[38] The authors find that members of parliament provide more local public goods primarily to members of their ethnicity in their electoral districts, when ethnic groups are geographically segregated. Amanda Lea Robinson argues that ethnic diversity is associated with lower levels of trust.[39] The author finds that citizens of ethnically diverse states express, on average, more ethnocentric trust. The authors also show that diversity lowers intergroup trust at the national level only when ethnic groups are spatially segregated.

NOTES

1. Des Forges. *Leave None to Tell the Story: Genocide in Rwanda.*

2. Bertolt, translated by John Willett. "When Evil-doing Comes Like Falling Rain." https://list.uvm.edu/cgi-bin/wa?A2=POETRY;39dfb3d5.1902

3. Nettle. "Explaining Global Patterns of Language Diversity." *Journal of Anthropological Archaeology*: 354–74.

4. Cashdan. "Ethnic Diversity and Its Environmental Determinants." *American Anthropologist*: 968–991.

5. Mace and Pagel. "A Latitudinal Gradient in the Density of Human Languages in North America." *Proceedings of the Royal Society*: 117–21. Ruth and Currie. "The Evolution of Ethnolinguistic Diversity." *Advances in Complex Systems*: 1–20. Moore, Manne, Brooks, Burgess, Davies, Rahbek, Williams, and Balmford. "The Distribution of Cultural and Biological Diversity in Africa." *Proceedings of the Royal Society*: 1645–53. Maffi. "Linguistic, Cultural and Biological Diversity." *Annual Review of Anthropology*: 599–617. Ahlerup and Olsson. "The Roots of Ethnic Diversity." *Journal of Economic Growth*: 71–102.

6. Michalopolous. "The Origins of Ethnolinguistic Diversity." *American Economic Review*: 508–1539.

7. Collier and Hoeffler. "On Economic Causes of Civil War." *Oxford Economic Papers*: 563–573.

8. Collier and Hoeffler. "Greed and Grievance in Civil War." *Oxford Economic Papers*: 563–595.

9. Fearon and Laitin. "Ethnicity, Insurgency, and Civil War." *American Political Science Review*: 75–90.

10. Alesina, Baqir, and Easterly. "Public Goods and Ethnic Divisions." *The Quarterly Journal of Economics*: 1243–1284.

11. Sturm and De Haan. "Income Inequality, Capitalism, and Ethno-linguistic Fractionalization." *The American Economic Review: Papers and Proceedings*: 593–97.

12. Glaeser. "The Political Economy of Hatred." *The Quarterly Journal of Economics*: 45–86.

13. Alesina and La Ferrara. "Participation in Heterogeneous Communities." *The Quarterly Journal of Economics*: 847–904.

14. Alesina, Gennaioli, and Lovo. "Public Goods and Ethnic Diversity." *Economica*: 32–66.

15. Easterly and Levine. "Africa's Growth Tragedy: Policies and Ethnic Divisions." *The Quarterly Journal of Economics*: 1203–1250.

16. Alesina, Devleeschauwer, Easterly, Kurlat, and Wacziarg. "Fractionalization." *Journal of Economic Growth*: 155–194.

17. Churchill and Smyth. "Ethnic Diversity and Poverty." *World Development*: 285–302.

18. Easterly. "Can Institutions Resolve Ethnic Conflict?" *Economic Development and Cultural Change*: 687–706.

19. Collier. "Ethnicity, Politics, and Economic Performance." *Economics and Politics*: 225–245.

20. Tan. "No One True Path: Uncovering the Interplay between Geography, Institutions, and Fractionalization in Economic Development." *Journal of Applied Econometrics*: 1100–1127.

21. Campos, Saleh, and Kuzeyev. "Dynamic Ethnic Fractionalization and Economic Growth." *The Journal of International Trade and Economic Development*: 129–152.

22. Campos and Kuzeyev. "On the Dynamics of Ethnic Fractionalization." *American Journal of Political Science*: 620–639.

23. Desmet, Ortuño-Ortín, and Wacziarg. "Culture, Ethnicity, and Diversity." *The American Economic Review*: 2479–2513.

24. Montalvo and Reynal-Querol. "Ethnic Diversity and Economic Development." *Journal of Development Economics*: 293–323.

25. Montalvo and Reynal-Querol. "Ethnic Polarization and the Duration of Civil Wars." *Economics of Governance*: 123–143.

26. Reynal-Querol and Montalvo. "Discrete Polarization with an Application to the Determinants of Genocide." *The Economic Journal*: 1835–1865.

27. Reynal-Querol. "Ethnicity, Political Systems, and Civil Wars." *Journal of Conflict Resolution*: 29–54.

28. Montalvo and Reynal-Querol. "Religious Polarization and Economic Development." *Economics Letters*: 201–210.

29. Esteban, Mayoral, and Ray. "Ethnicity and Conflict: An Empirical Study." *The American Economic Review*: 1310–1342.

30. Alesina, Michalopoulos, and Papaioannou. "Ethnic Inequality." *Journal of Political Economy*: 428–488.

31. Baldwin and Huber. "Economic versus Cultural Differences." *American Political Science Review*: 644–662.

32. Franck and Rainer. "Does the Leader's Ethnicity Matter? Ethnic Favoritism, Education, and Health in Sub Saharan Africa." *American Political Science Review*: 294–325.

33. Dickens. "Ethnolinguistic Favoritism in African Politics." *American Economic Journal: Applied Economics*: 370–402.

34. Burgess, Jedwab, Miguel, Morjaria, and Padró i Miquel. "The Value of Democracy: Evidence from Road Building in Kenya." *American Economic Review*: 1817–1851.

35. Fearon, Kasara, and Laitin. "Ethnic Minority Rule and Civil War Onset." *American Political Science Review*: 187–193.

36. Ahlerup, Baskaran, and Bigsten. "Government Impartiality and Sustained Growth in Sub-Saharan Africa." *World Development*: 54–69.

37. Alesina and Zhuravskaya. "Segregation and the Quality of Government in a Cross Section of Countries." *The American Economic Review*: 1872–1911.

38. Robinson, Ejdemyr, and Kramon. "Segregation, Ethnic Favoritism, and the Strategic Targeting of Local Public Goods." *Comparative Political Studies*: 1111–1143.

39. Robinson. "Ethnic Diversity, Segregation and Ethnocentric Trust in Africa." *British Journal of Political Science*: 217–239.

Chapter Fifteen

Climbing the Social Ladder

ANATOMY OF INEQUALITY

According to some, income inequality is a natural outcome in life. People have different abilities, attributes, talents, aptitudes, aims, aspirations, and ambitions. Some people are smarter than others, some are more fortunate than others, some work harder than others, some are more adventurous than others, some are thriftier than others, and some have more self-discipline than others. Even if some share similar characteristics, different circumstances can lead to distinct life experiences and divergent outcomes. Thus, unequal economic outcomes seem a natural and organic component of life. In addition, income inequality may also be perceived as fair if it stems from a situation where more labor and higher productivity are rewarded accordingly.

On the other hand, the extent of income inequality observed in some societies is disturbing to those who feel it is not sufficiently justified by the differences in inclinations or circumstances. In this context, these disparities could be either an outcome of a system that is tilted in favor of some on the expense of others, or a consequence of favorable circumstances for some that are not enjoyed by others, or the result of unequal opportunities in life. The advocates of this point of view argue that the world has been growing more unequal to an extent that cannot be explained exclusively by differences in effort or talent. For instance, a study by Oxfam concludes that[1] "The combined fortunes of the world's 26 richest individuals reached $1.4 trillion last year—the same amount as the total wealth of the 3.8 billion poorest people." Historian Niall Ferguson also refers to the rising inequalities in the twenty-first century as he states that[2] "And, since the turn of the century, that bottom half has received just 1 per cent of the total increase in global wealth, while 50 per cent of that increase has gone to the top 1 per cent." This level of income inequality can lead to a situation where some cannot fulfill their full potential while others would not even try from desperation to the detriment of the entire economy.

Historians also elaborate on the part that income inequality played in human history. For instance, Peter Turchin directs our attention to the role of lower income inequality in empire building as he states that[3]

> Vertical integration—lack of glaring barriers between the aristocracy and the commons—seems to be a general characteristic of successful imperial nations during their early phase. To cite another example from antiquity, the lifestyle of the royal family of Macedon before the Persian conquests was also very modest. The mothers and sisters of the kings cooked the food and wove the cloth. When Alexander was conquering the Persian Empire, he wore homespun clothes made by his sisters. During the campaigns, Alexander ate the same food and slept under the same conditions as his soldiers.

Turchin continues to offer another example from the heydays of the Roman Empire:[4]

> The frugal lifestyle of the senatorial aristocracy in early Rome also did not distinguish them greatly from the common citizens. Overseas trade during the early Republic was at a low ebb, so hardly any oriental luxuries were imported to serve as goods for conspicuous consumption. The only difference in clothing that distinguished senators from the rest of citizens was the broad purple stripe on their toga. Roman historians of the later age stressed the modest way of life, even poverty of the leading citizens.

This chapter focuses on the effect of income inequality on economic performance. Income distribution and its effect on economic outcomes have been a source of concern for social scientists. In this context, there are two streams of literature. One argues that income inequality is conducive to economic growth, while the other advocates the idea that the prevalent disparities call for an intervention to achieve the desired outcomes. According to Nobel laureate Simon Kuznets, these attempts struggle in a[5] "field of study that has been plagued by looseness in definitions, unusual scarcity of data, and pressure of strongly held opinions." This chapter complements the previous two chapters that focus on conflict, since income inequality can lead to distributional conflict.

Before delving into the economic consequences of income distribution, it is essential to shed light on the geographic origins of income inequality. As discussed earlier, some scholars argue that soil and climate predisposed different areas in the new world to varying degrees of inequality. For example, some climate and soil are more amenable to certain crops that can be efficiently produced in plantations featuring the use of slaves or indigenous labor. Therefore, the population of these countries came to be dominated by slaves of African descent and Europeans who were tempted by the economic returns from the production of these valuable commodities. The disparities in human capital between these two groups contributed to a high level of inequality. In contrast, soil and climate in other areas were more amenable to the cultivation of other crops that can grow on smaller family farms with laborers of European descent who had high levels of human capital. This promoted the rise of a broad middle class in which power and wealth were more equally distributed.

INEQUALITY HINDERS GROWTH

A vast literature argues that greater egalitarian conditions are a prerequisite for economic growth, and that income inequality adversely affects economic performance. In the words of Aristotle,[6] "Thus it is manifest that the best political community is formed by citizens of the middle class, and that those states are likely to be well-administered, in which the middle class is large, and stronger if possible than the other classes." This conclusion is based on two arguments. The first pertains to credit market imperfections and the second has political economy undertones.

In an economy with a high level of income inequality and credit constraints, the majority will have no access to credit to finance their investment in human capital which ultimately affects their educational attainment and occupational choices. Alternatively, income redistribution allows the poor to invest more in human capital than their endowment would allow. This would enhance productivity and economic growth. Thus, equality alleviates the adverse effect of credit constraints on the accumulation of human capital.

There are also some political economy arguments that advocate that income inequality hinders economic growth. In this context, the incentives for accumulation of physical capital, human capital, and knowledge hinge on the ability of individuals to appropriate the return on their investment. However, in an economy with a high level of income inequality most voters may use the political system to vote for greater government intervention in their favor through higher taxation and redistribution. This can be distorting to the incentives for investment and can hinder economic growth. On the other hand, the more equitable the economy the better endowed the median voter with capital, and thus the lower the level of capital taxation. This, in turn, enhances capital accumulation and economic growth. In economies where the majority of voters favor redistribution, any lobbying efforts to impede these preferences from being translated into policies exhaust scarce resources and promote corruption and rent seeking. This is the case assuming that the system of governance is sufficiently democratic such that the will of the people is reflected in policymaking.

Income disparities can also instigate discontent by the poor who may be exasperated with the absence of distributive justice. This can lead the disgruntled poor to engage in protests, labor strikes, civil disobedience, a civil war, or other violent acts. This may lead to political instability that is detrimental to economic growth. On the other hand, redistribution toward egalitarian conditions can ease social tensions to the benefit of the entire economy.

Income inequality can also have a detrimental effect on social capital. A high level of income inequality can decrease the level of trust and social solidarity in a society. If a skewed income distribution is seen as a way of a few to amass wealth on the expense of the rest, a fissure will be created in the social fabric that is hard to heal. Historian Peter Turchin turns our attention to[7] "the corrosive effect that glaring inequality has on the willingness of people to cooperate, which in turn underlies the capacity of societies for collective action." He also asserts that incipient imperial nations are egalitarian in nature while greater disparities undermine cooperation and cause empires to succumb to adversaries with higher levels of solidarity.

Turchin also attributes to income inequality a role in the process of "Emperiopathosis" or the decline and fall of empires. He proposes that the internal stability and peace that empires impose contain within them the seeds of chaos and collapse. Initially, stability and peace bring prosperity and an increase in population. This demographic change leads to overpopulation, which causes wages of the commoners to decline but makes the landed elite wealthier with increased rents. As the elite increase in numbers, they eventually struggle with declining incomes. The elite turn to the state for assistance which they will be denied since tax collection dwindles due to the impoverished state of the population. When the state finances collapse, it loses control of law enforcement. Strife escalates between the elite and brings in its wake famine, war, pestilence, and bloodshed. Afterward, population growth declines. This causes the income of the commoners to recover with the increase in wages, and the fortunes of the upper classes to deteriorate with the decrease in rents. This decreases the numbers of the elite which causes their competition to subside allowing for the restoration of law and order. Stability and peace bring prosperity and another cycle begins.

INEQUALITY ENHANCES GROWTH

Another stream of literature disputes the previous arguments and asserts that income inequality is conducive to economic growth. Studies of consumption and saving behavior propose a channel in which income inequality has a stimulating effect on the economy. According to the precautionary saving incentive, consumers with small asset stocks tend to compress their consumption so that their marginal propensity to consume out of wealth is higher than that of those holding larger asset stocks. This means that the marginal propensity to save of the poor is lower than that of the wealthy.[8] The implication is that if economic growth is proportional to aggregate saving, then economies with higher income inequality will tend to grow faster. This is because wealth is concentrated in the hands of the few who save more.

Agents are also heterogeneous in their abilities, talents, and effort. These differences ought to be reflected in the return to their labor to create incentives for hard work, productivity, and innovation. If the return is not consistent with these differences, then economic agents will believe that there are other factors at work such as luck, cronyism, or connections. Thus, the incentive to put forth their best effort will be compromised.

In this context, there is one study by Kristin Forbes who attempts to challenge the common belief that income inequality has an adverse effect on economic growth.[9] The author finds that an increase in a country's level of income inequality has a significant positive association with subsequent economic growth in the short and medium terms.

A RECONCILIATION

As an attempt to reconcile these two streams, Oded Galor and Omer Moav offer a unified approach.[10] Their proposition is that in the early stages of development, physical capital accumulation is the primary source of economic growth. Saving provides the funds to finance investment in physical capital. In this case, income inequality enhances economic growth by concentrating income in the hands of those whose marginal propensity to save is higher. Thus, income inequality can enhance physical capital accumulation and economic growth at this stage of development. In later stages of development, physical capital is replaced by human capital as the engine of economic growth. Accordingly, egalitarian conditions alleviate the adverse effects of credit constraints on human capital accumulation and promote a growth process. Thus, redistribution allows the poor to invest in human capital which enhances economic growth at this stage of development.

ONE'S FAIR SHARE OF A GROWING PIE

It is worth noting that scholars distinguish between inequality of outcomes and inequality of opportunity. The former reflects the outcome of individual choices, collective actions, societal structures, political ideologies, economic systems, social norms, cultural biases, and implemented policies in an economy. The latter reflects the opportunities made available to individuals and households that they can choose to take advantage of to be able to climb the income ladder. Thus, social mobility can become a feature of societies that have a higher level of equal opportunity. Unfortunately, it is hard to quantify income mobility at a scale that would allow scholars to use in an analytical study to determine its effect on economic outcomes. Alternatively, there are plentiful ways of quantifying income inequality. Therefore, the studies that are discussed in this section focus exclusively on the effect of income inequality on economic outcomes.

Several studies provide evidence that income inequality hinders economic growth. For instance, Alberto Alesina and Dani Rodrik develop a model of endogenous growth with distributive conflict between agents.[11] The authors find that there is a strong demand for higher taxation and income redistribution in inegalitarian societies leading to lower economic growth. The authors test their predictions and show that inequality in land ownership and income is negatively correlated with subsequent economic growth.

Alberto Alesina and Roberto Perotti attempt to identify the channels from income inequality to economic growth. The authors find that income inequality increases sociopolitical instability and economic uncertainty that deter investment which is a primary engine of economic growth.[12] Roberto Perotti explores the relationship between income distribution, democratic institutions, and economic growth.[13] The author finds a positive association between equality and economic growth particularly in democracies, and that unequal societies tend to suffer from sociopolitical instability which leads to lower investment and economic growth. Torsten Persson and Guido Tabellini address the question of whether inequality is harmful for economic growth.[14] The authors develop a theoretical setup that predicts that decision makers in economies with distributional conflict adopt economic policies that tax investment to redistribute income. The authors test these predictions and find a significant adverse effect of income inequality on economic growth, which is only observed in democracies.

William Easterly examines whether income inequality, predicted by the agricultural endowment, affects economic development.[15] The author uses the abundance of land suitable for wheat, compared to sugarcane, as an instrument for structural inequality. The intuition is that wheat is grown in family farms which support the rise of a broad middle class, while sugarcane production features economies of scale and the use of slave labor which increases income inequality. The author finds that income inequality, predicted by these natural endowments, acts as a barrier to economic prosperity due to its adverse effect on institutional quality and schooling. In another contribution,

William Easterly defines a middle-class consensus as a high share of income for the middle class and a low degree of ethnic divisions.[16] The author finds that the middle-class consensus is associated with higher income, higher economic growth, higher human capital, better infrastructure, better economic policies, more political stability, and better democratic practices.

In a popular study, Klaus Deininger and Lyn Squire compile a new data set on income inequality and land distribution.[17] The authors show that there is a strong negative association between initial land inequality and long-term economic growth especially for poor countries. George Clarke shows evidence that strongly supports the view that income inequality is negatively correlated with economic growth in both democracies and non-democracies.[18] Abhijit Banerjee and Esther Duflo examine the connection between income inequality and economic growth without imposing a linear structure on the estimation.[19] The authors show that "the growth rate is an inverted U-shaped function of net changes in inequality: changes in inequality (in any direction) are associated with reduced growth in the next period."

Some studies argue that the effect of income inequality on economic performance depends on the characteristics of the country. For instance, Robert Barro provides evidence from a broad panel of countries that the effect of income inequality depends on the level of economic development such that higher income inequality decreases growth in poor countries and increases it in high income ones.[20] Sherif Khalifa and Sherine El Hag attempt to test the hypothesis that the effect of income inequality on economic growth depends on the country's stage of development.[21] The analysis suggests that there is a statistically significant threshold income per capita, below which income inequality hinders economic growth and above which the effect is not statistically significant.

Some studies find that the adverse effect of income inequality on economic growth goes through the channel of the quality of institutions. This is because the economic elite can convert their immense wealth into de facto political power to protect their economic interests. Thus, the elite can use their acquired political clout to influence the institutional structure of the country. For instance, Phillip Keefer and Stephen Knack find that income disparities and land inequality have an adverse effect on the security of contractual and property rights.[22] When the authors control for property rights, the effect of income inequality on economic growth diminishes considerably. Md. Rabiul Islam finds that higher wealth inequality is associated with lower economic freedom, smaller government size, less property protection, less trade openness, and higher regulatory environment.[23] Tim Krieger and Daniel Meierrieks show that income inequality is negatively related to those components of economic freedom pertinent to international trade, government regulation, the rule of law, and property rights protection.[24]

Another stream of literature argues that the negative effect of income inequality on economic growth goes through the channel of human capital. For instance, Kevin Sylwester shows that income inequality increases the expenditure on public education as a portion of Gross Domestic Product, which is positively associated with future economic growth.[25] The author, however, finds that the contemporaneous effect of income inequality on economic growth is negative which implies that the cost that income inequality exerts upon economic outcomes is short term. Other studies find that historical income inequality has a persistent effect on current levels of human capital as well. For instance, Joerg Baten and Dácil Juif attempt to test the influence of land inequality on human capital formation during the period from 1820 C.E. to 2000 C.E.[26] Their analysis shows that early land inequality has a detrimental causal influence on mathematics and science education even a century later. Andros Kourtellos, Ioanna Stylianou, and Chih Ming investigate whether historical higher levels of land inequality led to longer delays in the implementation of policies aimed at promoting educational attainment, especially the extension of primary schooling.[27] Using a historical dataset, the authors find that land inequality is a critical factor of the delays in schooling.

NOTES

1. https://www.cnn.com/2019/01/20/business/oxfam-billionaires-davos/index.html
2. Ferguson. *The Square and the Tower* (p. 360).
3. Turchin. *War and Peace and War: The Rise and Fall of Empires* (pp.161–162).
4. Ibid. (p. 161).
5. Kuznets. "Economic Growth and Income Inequality." *The American Economic Review*: 1–28.
6. Jowett. *Politica* (p. 1295).
7. Turchin. *War and Peace and War: The Rise and Fall of Empires* (p. 261).
8. Carroll. "Why do the Rich Save So Much?" In *Does Atlas Shrug?: Economic Consequences of Taxing the Rich*, edited by J. Slemrod. Cambridge: Cambridge University Press.
9. Forbes. "A Reassessment of the Relationship between Inequality and Growth." *The American Economic Review*: 869–887.
10. Galor and Moav. "From Physical to Human Capital Accumulation: Inequality and the Process of Development." *Review of Economic Studies*: 1001–1026.
11. Alesina and Rodrik. "Distributive Politics and Economic Growth." *The Quarterly Journal of Economics*: 465–490.
12. Alesina and Perotti. "Income Distribution, Political Instability, and Investment." *European Economic Review*: 1203–1228.

13. Perotti. "Growth, Income Distribution, and Democracy." *Journal of Economic Growth*: 149–187.

14. Persson and Tabellini. "Is Inequality Harmful for Growth?" *The American Economic Review*: 600–621.

15. Easterly. "Inequality Does Cause Underdevelopment: Insights from a New Instrument." *Journal of Development Economics*: 755–776.

16. Easterly. "The Middle-Class Consensus and Economic Development." *Journal of Economic Growth*: 317–335.

17. Deininger and Squire. "New Ways of Looking at Old Issues: Inequality and Growth." *Journal of Development Economics*: 259–287.

18. Clarke. "More Evidence on Income Distribution and Growth." *Journal of Development Economics*: 403–427.

19. Banerjee and Duflo. "Inequality and Growth: What Can the Data Say?" *Journal of Economic Growth*: 267–299.

20. Barro. "Inequality and Growth in a Panel of Countries." *Journal of Economic Growth*: 5–32.

21. Khalifa and El Hag. "Income Disparities, Economic Growth and Development as a Threshold." *Journal of Economic Development*: 23–36.

22. Keefer and Knack. "Polarization, Politics and Property Rights." *Public Choice*: 127–154.

23. Rabiul Islam. "Wealth Inequality, Democracy and Economic Freedom." *Journal of Comparative Economics*: 920–935.

24. Krieger and Meierrieks. "Political Capitalism: The Interaction between Income Inequality, Economic Freedom and Democracy." *European Journal of Political Economy*: 115–132.

25. Sylwester. "Income Inequality, Education Expenditures, and Growth." *Journal of Development Economics*: 379–398.

26. Baten and Juif. "A Story of Large Landowners and Math Skills." *Journal of Comparative Economics*: 375–401.

27. Kourtellos, Stylianou, and Tan. "Failure to Launch? The Role of Land Inequality in Transition Delays." *European Economic Review*: 98–113.

Chapter Sixteen

Echoes of the Past

Confucius once said "study the past if you would define the future." That is, if we want to understand the present and foresee the future we must reminisce about the past. In a similar vein, some scholars argue that humans cross some historical junctures that prove to have a lasting impact on the trajectories of nations. These events happened a long time ago but still shape our lives today. In this sense, we are products of our past to a certain extent. This chapter and the following one focus on few of these decisive events such as the agricultural transition, the colonial expansion, the slave trade, state antiquity, the Protestant Reformation, and others.

AGRICULTURAL TRANSITION

The Neolithic Revolution was the wide scale transition of humans from a lifestyle of hunting and gathering to a way of life that featured settled agriculture. During the ensuing millennia, this monumental transition would transform the hunter-gatherers that had heretofore dominated human history into sedentary societies. This transformation allowed the emergence of large population centers and sprawling human settlements. Settled societies changed their way of life through specialized crop cultivation and developing agricultural techniques that allowed the production of surplus food. These significant developments provided the basis for densely populated settlements, specialization and division of labor, trade and commerce, art and architecture, centralized administrations, political structures, state formation, hierarchical ideologies, property ownership, pottery, polished tools, writing, astronomy and countless other human achievements.

Some studies emphasize the effect of climate on the transition to agriculture. After 200,000 years of hunting and gathering, agriculture was invented independently in different continents. Archaeologists agree that this occurred in the Fertile Crescent, sub-Saharan Africa, North and South China, the

Andes, Mexico, and North America. Some argue that the advent of agriculture was triggered by an increase in climatic seasonality which peaked shortly before the first archaeological evidence for agriculture. Survival of hunter-gatherers was harder with harsher winters and drier summers. Those affected by these climatic fluctuations reacted by storing food to smooth their consumption. This, in turn, forced them to abandon their lifestyles as they had to settle adjacent to their stationary granaries. The sedentary lifestyle and food storage made it easier for them to adopt farming. Harvey Weiss and Raymond Bradley elaborate on this process in an article in *Science*:[1]

> About 12,000 years ago, the Natufians abandoned seasonally nomadic hunting and gathering activities that required relatively low inputs of labor to sustain low population densities and replaced these with new labor-intensive subsistence strategies of plant cultivation and animal husbandry. The consequences of this agricultural revolution, which was key to the emergence of civilization, included orders of magnitude increases in population growth and full-time craft specialization and class formation, each the result of the ability to generate and deploy agricultural surpluses. What made the Natufians change their lifestyle so drastically? Thanks to better dating control and improved paleoclimatic interpretations, it is now clear that this transition coincided with the Younger Dryas climate episode about 12,900 to 11,600 years ago. Following the end of the last glacial period, when southwest Asia was dominated by arid steppe vegetation, a shift to increased seasonality (warm, wet winters and hot, dry summers) led to the development of an open oak terebinth parkland of woods and wild cereals across the interior Levant and northern Mesopotamia. This was the environment exploited initially by the hunting and gathering Natufian communities. When cooler and drier conditions abruptly returned during the Younger Dryas, the harvests of wild resources dwindled, and foraging for these resources could not sustain Natufian subsistence. They were forced to transfer settlement and wild cereals to adjacent new locales where intentional cultivation was possible.

Andrea Matranga tests this hypothesis against a global dataset of climate conditions and Neolithic adoption dates.[2] According to the author,

> the patterns of climatic seasonality experience on Earth depend chiefly on the shape of Earth's orbit, as described by three parameters: axial tilt, eccentricity, and precession. During the Ice Age, the Earth's axis of rotation was less tilted, and its orbit was less elliptic. Moreover, when the northern hemisphere was tilted towards the Sun, the planet was at its aphelion—the furthest point from the Sun along its orbit. As a result, the two effects partially canceled out, and climate was not very seasonal. Between 22,000 and 12,000 BP, changes in these parameters made global climate patterns become steadily more seasonal.

The author finds that the introduction and adoption of agriculture were both systematically faster in locations exposed to higher climate seasonality. The author also shows that farming spread faster in highly seasonal locations, such that one extra standard deviation of temperature seasonality is associated with adopting agriculture 1,500 years earlier.

In another insightful contribution, Quamrul Ashraf and Stelios Michalopoulos probe into the climatic origins of the diffusion of agriculture across countries and archaeological sites.[3] The authors argue that societies that faced climatic fluctuations adopted survival strategies by accumulating knowledge complementary to agricultural practices. This facilitated the adoption of farming when the technology diffused from the Neolithic frontier. Consistent with the predictions of their theory, their analysis demonstrates a highly statistically significant association between the standard deviation of temperature and the timing of the transition into agriculture.

These studies establish the geographic origins of the transition to agriculture. On the other hand, several studies investigate whether the early adoption of agriculture affected contemporary economic conditions. The argument is that this dramatic change had a lasting imprint on those societies that experienced it earlier than others. On one hand, the earlier the transition to agricultural production, the longer the period of accumulation of knowledge, the earlier the transition to industrialization, and the higher the level of current economic development. On the other hand, early transition was also accompanied by extractive institutions, autocratic states, collectivist cultures, and income disparities.

In this context, some studies find a beneficial effect of the early transition to agriculture. For instance, Ola Olsson and Douglas Hibbs attempt to determine whether the factors that influenced the transition to agricultural production also influenced current economic development.[4] The authors show that some geographic factors and biogeographic conditions, or the distribution of heavy seeded plants and large domesticable animals, exerted influence on the location and timing of the transition to agriculture. Their evidence also indicates substantial effects of geography and biogeography on contemporary economic development. In another article, the authors state that[5]

The most important event in human economic history before the industrial revolution was the Neolithic transition from a nomadic hunter-gatherer lifestyle to sedentary agriculture, beginning 10,000 years ago. The transition made possible the human population explosion, the rise of non-food-producing specialists, and the acceleration of technological progress that led eventually to the industrial revolution. But the transition occurred at different times in different regions of the world, with big consequences for the present-day economic conditions of populations indigenous to each region.

Louis Putterman extends this analysis by introducing a new set of estimates for the year of transition to agriculture for a large set of countries.[6] The author finds weaker estimates on the effect of the timing of transition on current income than the ones found by the seminal study by Ola Olsson and Douglas Hibbs. The author argues that a better indicator of the time since transition in a country is a weighted average of the values applicable to the countries its people came from. The argument is that the transition to agriculture is associated with a "lengthy development of human capabilities that are associated with the growth of civilizations." The analysis shows that this adjusted indicator achieves a better fit in the analysis than the one without the adjustment. Michael Bleaney and Arcangelo Dimico test the hypothesis that prehistoric biogeography, or the availability of wild grasses and large domesticable animal species, determined the date of the transition to agriculture and thereby influences current economic outcomes.[7] The authors find that the date of transition to agriculture is correlated with prehistoric biogeography, and that the factors conducive to current economic development include an early transition to agriculture, institutional quality, access to the sea and a low incidence of Malaria.

In an insightful study, Justin Cook attempts to explain differences in population density in 1500 C.E. as a function of a country's frequency of lactase persistence.[8] The author argues that a significant adaptation to the agricultural lifestyle is the ability to consume milk, or to be lactase persistent, which provided advantages to the diet of these societies. The increased productivity of lactase persistent workers led to a temporary increase in income and a permanent increase in population. The author shows that the frequency of lactase persistence is positively associated with population density in 1500 C.E., which is an indicator of economic development at the time.

On the other hand, some studies argue that an early transition to agriculture was not beneficial to current economic conditions. This is because the advent of agriculture and the introduction of farming practices led to extractive institutions, autocratic governance, extensive corruption, and social disparities. There are few possible transmission channels between the transition to agriculture and these low-quality institutions. First, the adoption of agriculture in river valleys was only possible through coordinated efforts in the construction of dikes, levees, dams, fields, plantations, and orchards. These collective actions led to the emergence of a centralized authority with immense powers. Second, these river valleys became densely populated agricultural settlements with a large accumulation of wealth due to the production of food surplus. Such wealth became a tempting target for neighboring populations. Being under constant threat by foreigners, the form of government tilted toward a more autocratic military rule. Finally, agricultural land in river valleys was under constant threat of salinization which led to crop shifts and abandonment of settlements. These ecological failures and the ensuing drastic changes have often induced internal strife and social collapse.

Building on this intuition, Ola Olsson and Christopher Paik argue that communities that adopted agriculture early have autocratic systems with social inequality, while late adopters have egalitarian societies with better property rights.[9] The authors provide evidence for these observations by showing that time since transition to agriculture has a negative correlation with contemporary levels of income and institutions, and a positive association with early statehood, ubiquitous corruption, autocratic systems, and extensive inequality. In a similar vein, Christopher Paik provides evidence that the adoption of agriculture affected contemporary institutions by influencing early ones.[10] The author argues that lands with vegetation suitable for agriculture experienced higher levels of extraction compared to ones that needed more effort in cultivation. The analysis suggests that areas that experienced early adoption of agriculture developed extractive institutions and centralized political systems with hierarchical structures that persisted over time.

Some studies also examine the effect of the agricultural transition on some cultural traits that have economic consequences. For instance, Ola Olsson and Christopher Paik explore the effect of the adoption of agriculture on contemporary cultural norms of collectivism.[11] The authors argue that the advent of agriculture was accompanied by collectivist values because early farming was characterized by a high chance of predation from others and prevalence of infectious diseases. These societies became collectivist in nature to be able to deal with adversity, which triggered an exodus of individualistic farmers to set up communities in peripheral areas and frontier territories. This caused the initial cultural divergence which persisted over generations. Along the lines of this intuition, the authors provide evidence that areas that adopted agriculture early value obedience and feel less in control of their lives.

STATE ANTIQUITY

Some scholars argue that the experience of the state, determined by its longevity or period in existence, can affect economic outcomes today. State history refers to the duration of experience with statehood, the length of exposure to state level institutions, and the protracted presence of state structures. Some studies argue that societies with a long-established state usually enjoy a head start. This early start confers upon their state institutions and state personnel advantages compared to newer states. Through a process of learning by doing, older states will have a wider pool of experienced public personnel who can fulfill their duties competently. In addition, the continuous operation of state institutions allows the development of bureaucratic regimen and hierarchical discipline. This can enhance the organizational effectiveness of public administration, which is critical for promoting economic, political, legal, social, cultural, and financial development.

Before delving into the effect of state formation on current economic outcomes, we will explore its geographic origins. Some studies find that state formation followed the transition to agriculture, which was influenced by geographic factors as discussed earlier.[12] First, this transition that allowed for the domestication of storable crops created a food surplus. This contributed to the emergence of an elite class that became sufficiently powerful to be able to extract this surplus. The ensuing stratification of society ultimately led to the formation of the state as an instrument for the elite to preserve and expand its powers, perks, and perquisites. Second, the transition to agriculture led to settled societies with higher population density. This required an elevated degree of cooperation, coordination and centralized decision making for the society to be functional. Densely settled populations also generated social pressure, thereby accentuating the need for the emergence of an authority able to contain any turmoil or tumultuous events.

Other scholars offer an alternative explanation, given that the adoption of agriculture in some areas did not lead to state formation. According to their view, the emergence of hierarchy and state structures depends on the ability of the elite to appropriate food crops from farmers. In the case of a community of farmers who cultivate a crop which is highly perishable, it may be impossible for anyone to appropriate the produce since the crop cannot be stored after the harvest. On the other hand, in a farming community growing a grain that has to be stored for later use, the produce could be easily confiscated by an elite or a tax collector. Thus, differences in the suitability of land for crops that are appropriable can lead to differences in the formation of hierarchical state institutions. Building on this intuition, Joram Mayshar, Omer Moav, Zvika Neeman and Luigi Pascali show that land suitability for cereals, which are storable, compared to the suitability for tubers, which are perishable, explains the formation of hierarchical institutions and states, whereas land productivity does not.[13]

Another argument on the effect of the natural environment on state formation posits that state formation was expedited in areas with a high level of land and climate variability. This is because differences in the comparative advantage of agricultural production across these areas, driven by these variations, created incentives for a central government to emerge. The purpose of the state in this case was to develop the essential infrastructure, in terms of trade routes, and the necessary institutions, in terms of protection of trade transactions, that would facilitate commercial exchange between these different areas. Building on this intuition, Anastasia Litina shows that the advent of statehood was expedited in areas characterized by a higher degree of variability in land and climatic conditions, and that the role of the state operates partly through the facilitation of commercial exchange.[14]

After this exposition of the geographic origins of state formation, we can now turn into its effect on current economic outcomes. In this context, some studies show that older states enjoyed advantages that newer ones did not. For instance, Louis Putterman, Areendam Chanda, and Valerie Bockstette develop an index of the depth of experience with state institutions, that they refer to as "state antiquity," for a large set of countries.[15] The authors show that state antiquity has a significant positive effect on economic growth, output per worker, political stability, and institutional quality. Louis Putterman and Areendam Chanda show that early states, like China and India, have been experiencing accelerated economic growth lately.[16] The authors show that state history and early transition to agriculture have a positive effect on historical economic development captured by urbanization rates and population density in 1500 C.E. The analysis also shows a reversal of this fortune for these early starters during the era of European expansion until 1980 C.E. Thus, the analysis shows that old agrarian societies began to catch up lately with earlier industrializers while the newer states experienced slower economic growth.

Louis Putterman, Oana Borcan, and Ola Olsson construct a dataset on state history from state emergence before the Common Era to 2000 C.E.[17] The authors outline a framework where accumulated state experience enhances aggregate productivity, while newer inexperienced states can achieve higher productivity by learning from older ones. The authors provide empirical evidence for their model prediction that newer states can enjoy a higher level of economic development compared to older ones.

Some studies also argue that state history influences the timing of colonization and its subsequent effects. For instance, Louis Putterman, Arhan Ertan, and Martin Fiszbein study the determinants of the occurrence and timing of colonization by western European powers.[18] The authors show that societies who were less likely to be colonized had longer histories of agriculture and statehood and higher levels of technology adoption in 1500 C.E. James Ang and Per Fredriksson argue that countries with longer state history at the time of colonization were better able to implement the legal practices transplanted by their colonizers.[19] The authors also show that some differences between common law countries and civil law countries are inflated by a longer statehood experience.

Besides economic development, some studies explore the association between state history and financial development. The argument is that the sophistication of financial systems is the outcome of a process defined by the ability of the state to administer its treasury, to regulate financial markets and institutions, and to draft legislations for financial transactions. Long standing state institutions, with experienced civil servants, are better equipped to formulate laws that contribute to financial development. These states are also expected to be more competent in the use of public funds, tax collection, and government administration which are critical for the emergence of the contemporary financial architecture.

In this context, James Ang investigates whether differences in financial development between countries can be explained by the depth of state experience.[20] The author shows a significant positive effect of state antiquity on the ratio of private credit to Gross Domestic Product, as an indicator that captures financial development. James Ang and Per Fredriksson expand this analysis to examine the relationship between state history, legal origins, and financial development.[21] The authors find that countries with adaptable civil law exhibit lower financial development compared to common law ones. However, the longer the history of statehood in these countries the higher their level of financial development.

Other studies examine the effect of state history on the extent of ethnic diversity and the likelihood of conflict. The argument is that national identity is considered the linchpin in the process of state consolidation as it offers a common ground between citizens. Thus, countries that have gone through a lengthy state-formation process are better able to forge a common identity which diminishes the degree of stratification. In this context, Michael Bleaney and Arcangelo Dimico find that ethnic fractionalization is higher in less historically legitimate states and, to a lesser extent, in states with a shorter history.[22]

The accumulation of experience with state institutions may also lead to increased state capacity over time. These factors allow these countries to be better equipped to maintain law and order, to have efficient law enforcement, to be better able to allocate scarce resources, to be better able to protect property, and to have legal courts capable of settling disputes peacefully. This may decrease the likelihood of conflict. In this context, Emilio Depetris-Chauvin show that the historical exposure to centralized institutions has a strong causal effect on the likelihood of conflict, and that countries with a long state history are less prone to experience conflict when hit by an adverse agricultural productivity shock.[23]

SLAVE TRADE

Various studies investigate the long-term effects of the slave trade. Some of these studies find that the slave trade adversely affects current economic development. The proposed channels include the effect of the slave trade on labor supply, social capital, income inequality, armed conflict, and ethnic stratification. From 1400 C.E. to 1900 C.E., the African continent experienced four slave trades through the Atlantic Ocean, the Sahara Desert, the Red Sea, and the Indian Ocean. Millions of slaves were exported from Africa in the most modest estimates. These estimates do not even include those who perished during the raids or those who died during the journey to the final destination. By 1850 C.E., Africa's population was only half of what it would have been had the slave trades not taken place. This affected labor supply and ultimately production in Africa. African historian Elikia M'bokolo wrote that[24]

> The African continent was bled of its human resources via all possible routes. Across the Sahara, through the Red Sea, from the Indian Ocean ports and across the Atlantic. At least ten centuries of slavery for the benefit of the Muslim countries (from the ninth to the nineteenth). Then more than four centuries (from the end of the fifteenth to the nineteenth) of a regular slave trade to build the Americas and the prosperity of the Christian states of Europe. The figures, even where hotly disputed, make your head spin. Four million slaves exported via the Red Sea, another four million through the Swahili ports of the Indian Ocean, perhaps as many as nine million along the trans-Saharan caravan route, and eleven to twenty million (depending on the author) across the Atlantic Ocean.

The extent of slave shipments in an area was affected by climatic conditions as a higher level of slave exports was observed in colder years than in warmer ones. This is because higher temperatures were accompanied by an increased cost of raiding to capture those who were about to be shackled. Warmer temperatures decrease agricultural productivity and increase fatalities due to food shortages and disease burdens. These factors led to a drop in the availability of slaves and the provisions to feed them, which made slave exports untenable. Along the lines of this intuition, James Fenske and Namrata Kala consider the variation in weather conditions in Africa during the time of the trans-Atlantic slave trade.[25] The authors find a considerable decline in the recorded quantity of shipped slaves from ports in warmer years. The study also suggests that areas around ports that experienced cold temperature shocks, which increased slave trade, are poorer today.

Other scholars argue that terrain ruggedness bestowed some advantages on the areas that are defined by this topographic characteristic. This could be seen in the effect of topography on the slave trade. Enslavement occurred through raids by one group on another. For those fleeing captivity, rugged terrain offered protection from those attempting to capture them. In this case, caves and dunes served as a hideaway while hills and cliffs acted as lookout posts. Thus, terrain ruggedness conferred advantages by helping areas avoid the adverse long-term consequences of the slave trade. To test the blessing of furrowed terrain, Nathan Nunn and Diego Puga examine the effect of terrain ruggedness on slave exports and subsequently on current economic development.[26] The authors find that terrain ruggedness was a blessing for current economic development by curbing the slave trade in parts of Africa.

Slavery had a persistent effect on countries afflicted by this abominable sort of trade. Some studies explore the effect of the slave trade on current economic outcomes in Africa. For instance, Nathan Nunn examines whether the slave trade can explain Africa's current underdevelopment.[27] The author uses data from historical documents and shipping records to construct estimates of the number of slave exports from each country during the period from 1400 C.E. to 1900 C.E. The author finds a negative association between the number of slaves exported from a country and current economic development. Daron Acemoglu, Camilo García-Jimeno and James Robinson examine the effect of slavery on economic development in Colombia.[28] The study compares areas with gold extraction activities, which were a source of demand for slave labor during the seventeenth and eighteenth centuries, to other areas. The authors find that the historical presence of slavery is associated with higher poverty levels, higher land inequality, lower school enrollment, lower vaccination coverage, and worse public good provision.

Slaves were also captured through raids of one group on another in lots of cases. Thus, ties between communities were weakened and trust between societies was depleted. This situation, in turn, impeded the formation of larger communities, broader ethnic identities, and cohesive state structures. Thus, the slave trade was a critical factor in Africa's high level of ethnic diversity, low levels of social trust, high frequency of conflicts and fragile states today.

When it comes to the effect of slavery on trust, Nathan Nunn and Leonard Wantchekon combine contemporary survey data on trust with historical information on slave shipments to show that current differences in trust levels within Africa can be traced back to the slave trade.[29] The authors provide evidence that individuals' trust in relatives, neighbors, co-ethnics, and local government is lower if their ancestors were heavily affected by the slave trade. The authors conclude that the 400 years of insecurity due to the slave trade caused distrust sentiments to evolve and to be transmitted from parents to offspring over time.

Some studies explore the effect of slavery on ethnic stratification. For instance, Warren Whatley and Rob Gillezeau argue that the slave trade[30] "constrained the geographic scope of authority and increased the salience of ethnic identity." Their analysis shows an economically and statistically significant positive association between the number of ethnicities in the present and the number of slave exports in the past. Since the slave trade intensified ethnic divisions in Africa, some studies argue that slavery also increased the likelihood of conflict while other studies argue that the termination of the slave trade was another factor that contributed to an increase in conflict in Africa. For instance, James Fenske and Namrata Kala find that one of the determinants of the increase in conflicts in Africa is the suppression of the slave trade after 1807 C.E.[31] The authors argue that this is because the demand for slaves could only be satisfied through the violent seizure and enslavement of war captives. In addition, states that derived income from the slave trade found their power weakened and thus resorted to the spoils of war to preserve their status. When it comes to the effect of slavery on state fragility, Dirk Bezemer, Jutta Bolt, and Robert Lensink examine the long-term effect of Africa's indigenous slavery on economic and political development.[32] Using anthropological data, the authors find that slavery led to lower current income levels as it hindered the development of capable and accountable states in Africa.

Finally, some studies examine the effect of the use of slaves on current income inequality in the destination countries. This is because the descendants of these slaves became the underprivileged communities who continue to deal with the stigma even after the abolition of slavery and the suspension of the slave trades. In this context, Rodrigo Soares, Juliano Assunção, and Tomás Goulart compile a database on the number of African slaves in each destination country to examine the effect of slavery on the levels of income inequality observed across the globe today.[33] The authors find that the slavery indicators are highly correlated with current levels of income inequality.

PROTESTANT REFORMATION

Examining the effect of religious affiliation complemented the analysis of the effect of religiosity discussed earlier. Lots of these studies find a particular positive association between the share of Protestants in a country and economic performance. In this context, it is inconceivable to attribute the affiliation to a specific faith to geographic conditions. However, the reformation as a challenge to established clerical authority can provide an opportunity for exploring the effect of climate change on historical events that have long lasting consequences.

Several historical studies claim that one of the causes of the reformation is the bubonic plague of 1347 C.E.–1353 C.E. which decimated the population in Europe, in addition to the other factors related to the corruption in the church, the emergence of the nation state, the decline of Latin as a language of intellect, and the renaissance. In the words of historian Niall Ferguson,[34] "The population of the entire Eurasian land mass was devastated in the fourteenth century by the Black death, the bubonic plague caused by the flea borne bacterium *Yersinia Pestis*, which was transmitted along the Eurasian trade networks described above." He adds, "But the impact was very different in Europe, where roughly half of the population died (including perhaps three quarters of the population of Southern Europe), compared with Asia." The Church suffered greatly during the plague as the monasteries proved to be ideal breeding grounds for the plague. Priests and monks contracted the disease as they gave the last rites to those in their death bed. This led to a shortage in clergy which caused the Church to hastily train new clerics to serve the community's spiritual needs, especially as they came to terms with the trauma of the Black Death. This meant that many unsuitable individuals became clerics leading to a drop in standards among priests and prelates. The Church became inept and corrupt which led believers to gradually turn away from the church in apprehension with the clergy's worldliness. This was decisive in the emergence of both the renaissance and the reformation.

In this context, an influential study finds that the Black Death originated in Asia and arrived in Europe through the land and sea trade routes of the Silk Road.[35] This pandemic was the consequence of the introduction of Yersinia pestis, after which the disease established itself in European rodents and continued to cause outbreaks over four centuries until it disappeared in the early nineteenth century. The authors of this study provide evidence for repeated climate-driven introductions of the bacterium into European ports. In particular, the study shows that climate-driven outbreaks of Yersinia pestis in Asian rodent reservoirs are "significantly associated with new waves of plague arriving at Europe through its maritime trade network with Asia." Hence, climatic factors contributed to the recurrence of the plague which was one of the critical factors leading to the reformation.

In this context, scholars are interested in studying the contention, advocated by Max Weber, that the Protestant Reformation was critical to the rise of capitalism.[36] Weber claims in *The Protestant Ethic and the Spirit of Capitalism* that the reformation nourished and nurtured attitudes that were conducive to the inception of capitalism such as hard work, self-reliance, less support for government intervention, a worldly asceticism focused on efficient economic activity, thrift, and non-ostentatious accumulation of wealth. Max Weber proclaims that[37] "what was definitely new was the estimation of fulfillment of duty within secular callings as being of the absolutely highest level possible for moral activity. It was this that led, inevitably, to the idea of the religious significance of secular everyday labor and gave rise to the concept of the calling." Weber saw these qualities as the bedrock of modern capitalism. As Anthony Padgen puts it,[38] "The Reformation—although it was never one movement but many—had begun. It unleashed a conflagration upon Europe, far greater and far more radical than any Luther himself had ever intended." In this context, several studies examine the repercussions of the Protestant Reformation on educational attainment, employment, work ethics, entrepreneurship, and economic performance.[39]

Some studies provide a view that argues that the Protestant Reformation did not induce the work ethics that Max Weber claimed to be fundamental for the rise of capitalism, but rather encouraged the accumulation of human capital as an unintended consequence of the admonitions to learn to read the testaments. The subsequent increase in educational attainment contributed to better economic outcomes. It is also worth mentioning that this process coincided with the introduction of the printing press at the time. Niall Ferguson states that[40] "Printing was crucial to the Reformation's success. Cities with at least one printing press in 1500 were significantly more likely to adopt Protestantism than cities without printing, but it was cities with multiple competing printers that were more likely to turn Protestant."

In this context, Sascha Becker and Ludger Woessmann posit that an unintended side effect of Luther's exhortations to read the Bible was that Protestants acquired literacy skills that were crucial for economic development.[41] The authors test their proposition using county-level data from nineteenth century Prussia and find that Protestantism led to higher economic prosperity and better educational attainment. In another related contribution, Sascha Becker and Ludger Woessmann show that Protestantism had a positive effect on school supply and educational enrollment across Prussian counties before industrialization in 1816 C.E.[42] The authors find that school enrollment in Protestant counties was about 25 percentage points higher than in the entirely Catholic counties. The authors conclude that their finding supports an interpretation where Martin Luther's appeal to read the Bible created the human capital that induced industrial development and rejects the alternative that the better education in Protestant areas was only a consequence of increased demand for it due to industrialization. Sascha Becker and Ludger Woessmann also examine the effect of the Reformation on the gender gap in basic education using county and town-level data on school enrollment from the first Prussian census of 1816 C.E.[43] Their analysis suggests that Protestantism was a driving force in the advancement of female education in Prussia as Luther urged girls and boys to study the Gospel. The authors show that a larger share of Protestants in a county or a town was associated with a larger share of girls in the total school population.

Another group of scholars extended this analysis to how Protestantism impacted spending on schooling and school performance. For instance, Timo Boppart, Josef Falkinger and Volker Grossman examine whether Protestants were more literate than Catholics due to the enticement to recite the Bible.[44] The authors use historical Swiss data which allows for the distinction between different cognitive abilities such as reading, writing, numeracy, and history. The authors show that Protestants acquired better cognitive abilities, especially reading, at the time of industrialization consistently with the impetus to read their holy book. Timo Boppart, Josef Falkinger, Volker

Grossman, Ulrich Woitek, and Gabriela Wüthrich examine how the affiliation to Protestantism affects public spending on schooling and educational performance.[45] The authors employ a data set from Swiss districts for the last quarter of the nineteenth century on public school inputs, scores from pedagogical examinations of conscripts, and outcomes of political referenda that capture support for conservative versus progressive values. The authors find that Catholic districts show lower educational performance and less spending on primary schooling than Protestant districts, but only in a milieu where conservative political attitudes were predominant.

Other studies focus on the effect of Protestantism on the entrepreneurial spirit that is critical for the economic success of a capitalist society. For instance, Luca Nunziata and Lorenzo Rocco examine whether Protestantism favors entrepreneurship compared to Catholicism using Swiss census data.[46] The authors find that Protestantism is associated with a higher propensity for entrepreneurship than Catholicism.

Some studies argue that it is not Protestantism that promoted work ethics, but rather it is those with higher work ethic who selected to become Protestants. For instance, André van Hoorn and Robbert Maseland examine the relation between Protestantism and the effect of unemployment on individuals' subjective well-being.[47] The authors find that unemployment has an adverse effect on subjective well-being in general, but that it affects individuals living in Protestant areas more. Thus, they conclude that this reflects a process of self-selection in which people with a stronger work ethic have disproportionately converted to Protestantism because it offered a framework for their ethical predispositions. Other studies argue that it is a social ethic and not a work ethic that contributed to the favorable effect of Protestantism. For instance, Benito Arruñada concludes that Protestantism seems propitious to economic outcomes, not because of the work ethic but by promoting a social ethic where individuals are willing to exert effort in informal social pressure that facilitates formal legal enforcement and lowers the cost of impersonal exchange.[48]

Others argue that the favorable effect of Protestantism occurs through its unintended promotion of secularization. For instance, Davide Cantoni, Jeremiah Dittmar, and Noam Yuchtman study the effect of the Protestant Reformation on the allocation of resources between the religious and secular sectors in Germany.[49] The authors find that during the reformation, secular authorities expropriated monasteries with enormous amounts of wealth which was then used to expand construction for secular administrative purposes. This shifted the demand for labor such that graduates from Protestant universities increasingly entered secular administrative occupations while students at Protestant universities shifted from the study of theology toward secular degrees especially ones that prepared students for public sector jobs.

Thus, the reformation played an important role in the secularization and the economic development of the West. The authors conclude that "the realloca-tion of resources (particularly upper-tail human capital) and the weakening of religious elites might have set in motion a process of cultural and intellectual change that culminated in the Enlightenment, the scientific revolution, and modern economic growth." This supports the arguments of historians such as Niall Ferguson who states that[50]

> After Luther's revolution, Protestant states began to show signs of greater eco-nomic dynamism. Why was this? One answer is that, despite Luther's desire to purify the Church, the Reformation led to a large scale reallocation of resources from religious to secular activities. Two thirds of monasteries were closed in the Protestant territories of Germany, the lands and other assets mostly appropriated by secular rulers and sold to wealthy subjects, as also happened in England. A rising share of university students gave up thoughts of the monastic life, turning their attention to more worldly vocations. Church building diminished; secular construction increased.

NOTES

1. Weiss and Bradley. "What Drives Societal Collapse?" *Science*: 609–610.

2. Matranga. "The Ant and the Grasshopper: Seasonality and the Invention of Agriculture." Manuscript.

3. Ashraf and Michalopoulos. "Climatic Fluctuations and the Diffusion of Agriculture." *The Review of Economics and Statistics*: 589–609.

4. Olsson and Hibbs. "Biogeography and Long-Run Economic Development." *European Economic Review*: 909–938.

5. Olsson and Hibbs. "Geography, Biogeography, and Why some Countries are Rich, and others are Poor." *PNAS*: 3715–3720.

6. Putterman. "Agriculture, Diffusion and Development: Ripple Effects of the Neolithic Revolution." *Economica*: 729–748.

7. Bleaney and Dimico. "Biogeographical Conditions, the Transition to Agriculture and Long-Run Growth." *European Economic Review*: 943–954.

8. Cook. "The Role of Lactose Persistence in Pre-colonial Development." *Journal of Economic Growth*: 369–406.

9. Olsson and Paik. "A Western Reversal Since the Neolithic? The Long-Run Impact of Early Agriculture." *The Journal of Economic History*: 100–135.

10. Paik. "Historical Underpinnings of Institutions: Evidence from the Neolithic Revolution." Manuscript.

11. Olsson and Paik. "Long-Run Cultural Divergence: Evidence from the Neolithic Revolution." *Journal of Development Economics*: 197–213.

12. Petersen and Skaaning. "Ultimate Causes of State Formation: The Significance of Biogeography, Diffusion, and Neolithic Revolutions." *Historical Social Research*: 200–226.

13. Mayshar, Moav, Neeman, and Pascali. "Cereals, Appropriability and Hierarchy." Manuscript.

14. Litina. "The Geographical Origins of Early State Formation." Center for Research in Economics and Management Paper 28.

15. Bockstette, Chanda, and Putterman. "States and Markets: The Advantage of an Early Start." *Journal of Economic Growth*: 347–369.

16. Chanda and Putterman. "Early Starts, Reversals and Catch-up in the Process of Economic Development." *Scandinavian Journal of Economics*: 387–413.

17. Borcan, Olsson, and Putterman. "State History and Economic Development." *Journal of Economic Growth*: 1–40.

18. Ertan, Putterman, and Fiszbein. "Who was Colonized and When? A Cross-Country Analysis of Determinants." *European Economic Review*: 165–184.

19. Ang and Per Fredriksson. "Statehood Experience, Legal Traditions, and Climate Change Policies." *Economic Inquiry*: 1511–1537.

20. Ang. "Are Modern Financial Systems Shaped by State Antiquity?" *Journal of Banking and Finance*: 4038–4058.

21. Ang and Per Fredriksson. "State History, Legal Adaptability and Financial Development." *Journal of Banking and Finance*: 169–191.

22. Bleaney and Dimico. "State History, Historical Legitimacy and Modern Ethnic Diversity." *European Journal of Political Economy*: 159–170.

23. Depetris-Chauvin. "State History and Contemporary Conflict." Documentos de Trabajo 475, Instituto de Economia, Pontificia Universidad Católica de Chile.

24. M'bokolo. "The Impact of the Slave Trade on Africa." Le Monde Diplomatique, April 1998.

25. Fenske and Kala. "Climate and Slave Trade." *Journal of Development Economics*: 19–32.

26. Nunn and Puga. "Ruggedness: The Blessing of Bad Geography in Africa." *The Review of Economics and Statistics*: 20–36.

27. Nunn. "The Long-Term Effects of Africa's Slave Trade." *The Quarterly Journal of Economics*: 139–176.

28. Acemoglu, García-Jimeno, and Robinson. "Finding Eldorado: Slavery and Long-Run Development in Colombia." *Journal of Comparative Economics*: 534–564.

29. Nunn and Wantchekon. "The Slave Trade and the Origins of Mistrust in Africa." *The American Economic Review*: 3221–3252.

30. Whatley and Gillezeau. "The Impact of the Transatlantic Slave Trade on Ethnic Stratification in Africa." *American Economic Review: Papers & Proceedings*: 571–576.

31. Fenske and Kala. "1807: Economic Shocks, Conflict and the Slave Trade." *Journal of Development Economics*: 66–76.

32. Bezemer, Bolt, and Lensink. "Slavery, Statehood, and Economic Development in Sub-Saharan Africa." *World Development*: 148–163.

33. Soares, Assunção, and Goulart. "A Note on Slavery and the Roots of Inequality." *Journal of Comparative Economics*: 565–580.

34. Ferguson. *The Square and the Tower* (p. 65).

35. Schmid, Büntgen, Easterday, Ginzler, Walløe, Bramanti, and Tenseth. "Climate-Driven Introduction of the Black Death and Successive Plague Reintroductions into Europe." *PNAS*: 3020–3025.

36. Weber. *The Protestant Ethic and the Spirit of Capitalism and Other Writings*.

37. Ibid.

38. Pagden. *Worlds at War: The 2,500 Year Struggle between East and West* (p. 303).

39. Beker, Pfaff, and Rubin. "Causes and Consequences of the Protestant Reformation." *Explorations in Economic History*: 1–25.

40. Ferguson. *The Square and the Tower* (p. 83).

41. Becker and Woessmann. "Was Weber Wrong? A Human Capital Theory of Protestant Economic History." *The Quarterly Journal of Economics*: 531–596.

42. Sascha and Woessmann. "The Effect of Protestantism on Education before the Industrialization." *Economics Letters*: 224–228.

43. Becker and Woessmann. "Luther and the Girls: Religious Denomination and the Female Education Gap in Nineteenth-Century Prussia." *The Scandinavian Journal of Economics*: 777–805.

44. Boppart, Falkinger, and Grossman. "Protestantism and Education: Reading (The Bible) and Other Skills." *Economic Inquiry*: 874–895.

45. Boppart, Falkinger, Grossman, Woitek, and Wüthrich. "Under Which Conditions Does Religion Affect Educational Outcomes?" *Explorations in Economic History*: 242–266.

46. Nunziata and Rocco. "A Tale of Minorities: Evidence on Religious Ethics and Entrepreneurship." *Journal of Economic Growth*: 189–224.

47. van Hoorn and Maseland. "Does a Protestant Work Ethic Exist?" *Journal of Economic Behavior & Organization*: 1–12.

48. Arruñada. "Protestants and Catholics: Similar Work Ethic, Different Social Ethic." *The Economic Journal*: 890–918.

49. Cantoni, Dittmar, and Yuchtman. "Religious Competition and Reallocation: The Political Economy of Secularization in the Protestant Reformation." *The Quarterly Journal of Economics*: 2037–2096.

50. Ferguson. *The Square and the Tower* (p. 93).

Chapter Seventeen

The Big Scramble, the Great Loot

Colonialism is another episode in human history that attracted a lot of attention. Scholars continue to study the long-lasting effects of colonialism on the economies of the colonized countries after independence. Even though there are conflicting opinions on the impact of the colonial expansion, there is a consensus that colonialism had its indelible mark on the conquered nations. For instance, historian Paul Bairoch asserts that[1] "there is no doubt that a large number of negative structural features of the process of economic underdevelopment have historical roots going back to European colonization." Anthony Pagden also states that[2] "the older forms of imperialisms are no more, even if many of the wounds they left behind have still not healed."

The invasion of other countries, and the subjugation of other nations, has been a recurrent theme in human history since time immemorial. European colonialism, however, started with the age of discovery when Spain and Portugal stumbled into the Americas, followed by Britain and France, where they established settlements and occupied large stretches of land. This colonial expansion in the new world was curtailed in the late eighteenth and early nineteenth centuries by the American revolutionary war and the Latin American wars of independence. Afterward, new colonies were established elsewhere in other corners of the world especially with the expansion of the British and French empires. After the First World War, the victorious allies divided the colonies of the defeated Germany and Ottoman Empire between them. After the Second World War, decolonization started as many colonial powers were significantly drained by the end of the war. During the decades that followed, colonized countries gained their independence sometimes by carrying arms and other times by going to the negotiations table. In this context, Scott Anderson describes the sentiments of the colonial powers toward the demands of the colonized nations for independence:[3]

For many Europeans, steeped in condescension of the late imperial age, independence didn't mean letting native peoples actually govern themselves, but something far more paternalistic: a new round of "the white man's burden," the tutoring—and, of course, the exploiting—of native peoples until they might sufficiently grasp the ways of modern civilization to stand on their own at some indeterminate point in the future.

When independence was attained eventually, it was the fig leaf that covered a more sinister form of persistent exploitation. This is referred to as "neocolonialism" which is a term first coined by the French philosopher Jean-Paul Sartre who described the third world as follows:[4]

> we know too that enslaved peoples are still to be found there, together with some who have achieved a simulacrum of phony independence, others who are still fighting to attain sovereignty and others again who have obtained complete freedom but who live under the constant menace of imperialist aggression. These differences are born of colonial history, in other words of oppression. Here, the mother country is satisfied to keep some feudal rulers in her pay; there, dividing and ruling she has created a native bourgeoisie, sham from beginning to end; elsewhere she has played a double game: the colony is planted with settlers and exploited at the same time.

Some scholars argue that during the colonial era, colonies were exposed to devastating forms of exploitation that they were not able to recover from until the present day. These countries faced the expropriation of their natural wealth; the extraction of their resources; the use of their manpower for imperial military follies; the use of their labor force to the economic benefit of the metropole; the distortion of their educational systems to produce clerks for colonial administrations; the introduction of extractive institutions to facilitate exploitation by the colonial masters; the transplantation of some cultural elements of the colonizer such as language and religion to guarantee that the colony continues to be a vassal state even after independence; the transplantation of legal systems; the delineation of borders haphazardly without any consideration for the demographic composition of the colonies; the initiation of tensions between various ethnic and linguistic groups that led to subsequent ethnolinguistic conflicts; the demise of scores of nationalists who fought for their countries' independence; and the creation of a westernized elite class that continue to rule after independence with the aim of promoting their personal interests on the expense of the rest of the population.

Thus, the conventional wisdom is that colonization led to an economic drain of the colonies. In this context, colonial exploitation diminished indigenous physical capital accumulation which hampered the colonies' future economic prospects. The colonial practices also included forced labor and even enslavement of some indigenous people. The impact of these practices, combined with the distortion of educational policies, decreased the incentives for human capital accumulation. The adverse effects of colonialism on physical capital and human capital hindered economic growth. In the words of Frantz Fanon in his classic *The Wretched of the Earth*: "Colonialism hardly ever exploits the whole of a country. It contents itself with bringing to light the natural resources, which it extracts, and exports to meet the needs of the mother country's industries, thereby allowing certain sectors of the colony to become relatively rich. But the rest of the colony follows its path of under-development and poverty, or at all events sinks into it more deeply."

On the other hand, some argue that colonial powers brought some benefits to their colonies which they would not have enjoyed otherwise. In this context, colonial powers built an elaborate web of infrastructure that lasted after independence, facilitated the integration of the colonies into the world economic system, connected the colonies to international markets through trade and commerce, channeled foreign capital into their colonies, introduced cultural modes and promoted a modernization process that allowed the colony's people to become members of the contemporary world, encouraged the incorporation of western ideals such as democratic governance and political freedoms, and transplanted legal traditions that continue to serve as a frame of reference for legislation even after independence. In the words of Ian Smith, "I would say colonialism is a wonderful thing. It spread civilization to Africa. Before it they had no written language, no wheel as we know it, no schools, no hospitals, not even normal clothing." According to this view, colonialism was conducive to the long run growth potential of the colonies.

Given the conflicting points of view on the overall effect of colonialism on economic outcomes, an empirical analysis driven by data is imperative. This chapter discusses the latest findings of some studies that focus on the effect of colonialism on economic performance, and whether there is an economic pecking order among the colonizers. In this context, colonialism can be captured by indicators of the identity of the colonial power, the duration of the colonial period, the degree of economic penetration of the colonial era, and whether the colonial rule was direct or indirect.

As discussed earlier, colonialism was driven by geographic factors as discussed earlier. Colonial powers aimed to dominate other territories in order to extract natural assets and valuable commodities that were not abundantly available, but badly needed, in their territories. It is also worth noting that some studies argue that the type of colonialism was determined by climatic and ecological conditions as well.[5] In areas where the climate-induced disease environment was not favorable to Europeans, there was less incentive to settle. In these areas, Europeans extracted resources without settlement. In other areas where ecological conditions allowed for the survival of Europeans, they established settlements where life was modeled after their home country.

THE NON-WHITE MAN'S BURDEN

A plethora of studies explore the effect of colonialism on economic outcomes. The purpose of these studies is to examine whether the so-called white man's burden, that justifies imperialism as a way of civilizing not so civilized people, became a persistent burden on the non-white man. The "white man's burden" proposes that the white race is morally obligated to rule other people to ensure their progress. This concept is best articulated by Rudyard Kipling's notorious poem:[6]

> Take up the White Man's burden
> Send forth the best ye breed
> Go bind your sons to exile
> To serve your captives' need;
> To wait in heavy harness,
> On fluttered folk and wild
> Your new-caught, sullen peoples,
> Half-devil and half-child.

Some earlier studies find a favorable effect of colonialism on economic outcomes. For instance, Robin Grier examines the effect of the duration of the colonial period and the identity of the colonial power on economic outcomes.[7] The author finds that colonies that were subjugated for longer periods of time tend to perform better after independence. The author also shows that former British colonies outperform their French counterparts, because the former were more successful in educating their dependents than the latter. James Feyrer and Bruce Sacerdote examine the effect of colonialism on economic development using a new dataset of islands throughout the Atlantic, Pacific, and Indian Oceans.[8] The authors show a robust positive association between the number of years spent as a European colony and current economic development. They also find that years under American, British, French, and Dutch colonial rule have more beneficial economic effects than those spent under Spanish or Portuguese domination.

Later studies find that the economies that were exposed to colonialism had to continue carrying the brunt of it even after gaining their independence. For instance, Graziella Bertocchi and Fabio Canova investigate whether the colonial heritage, captured by the identity of the metropolitan ruler and by the degree of economic penetration, influenced the growth trajectories of African countries.[9] The authors find that British and French colonies performed better than others, that a lower degree of economic penetration has a positive effect on economic growth, and that there are growth gains from decolonization. Kevin Sylwester examines the effect of colonization on economic growth in sub-Saharan Africa.[10] For each period considered, the author distinguishes between countries that gained independence before, during or after that period. The author finds that newly independent countries grew slower than those that gained their independence previously, but faster than those that continued to be colonies. Miriam Bruhn and Francisco Gallego compare the economic effects of different colonial activities: the bad, the good, and the ugly.[11] Bad colonial activities include those that displayed economies of scale and exploitation of labor, such as mining and sugar production. Good colonial activities include those that did not display economies of scale, such as the production of subsistence crops and cattle breeding. Ugly colonial activities are those performed with forced labor from the native populations. The authors provide evidence that bad colonial activities led to lower current economic development.

Besides the effect of colonization on income, some studies explore its effect on income inequality as well. For instance, Luis Angeles explores whether colonialism explains current differences in income inequality across countries.[12] The author shows that income inequality has been higher in colonies where the percentage of European settlers to total population was higher, as long as they remained a minority.

COLONIAL CLERKS

Some scholars argue that the effect of colonialism on current economic outcomes goes through the education channel. European colonizers and settlers brought their own human capital and educational systems that eventually affected their colonies. The colonial administrations were also in need of clerks and bureaucrats to perform tasks intended to accomplish the aims of the metropole. To prepare a compliant workforce, the colonial powers transformed the education system in such a way to serve its designs. The aim was to produce a clerk sufficiently competent in accomplishing the tasks assigned by colonial superiors, but not inquisitive enough to question or to oppose the purpose of these assignments. This entailed a drastic change in the teaching approach, the pedagogical style, the curriculum content, the instructional material, and the schools' design. These systems and structures persisted after independence and continued to preclude a country's ability to cultivate a culture of critical thinking and innovative creativity.

As an example, an article in *Nature* highlights the proceedings of the Ormsby-Gore Commission which was appointed by the British parliament to submit recommendations on how to accelerate economic development and improve living conditions in their African colonies.[13] The article states that "Since the scientific community in general has taken so little interest in the prosecution of research and the provision of essential scientific services in the Colonies, it is not surprising that successive Governments have ignored them when appointing committees to consider Colonial services and development." The article also referred to the findings of the Commission as "a report in striking contrast with previous reports on Colonial matters because of the exceptional prominence it gave to the dependence of economic progress on the generous provision of education and medical services, the adequate provision of scientific and technical services, and the prosecution of scientific research in connexion with social as well as purely economic problems." This is but an example of the neglect in the provision of proper education in the British colonies until a parliamentary commission sounded the alarm. There is no evidence that other colonies fared any better.

Based on this intuition, some studies attempt to explore the effect of colonialism on education. For instance, William Easterly and Ross Levine examine the hypothesis that Europeans brought human capital and human-capital-creating institutions that shape long run economic outcomes.[14] The authors find that the European share of the population during colonization is more positively associated with current economic development than the percentage of the population that is of European descent today. The authors conclude that this finding is consistent with human capital playing a critical role in the way that colonial European settlement affects current economic development. Elise Huillery examines the extent to which colonial public investments continue to influence current outcomes in West Africa.[15] The author shows that colonial public investments have been a strong determinant of a district's current development such that current educational performance is determined by colonial investments in schooling, current health performance is determined by colonial investments in medical care, and current infrastructure's development is determined by colonial public works.

Some studies also argue that colonial education affected the cultural attitudes in their colonies. For instance, James Fenske evaluates the effect of colonial education on polygamy in Africa, which is known to be associated with slow economic growth, low saving rates, and low investment in females' human capital.[16] The author shows that former colonial districts that had more teachers per capita during the early colonial period, and those that had missionary schooling, have lower practice of polygamy in the present. The author concludes that colonial and missionary education has been critical sources of cultural change compared to modern education.

POST-COLONIAL INSTITUTIONS

Several studies examine the effect of colonialism on the quality of institutions. Some of these studies posit that "settlement colonialism" had a different effect on the quality of institutions compared to "exploitation colonialism." For instance, Daron Acemoglu, Simon Johnson, and James Robinson examine the effect of institutions, in particular the protection against expropriation, on economic performance.[17] The authors find that lower settler mortality faced by soldiers, bishops, and sailors created incentives for Europeans to settle, and where they settled they established high quality institutions similar to those they enjoyed in their home countries. The opposite occurred in areas with higher settler mortality. The authors show that these institutions persisted until the present days. In another paper, Robert Masseland examines the claim that colonial history has left an enduring effect on Africa's economic development.[18] The author finds that the period of colonization, the identity of the colonizer, and the proportion of settlers are significant predictors of institutional quality and income per capita shortly after independence. The author, however, shows that the effect of these colonial legacies on institutional quality and economic development is disappearing in Africa.

Other studies find a connection between the form of colonial rule and the post-colonial quality of institutions in the colonies. For instance, Patricia Jones proposes that better paid colonial governors established better institutions than their lesser paid counterparts.[19] The author finds evidence that the colonies, with better paid colonial governors, developed better institutions captured by the rule of law, government effectiveness, and control of corruption. The data indicate that these early differences in colonial administration had a long-lasting effect on economic development. Rasmus Broms examines the effect of colonial revenue collection and current government effectiveness.[20] The argument is that the extent of revenue extraction, in the form of taxation, has been identified as a critical factor for successful state building, better quality institutions, and economic development. Using fiscal records from British colonies, the author shows that larger colonial revenues during the early twentieth century are associated with higher government quality today. Matthew Lange explores the effect of direct and indirect colonial rule on the postcolonial institutions in British colonies with low levels of European settlement.[21] The author uses the number of colonially recognized customary court cases by the total number of court cases in 1955 C.E. as an indicator that reflects the degree of indirect colonial rule. The analysis suggests that the extent of indirect colonial rule is strongly negatively associated with different indicators of postcolonial institutional outcomes such as political stability, bureaucratic effectiveness, regulatory burden, rule of law, lack of corruption, and democratic governance.

Some studies also consider the consequences of colonialism on the system of governance. The argument is that some colonies may have inherited the political institutions left by the colonial powers, may have attempted to mimic the political practices of their colonizers, or may have learned about the ideals of democracy and political freedoms during the period of colonization. Along the lines of this intuition, Ola Olsson examines the effect of colonial duration and time of independence on contemporary levels of democracy.[22] The author finds that there is a positive association between the duration of colonial rule and current democracy, which is mainly driven by the experience of former British colonies and by countries colonized after 1850 C.E.

PRE-COLONIAL INSTITUTIONS

Some scholars argue that in precolonial times, there were areas that had centralized systems of governance with hierarchy beyond the local level and where provincial traditional chiefs were accountable to a higher authority. In other areas, societies lived in politically fragmented areas without any coordination beyond the local realm. These are institutions that prevailed in days of yore but are observed to have an enduring effect on contemporary economic outcomes. In the former, colonial and postcolonial authorities were able to bargain with traditional leaders to coordinate policy with their communities. This led to a faster adoption of European policies, practices, and technologies. By contrast, there were many traditional power brokers in areas with politically fragmented groups. This rendered bargaining costly or infeasible to colonial and postcolonial powers. In those areas, local chiefs were often allowed to follow parochial policies which ultimately impeded modernization.

Based on this intuition, few studies examine the effect of precolonial centralized institutions on current economic outcomes. For instance, Nicola Gennaioli and Ilia Rainer assess whether stronger precolonial political institutions permitted colonial and postcolonial African governments to implement modernization programs.[23] Using anthropological data, the authors document a strong positive association between the provision of education, health, and infrastructure in African countries and the share of a country's population belonging to ethnic groups with centralized precolonial institutions. James Robinson and Philip Osafo-Kwaako show that precolonial political centralization, defined as jurisdictional hierarchy beyond local community, is associated with better provision of public goods and a higher level of economic development.[24]

Stelios Michalopolous and Elias Papaioannou assess the role of preco-lonial ethnic centralization in shaping economic conditions within African countries.[25] Using anthropological data, the authors show a strong association between precolonial ethnic political centralization and contemporary satellite images of luminosity at night that reflects current economic development at the local level. Luis Angeles and Aldo Elizalde argue that Amerindian groups with advanced precolonial institutions would have been able to protect their interests leading to better socioeconomic outcomes today in Latin America.[26] The authors construct a population-weighted average of the jurisdictional hierarchy beyond the local level index for Amerindian ethnic groups. The analysis shows that precolonial centralized institutions are positively associ-ated with the share of population who completed secondary school, years of schooling, primary education, secondary education, potable water, electric-ity, and income per capita, but is negatively related to infant mortality and poverty rates.

(NATIONS) WITHOUT BORDERS

Several studies examine the implications of the arbitrary borders charted by colonial powers. These studies focus on the consequences of the concocted lines drawn on the map which do not coincide with either the demographic composition of the people or with the geographic features of the land. These borders were designed in European capitals at a time when Europeans had barely settled in the continent and had limited knowledge of local condi-tions. In this context, Stelios Michalopoulos and Elias Papaioannou explore the consequences of ethnic partitioning along these borders that outlived the colonial era in Africa.[27] Their analysis suggests that the incidence, severity, and duration of political violence are higher for partitioned homelands, and that respondents of surveys identifying with split ethnicities are poorer. In another contribution, Stelios Michalopoulos and Elias Papaioannou compare the economic performance across adjoining areas belonging to the historical homeland of the same ethnic group but falling in different countries with different formal institutions.[28] The authors show that differences in national institutions across the border do not translate into differences in economic performance within partitioned ethnicities, and that national institutions do correlate with subnational development only when both partitions are close to the respective capital cities.

COLUMBIAN EXCHANGE

There is a large literature that attempts to link nutrition to multiple economic outcomes. Better nutrition, particularly early in life, is associated with better cognitive abilities, improvements in health conditions, and a lower burden of infectious disease. These outcomes lead in turn to significant gains in productivity. In this context, some scholars note that one factor that led to the historical increase in agricultural productivity within the old world is the addition of potato from the Americas. Potatoes provide more calories, vitamins, and nutrients per area of land sown than other staple crops. This inclusion of potatoes in the diets of the old world occurred within what is referred to as the Columbian exchange which took place after the European conquest of the new world.

Based on this intuition, Nathan Nunn and Nancy Qian estimate the impact of potatoes on population and urbanization in the old world.[29] The authors show that the introduction of the potato accounts for approximately one-quarter of the growth in old world population and urbanization between 1700 C.E. and 1900 C.E. In a complementary paper, Justin Cook explores the role of potatoes and milk in explaining the economic development experienced throughout the old world in the eighteenth and nineteenth centuries.[30] This is because milk is a dietary complement that provide essential minerals, proteins, and fatty acids that are absent in potatoes. Thus, countries that consume milk at a greater frequency benefit more from the introduction of potatoes. The author shows that the interaction term between the agricultural suitability of potatoes and the frequency of lactase persistence or lactose tolerance, as an estimate of the suitability of milk consumption, has a significant positive effect on population and urbanization.

Some studies also argue that the Columbian exchange influenced the likelihood of conflict in the old world. For instance, Nathan Nunn, Nancy Qian, and Murat Iyigun examine the implications of a permanent increase in agricultural productivity on conflict, exploiting the introduction of potatoes from the Americas to the old world.[31] The argument is that the introduction of potatoes improved agricultural productivity which increased real wages. This increased the opportunity cost for peasants to partake in conflict and decreased the need for rulers to engage in warfare given the swelling in their treasury from taxing labor income. The authors construct a dataset of battles in Europe, the Near East, and North Africa during the period between 1400 C.E. and 1900 C.E. and find that the introduction of potatoes decreased conflict for about two centuries.

NOTES

1. Bairoch. *Economics and World History: Myths and Paradoxes* (p. 8).

2. Pagden. *Worlds at War: The 2500 Year Struggle between East and West.*

3. Anderson. *Lawrence in Arabia: War, Deceit, Imperial Folly and the Making of the Modern Middle East* (p. 183).

4. Sartre. *Colonialism and Neocolonialism.*

5. Acemoglu, Johnson, and Robinson. "The Colonial Origins of Comparative Development." *American Economic Review*: 1369–1401.

6. Kipling. *The Collected Poems of Rudyard Kipling.*

7. Grier. "Colonial Legacies and Economic Growth." *Public Choice*: 317–335.

8. Feyrer and Sacerdote. "Colonialism and Modern Income." *The Review of Economics and Statistics*: 245–262.

9. Bertocchi and Canova. "Did Colonization Matter for Growth?" *European Economic Review*: 1851–1871.

10. Sylwester. "Decolonization and Economic Growth: The Case of Africa." *Journal of Economic Development*: 87–102.

11. Bruhn and Gallego. "Good, Bad, and Ugly Colonial Activities: Do They Matter for Economic Development?" *The Review of Economics and Statistics*: 433–461.

12. Angeles. "Income inequality and Colonialism." *European Economic Review*: 1155–1176.

13. Science and Imperial Affairs. *Nature* 129, 1–3, 1932. https://doi.org/10.1038/129001a0.

14. Easterly and Levine. "The European Origins of Economic Development." *Journal of Economic Growth*: 225–257.

15. Huillery. "History Matters: The Long-Term Impact of Colonial Public Investments in French West Africa." *American Economic Journal: Applied Economics*: 176–215.

16. Fenske. "African Polygamy: Past and Present." *Journal of Development Economics*: 58–73.

17. Acemoglu, Johnson, and Robinson. "The Colonial Origins of Comparative Development." *The American Economic Review*: 1369–1401.

18. Masseland. "Is Colonialism History? The Declining Impact of Colonial Legacies on African Institutional and Economic Development." *Journal of Institutional Economics*: 2, 259–287.

19. Jones. "History Matters: New Evidence on the Long Run Impact of Colonial Rule on Institutions." *Journal of Comparative Economics*: 181–200.

20. Broms. "Colonial Revenue Extraction and Modern-Day Government Quality in the British Empire." *World Development*: 269–280.

21. Lange. "British Colonial Legacies and Political Development." *World Development*: 905–922.

22. Olsson. "On the Democratic Legacy of Colonialism." *Journal of Comparative Economics*: 534–551.

23. Gennaioli and Rainer. "The Modern Impact of Precolonial Centralization in Africa." *Journal of Economic Growth*: 185–234.

24. Osafo-Kwaako and Robinson. "Political Centralization in Pre-Colonial Africa." *Journal of Comparative Economics*: 6–21.

25. Michalopolous and Papaioannou. "Pre-Colonial Ethnic Institutions and Contemporary African Development." *Econometrica*: 113–152.

26. Angeles and Elizalde. "Pre-colonial Institutions and Socioeconomic Development." *Journal of Development Economics*: 22–40.

27. Michalopoulos and Papaioannou. "The Long-Run Effects of the Scramble for Africa." *The American Economic Review*: 1802–1848.

28. Michalopoulos and Papaioannou. "National Institutions and Subnational Development in Africa." *The Quarterly Journal of Economics*: 151–213.

29. Nunn and Qian. "The Potato's Contribution to Population and Urbanization." *The Quarterly Journal of Economics*: 593–650.

30. Cook. "Potatoes, Milk, and the Old-World Population Boom." *Journal of Development Economics*: 123–138.

31. Iyigunt, Nunn, and Qian. "The Long Run Effects of Agricultural Productivity on Conflict, 1400–1900." National Bureau of Economic Research Working Paper 24066.

Chapter Eighteen

In a Flat World

PIED-À-TERRE SOMEWHERE

One of the geographic characteristics of a country is its location. A country's location can afford opportunities that can propel its economy to success or, otherwise, can act as an impediment on its path to prosperity. Location can be captured by the distance from a place of interest, or by the share of land or population in a certain area. This can refer to proximity to the coast, to navigable waterways, to rivers, or to a core economic hub. Access to the coast and navigable waterways lowers transportation costs and thus promotes trade and commercial exchange with other countries. Proximity to core markets refers to closeness to venues where considerable economic activities are conducted. This also facilitates integration, trade, globalization, and agglomeration. As Adam Smith stated,[1] "As by means of water carriage a more extensive market is opened to every sort of industry than what land carriage alone can afford it, so it is upon the sea-coast, and along the banks of navigable rivers that industry of every kind begins to sub-divide and improve itself, and it is frequently not till a long time after that those improvements extend themselves to the inland part of the country."

In this context, geography influenced the settlement of societies in particular locations which, in turn, determined their involvement in trade and commerce. The tendency of ancient societies to settle away from the coast is attributed to the fact that transportation was too costly to support commercial exchange. Thus, economic advantage came from agricultural productivity in river valleys with fertile soil rather than from access to trade routes and foreign markets. Therefore, early civilizations invariably emerged in river valleys such as those around the Nile, the Indus, the Tigris, the Euphrates, the Yellow, and the Yangtze rivers. Overtime, this led to high concentrations of inland populations that are partially cut off from trade and international markets. This is because areas far from the coast, and landlocked countries who do not have access to the coast, suffer from higher transportation costs compared to coastal areas. Affordable shipping costs are essential to facilitate international trade and integration into global markets.

Location may also influence the adoption of specific trade policies. A coastal economy faces a high elasticity of output to trade taxes, compared to a landlocked one. This implies that a one percentage increase in trade tariffs can lead to a more than one percentage decrease in output in coastal economies. Therefore, an inland policy maker may impose tariffs to generate larger government revenue, whereas a coastal sovereign is more likely to advocate policies that promote trade liberalization. These adopted trade policies affect the value and volume of trade flows with other economies.

Some studies focus on the effect of location on economic outcomes. For instance, Jeffrey Sachs, John Luke Gallup, and Andrew Mellinger examine the effect of location on economic development and income growth.[2] The authors show that both income per capita and economic growth are negatively associated with the distance to one of the core markets, and positively associated with the portion of population within hundred kilometers of the coast. Jeffrey Sachs, David Bloom, Paul Collier, and Christopher Udry explore the effect of coastal and inland population densities on economic growth.[3] The authors find that a higher coastal population is conducive to economic growth, while the inland population density does not have a statistically significant effect.

Topography is another geographic feature that characterizes a country's landscape in terms of elevation, the extent of steepness of inclines and slopes, and the degree of terrain ruggedness. In this context, rugged and irregular terrain can act as an impediment to trade and mobility between communities. This is because this type of landscape is harder to traverse which makes transportation of products slower and costlier as it may take longer to bypass these terrain obstacles. Thus, it becomes harder to engage in trade across this particular landscape. A flat terrain is usually more amenable to a passerby and, as such, is more opportune to commercial exchange.

A FLAT WORLD

Growing Flat and Flatly Growing

Globalization is a process through which economies around the world become more interdependent, interconnected, and integrated. The world has been in a continuous process of becoming more globalized because of the incessant technological advances in transportation and communication. The former makes the distance between two locations shorter compared to any other time. The latter allows information to travel from one location to another in no time. Both make us feel that we live in closer proximity than ever before. Famous writer and columnist Thomas Friedman even declared that "we saw the entire global economy at one time acting totally in sync. The real truth is the world is even flatter than I thought."

Historically, the world became more connected during such events as the imperial expansion, the colonial domination, the age of discovery, the extension of trade routes, the missionary expeditions, the waves of migration, the adoption of technologies and others. These events brought parts of the world closer together willingly or otherwise. Afterward, the steam locomotive, the steamship, the jet engine, and the telegraph were some of the advances that facilitated the integration between distant parts of the world. Nowadays, the internet and the mobile phones reflect the latest phenomenon in the telecommunications infrastructure. All these improvements generated further interdependence in economic, political, social, and cultural activities across the globe. Historian Niall Ferguson reminds us that[4]

> Globalization is sometimes discussed as if it were a spontaneous process brought about by private agents—firms and nongovernmental organizations. Economic historians chart with fascination the giddy growth of cross-border flows of goods, people and capital. Trade, migration and international lending all reached levels in relation to global output not seen again until the 1990s. A single monetary system—the gold standard—came to be adopted by nearly every major economy, encouraging later generations to look back on the pre-1914 decades as a literally golden age. In economic terms it doubtless was. The world economy grew faster between 1870 and 1913 than in any previous period. It is inconceivable, however, that such high levels of international economic integration would have come about in the absence of empires.

Though the origins of globalization are deeply rooted in history, we are witnessing the increasing connectivity of the world's economies in modern times. This is because the latest advances in technology are developing at such a fast pace and are being incorporated in our daily lives at an incomprehensible speed, making the world feel like a global village. Sociologist Anthony Giddens states that[5] "Globalization can thus be defined as the intensification of worldwide social relations which link distant localities in such a way that local happenings are shaped by events occurring many miles away and vice versa."

For some, globalization offer exciting opportunities that are not attainable otherwise. These include the expansion of markets, transfer of technology, capital mobility, and exchange of knowledge. Globalization also suggests a prospect of a world too interdependent to engage in war or conflict. In such an environment, those in disagreement wear the garb of diplomacy to settle their disputes. For others, globalization sounds like a bad omen as it increases concerns for intensification in wealth inequality, absolute poverty, unemployment, and environmental degradation. Nelson Mandela in one of his speeches warns us that[6]

> We often talk about the globalization of our world, referring to our world as a global village. Too often those descriptions refer solely to the free movement of goods and capital across the traditional barriers of national boundaries. Not often enough do we emphasize the globalization of responsibility. In this world where modern information and communications technology has put all of us in easy reach of one another, we do again share the responsibility for being the proverbial keeper of our brother or sister. Where globalization means, as it so often does, that the rich and powerful now have new means to further enrich and empower themselves at the cost of the poorer and weaker, we have a responsibility to protest in the name of universal freedom. Globalization opens up the marvelous opportunities for human beings across the globe to share with one another, and to share with greater equity in the advances of science, technology and industries. To allow it to have the opposite effect is to threaten freedom in the longer term.

This chapter focuses on the effect of the integration into the world trade system, as a form of globalization, on a country's economic outcomes. Early scholars argued that there are economic gains from trade. For instance, Adam Smith proposes that it was impossible for all countries to benefit simultaneously because the export of one country is another's import. Instead, he suggested that countries would gain simultaneously if they specialized in accordance with their absolute advantage and trade with each other. In this context, Adam Smith states that[7]

> If a foreign country can supply us with a commodity cheaper than we ourselves can make it, better buy it off them with some part of the produce of our own industry employed in a way in which we have some advantage. The general industry of the country, being always in proportion to the capital which employs it, will not thereby be diminished [. . .] but only left to find out the way in which it can be employed with the greatest advantage.

Other scholars argued that it is comparative advantage that determines the gains from trade. A country has a comparative advantage in producing a good compared to others if it can produce that item at a lower opportunity cost. In this context, David Ricardo studies two countries which produce two goods using one factor of production.[8] Ricardo argues that if each country specializes in the production of the good in which it has a comparative advantage, and exchanges it for the other good, each country will consume a larger bundle. Thus, each country can increase its consumption by exporting the good for which it has a comparative advantage while importing the other good.

Eli Heckscher and Bertil Ohlin extend these insights into a model of two countries, labor abundant and capital abundant, utilizing two factors of production, labor and capital, in order to produce a labor-intensive good and a capital-intensive one.[9] In this context, the benefits of trade are derived from differences in a country's endowment of labor and capital. The authors argue that a country could benefit from trade if it specializes in the production of the good that relies intensively on the abundant factor of production and exchanges that good for the other. In this context, if the labor-abundant country specializes in the production of the labor-intensive good, while the capital-abundant country specializes in the production of the capital-intensive good, trade between them will allow each country to consume a larger bundle. Thus, trade would make both countries better off.

Other scholars argue that international trade generates economic growth by encouraging technological advances.[10] Trade provides access to the technological knowledge of a country's trading partners, allows entrepreneurs and businesses access to wider markets, provides consumers with new products and inputs, and encourages research and development through increasing returns from innovation.

SHELTER THYSELF

On the other hand, there are arguments that free trade can stifle competition, suppress domestic investment and entrepreneurship, and hurt infant industries in developing countries. The infant industry argument has been used as one of the pretexts for trade protectionism. The core argument is that a new industry will experience difficulties in competing with established foreign competitors. This is because infant industries often do not have the economies of scale to decrease their production costs compared to their competitors. Thus, infant industries need to be protected until they can attain a similar level of economies of scale to be able to compete in a ferocious world market.

These arguments used to be voiced by some developing countries in the face of the unwavering tide of globalization. Nowadays, antagonistic sentiments to globalization are also stemming from developed countries. This is because profit maximizing firms in these countries relocate to an offshore site in a developing country to take advantage of lower production costs by outsourcing part of their operations. The low-cost products are then shipped back to consumers in developed countries who now have to deal with trade imbalances. This process destroys jobs in the developed world creating consternation among those who suffer its consequences. Thus, we observe a tide of anti-globalization in the developed world that used to strongly advocate for trade liberalization before.

No better way to conclude this discussion than by referring to the renowned American thinker Noam Chomsky who warned against the confusion between the opposition to the exploitation of people in the name of globalization and the desire for international solidarity:[11]

> The term "globalization" has been appropriated by the powerful to refer to a specific form of international economic integration, one based on investor rights, with the interests of people incidental. That is why the business press, in its more honest moments, refers to the "free trade agreements" as "free investment agreements" (Wall St. Journal). Accordingly, advocates of other forms of globalization are described as "anti-globalization"; and some, unfortunately, even accept this term, though it is a term of propaganda that should be dismissed with ridicule. No sane person is opposed to globalization, that is, international integration. Surely not the left and the workers movements, which were founded on the principle of international solidarity—that is, globalization in a form that attends to the rights of people, not private power systems.

A SPLENDID EXCHANGE

Several studies examine the effect of trade on economic outcomes. The literature focuses on the appropriate indicators of trade openness in the estimation of the effect of trade on economic outcomes, whether we should examine the effect of trade flows or trade policies, and whether the effect is different across countries and over different periods of time.

The first stream of literature focuses on the effect of trade on economic outcomes. For instance, Jeffery Sachs and Andrew Warner construct a trade openness dummy using trade policy criteria such as tariff barriers, non-tariff barriers, black-market exchange rate, state monopoly on exports and others.[12] The authors find that the trade openness dummy has a statistically significant positive effect on economic growth. Romain Wacziarg and Karen Welch attempt to examine the association between openness and economic growth around episodes of trade liberalization.[13] The authors argue that the openness dummy cannot capture the complexities of commerce, and use instead liberalization dates that indicate discrete shifts in trade policy. Their analysis suggests that countries that liberalized their trade experienced average annual growth rates that were about 1.5 percentage points higher. Joshua Aizenman and Mark Spiegel identify factors of economic takeoff, defined as a sustained period of high growth following stagnation.[14] The authors use the

Wacziarg-Welch improved indicator as a measure of de jure openness and use exports plus imports over Gross Domestic Product as an estimate of de facto openness. The authors find that de jure trade openness is positively associated with takeoffs while the de facto trade indicator is found to be a poor predictor of takeoffs.

David Dollar and Aart Kraay argue that the effect of trade openness and institutional quality on economic growth is uninformative because of the very high correlation between the two variables.[15] The authors instead examine the effect of changes in trade and in institutional quality on decadal growth rates. Their analysis provides evidence of a significant effect of trade on economic growth with a smaller role for institutional quality. In another contribution, David Dollar and Aart Kraay examine the effect of trade on inequality and poverty in a group of developing countries that have had large cuts in tariffs and large increases in trade volumes since 1980 C.E.[16] Their analysis shows that changes in trade volumes have a strong positive effect on economic growth, but no systematic effect on income inequality. The authors conclude that the increase in growth that accompanies expanded trade translates into a proportionate increase in the income of the poor.

Some scholars attempt to identify the direction of causality between trade and income. For instance, Jeffery Frankel and David Romer construct a predicted indicator of trade from the geographic features of the trading partners, such as the distance between them, whether they have common borders, their land size, their population size, and other factors.[17] Their analysis suggests that trade increases income by inducing the accumulation of physical capital and human capital. In a pertinent contribution, Douglas Irwin and Marko Tervio attempt to evaluate the findings of Jeffery Frankel and David Romer on trade's impact on income using data from the pre-World War I, the inter-war, and the post-World War II periods.[18] The authors find that the earlier findings are confirmed throughout the whole century.

Some studies compare the lagged versus the contemporaneous effect of trade on economic outcomes. For instance, David Greenaway, Wyn Morgan, and Peter Wright focus on the effect of trade liberalization on economic growth in a group of countries that liberalized after 1985 C.E.[19] Their analysis suggests that trade liberalization has been associated with a decline in economic growth. However, the authors argue that this finding relates only to contemporaneous effects but not dynamic ones which merit further exploration. To address this issue, the same authors examine in another paper the effect of trade liberalization on economic growth using a dynamic framework.[20] The authors find that liberalization has a favorable effect on economic growth but with a lag.

Halit Yanikkaya provides evidence that trade flows enhance economic growth through several channels such as technology transfer, scale economies, and comparative advantage.[21] Contrary to conventional wisdom, the analysis also shows that trade barriers are positively associated with economic growth especially for developing countries. Francisco Alcala and Antonio Ciccone find that international trade has an economically important and statistically significant positive causal effect on productivity using imports plus exports as a percentage of purchasing power parity Gross Domestic Product, which they argue is preferable to the standard nominal indicator.[22]

Even though the findings of these studies point to a favorable effect of trade on economic outcomes, other scholars warned that this could be because these studies focus on a specific period when globalization was taking over the world. Thus, some studies attempt to examine the effect of trade on economic outcomes during different historical episodes. For instance, Athanasios Vamvakidis compiles a data set from 1870 C.E. to 2000 C.E. on a variety of indicators for trade openness. The analysis shows that the association between trade openness and economic development has only become positive when globalization has expanded after 1970 C.E. In a similar vein, Kevin O'Rourke estimates the effect of tariffs on economic growth for the period between 1875 C.E. and 1914 C.E. when some countries adopted protectionist policies but also experienced steady economic growth.[23] The analysis suggests that tariffs were positively correlated with economic growth in these countries during that period. In response, Moritz Schularick and Solomos Solomou reassess the relationship between tariffs and economic growth between 1870 C.E. and 1914 C.E.[24] The authors do not find evidence that increased protectionism enhanced economic growth. The authors conclude that it is not that free trade was detrimental to economic growth, but rather that international economic policies seem to have mattered little to countries' economic growth during that time. Focusing on another historical period, Michael Clemens and Jeffery Williamson show that high tariffs were associated with fast economic growth before World War II and slow growth thereafter.[25]

NOTES

1. Smith. *An Inquiry into the Nature and Causes of the Wealth of Nations* (p. 44).

2. Gallup, Sachs, and Mellinger. "Geography and Economic Development." *International Regional Science Review*: 179–232.

3. Bloom, Sachs, Collier, and Udry. "Geography, Demography, and Economic Growth in Africa." *Brookings Papers on Economic Activity*: 207–295.

4. Ferguson. *The War of the World: Twentieth-Century Conflict and the Descent of the West* (pp. 105–106).

5. Giddens. *The Consequences of Modernity* (p. 64).

6. http://db.nelsonmandela.org/speeches/pub_view.asp?pg=item&ItemID=NMS919

7. Smith. *The Wealth of Nations* (p. 424).

8. Ricardo. *On the Principles of Political Economy and Taxation.*

9. Heckscher and Ohlin. *Heckscher-Ohlin Trade Theory.*

10. Grossman and Helpman. "Trade, Knowledge Spillovers, and Growth." *European Economic Review*: 517–526.

11. Lule. *Globalization and Media* (p. 31).

12. Sachs and Warner. "Economic Reform and the Process of Global Integration." *Brookings Papers on Economic Activity*: 1–118.

13. Wacziarg and Welch. "Trade Liberalization and Growth: New Evidence." *The World Bank Economic Review*: 187–231.

14. Aizenman and Spiegel. "Takeoffs." *Review of Development Economics*: 177–196.

15. Dollar and Kraay. "Institutions, Trade, and Growth." *Journal of Monetary Economics*: 133–162.

16. Dollar and Kraay. "Trade, Growth, and Poverty." *The Economic Journal*: F22–F49.

17. Frankel and Romer. "Does Trade Cause Growth?" *The American Economic Review*: 379–399.

18. Irwin and Tervio. "Does Trade Raise Income? Evidence from the Twentieth Century." *Journal of International Economics*: 1–18.

19. Greenaway, Morgan, and Wright. "Trade Liberalization and Growth in Developing Countries." *World Development*: 1885–1 892.

20. Greenaway, Morgan, and Wright. "Trade Liberalisation and Growth in Developing Countries." *Journal of Development Economics*: 229–244.

21. Yanikkaya. "Trade Openness and Economic Growth." *Journal of Development Economics*: 57– 89.

22. Alcala and Ciccone. "Trade and Productivity." *The Quarterly Journal of Economics*: 613– 646.

23. O'Rourke. "Tariffs and Growth in the Late Nineteenth Century." *The Economic Journal*: 456–483.

24. Schularick and Solomou. "Tariffs and Economic Growth in the First Era of Globalization." *Journal of Economic Growth*: 33–70.

25. Clemens and Williamson. "Why did the Tariff-Growth Correlation Change after 1950?" *Journal of Economic Growth*: 5–46.

Bibliography

Acemoglu, Daron, Francisco Gallego, and James Robinson. 2014. "Institutions, Human Capital and Development." *Annual Reviews of Economics*, 6: 875–912.

Acemoglu, Daron, and James Robinson. 2006. "De Facto Political Power and Institutional Persistence." *American Economic Review*, 96(2): 325–330.

Acemoglu, Daron, and James Robinson. 2008. "The Persistence and Change of Institutions in the Americas." *Southern Economic Journal*, 75(2): 282–299.

Acemoglu, Daron, and James Robinson. 2012. *Why Nations Fail: The Origins of Power, Prosperity, and Poverty*. Crown Publishers. (pp. 30, 31).

Acemoglu, Daron, and Simon Johnson. 2005. "Unbundling Institutions." *Journal of Political Economy*, 113(5): 949–995.

Acemoglu, Daron, and Thierry Verdier. 1998. "Property Rights, Corruption and the Allocation of Talent: A General Equilibrium Approach." *The Economic Journal*, 108(450): 1381–1403.

Acemoglu, Daron, and Thierry Verdier. 2000. "The Choice between Market Failures and Corruption." *The American Economic Review*, 90(1): 194–211.

Acemoglu, Daron, Camilo García-Jimeno, and James Robinson. 2012. "Finding Eldorado: Slavery and Long-Run Development in Colombia." *Journal of Comparative Economics*, 40: 534–564.

Acemoglu, Daron, James Robinson, and Thierry Verdier. 2017. "Asymmetric Growth and Institutions in an Interdependent World." *Journal of Political Economy*, 125 (5): 1245–1305.

Acemoglu, Daron, Simon Johnson, and James Robinson. 2001. "The Colonial Origins of Comparative Development: An Empirical Investigation." *American Economic Review*, 91(5): 1369–1401.

Acemoglu, Daron, Simon Johnson, and James Robinson. 2002. "Reversal of Fortune: Geography and Institutions in the Making of the Modern World Income Distribution." *The Quarterly Journal of Economics*, 117(5): 1231–1294.

Acemoglu, Daron, Simon Johnson, and James Robinson. 2005. "The Rise of Europe: Atlantic Trade, Institutional Change, and Economic Growth." *The American Economic Review*, 95(3): 545–579.

Acemoglu, Daron, Suresh Naidu, Pascual Restrepo, and James Robinson. 2019. "Democracy Does Cause Growth." *Journal of Political Economy*, 127(1): 47–100.

Ades, Alberto, and Hac Chua. 1997. "The Neighbor's Curse: Regional Instability and Economic Growth." *Journal of Economic Growth*, 2: 279–304.

Ager, Phillip, and Antonio Ciccone. 2018. "Agricultural Risk and the Spread of Religious Communities." *Journal of the European Economic Association*, 16(4): 1021–1068.

Aghion, Philippe, and Steven Durlauf. 2014. *Handbook of Economic Growth*. Volume 2. North Holland.

Aghion, Phillipe, Yann Algan, Pierre Cahuc and Andrei Shleifer. 2010. "Regulation and Distrust." *The Quarterly Journal of Economics*, 125(3): 1015–1049.

Ahlerup, Pelle, and Ola Olsson. 2011. "The Roots of Ethnic Diversity." *Journal of Economic Growth*, 17: 71–102.

Ahlerup, Pelle, Ola Olsson and David Yanagizawa. 2009. "Social Capital vs Institutions in the Growth Process." *European Journal of Political Economy*, 25: 1–14.

Ahlerup, Pelle, Thushyanthan Baskaran, and Arne Bigsten. 2016. "Government Impartiality and Sustained Growth in Sub-Saharan Africa." *World Development*, 83: 54–69.

Aidt, Toke, Jayasri Dutta, and Vania Senac. 2008. "Governance Regimes, Corruption and Growth: Theory and Evidence." *Journal of Comparative Economics*, 36: 195–220.

Aidt, Toke. 2009. "Corruption, Institutions and Economic Development." *Oxford Review of Economic Policy*, 25(2): 271–291.

Aisen, Ari, and Francisco José Veiga. 2006. "Does Political Instability Lead to Higher Inflation? A Panel Data Analysis." *Journal of Money, Credit, and Banking*, 38: 1379–1389.

Aisen, Ari, and Francisco José Veiga. 2008. "Political Instability and Inflation Volatility." *Public Choice*, 135(3–4): 207–223.

Aisen, Ari, and Francisco José Veiga. 2008. "The Political Economy of Seigniorage." *Journal of Development Economics*, 87: 29–50.

Aisen, Ari, and Francisco José Veiga. 2013. "How Does Political Instability Affect Economic Growth?" *European Journal of Political Economy*, 29: 151–167.

Aizenman, Joshua, and Mark Spiegel. 2010. "Takeoffs." *Review of Development Economics*, 14(2): 177–196.

Akçomak, Semih, and Bas ter Weel. 2009. "Social Capital, Innovation and Growth: Evidence from Europe." *European Economic Review*, 53(5): 544–567.

Akçomak, Semih, and Hanna Müller-Zick. 2018. "Trust and Inventive Activity in Europe: Causal, Spatial and Nonlinear Forces." *The Annals of Regional Science*, 60(3): 529–568.

Alcala, Francisco, and Antonio Ciccone. 2004. "Trade and Productivity." *The Quarterly Journal of Economics*, 119(2): 613–646.

Alesina, Alberto, and Dani Rodrik. 1994. "Distributive Politics and Economic Growth." *The Quarterly Journal of Economics*, 109(2): 465–490.

Alesina, Alberto, and Eakterina Zhuravskaya. 2011. "Segregation and the Quality of Government in a Cross Section of Countries." *The American Economic Review*, 101: 1872–1911.

Alesina, Alberto, and Eliana La Ferrara. 2000. "Participation in Heterogeneous Communities." *The Quarterly Journal of Economics*, 115(3): 847–904.

Alesina, Alberto, and Guido Tabellini. 1989. "External Debt, Capital Flight and Political Risk." *Journal of International Economics*, 27(3–4): 199–220.

Alesina, Alberto, and Guido Tabellini. 1990. "A Positive Theory of Fiscal Deficits and Government Debt." *The Review of Economic Studies*, 57(3): 403–414.

Alesina, Alberto, and Roberto Perotti. 1996. "Income Distribution, Political Instability, and Investment." *European Economic Review*, 40: 1203–1228.

Alesina, Alberto, Arnaud Devleeschauwer, William Easterly, Sergio Kurlat, and Romain Wacziarg. 2003. "Fractionalization." *Journal of Economic Growth*, 8: 155–194.

Alesina, Alberto, Caterina Gennaioli, and Stefania Lovo. 2018. "Public Goods and Ethnic Diversity: Evidence from Deforestation in Indonesia." *Economica*, 86(341): 32–66.

Alesina, Alberto, Paola Giuliano, and Nathan Nunn. 2013. "On the Origins of Gender Roles: Women and the Plough." *The Quarterly Journal of Economics*, 128(2): 469–530.

Alesina, Alberto, Reza Baqir and William Easterly. 1999. "Public Goods and Ethnic Divisions." *The Quarterly Journal of Economics*, 114(4): 1243–1284.

Alesina, Alberto, Stelios Michalopoulos, and Elias Papaioannou. 2016. "Ethnic Inequality." *Journal of Political Economy*, 124(2): 428–488.

Alesina, Alberto, Sule Ozler, Nouriel Roubini, and Phillip Swagel. 1996. "Political Instability and Economic Growth." *Journal of Economic Growth*, 1: 189–211.

Alexeev, Michael, and Robert Conrad. 2009. "The Elusive Curse of Oil." *The Review of Economics and Statistics*, 91(3): 586–598.

Algan, Yann, and Pierre Cahuc. 2010. "Inherited Trust and Growth." *The American Economic Review*, 100: 2060–2092.

Algan, Yann, Pierre Cahuc and Marc Sangnier. 2016. "Trust and the Welfare State: The Twin Peaks Curve." *The Economic Journal*, 126(593): 861–883.

Allison, Anthony. 2002. "The Discovery of Resistance to Malaria of Sickle-Cell Heterozygotes." *Biochemistry and Molecular Biology Education*, 30(5): 279–287.

Alsan, Marcella. 2015. "The Effect of the Tsetse Fly on African Development." *American Economic Review*, 105(1): 382–410.

Andersen, Thomas, Carl-Johan Dalgaard and Pablo Selaya. 2016. "Climate and the Emergence of Global Income Differences." *Review of Economic Studies*, 83: 1334–1363.

Anderson, Gary. 1988. "Mr. Smith and the Preachers: The Economics of Religion in the Wealth of Nations." *Journal of Political Economy*, 96(5): 1066–1088.

Anderson, Scott. 2014. *Lawrence in Arabia: War, Deceit, Imperial Folly and the Making of the Modern Middle East*. New York: Anchor Books.

Ang, James, and Per Fredriksson. 2017. "Statehood Experience, Legal Traditions, and Climate Change Policies." *Economic Inquiry*, 55(3): 1511–1537.

Ang, James, and Per Fredriksson. 2018. "State History, Legal Adaptability and Financial Development." *Journal of Banking and Finance*, 89: 169–191.

Ang, James. 2013. "Are Modern Financial Systems Shaped by State Antiquity?" *Journal of Banking and Finance*, 37: 4038–4058.

Angeles, Luis, and Aldo Elizalde. 2017. "Pre-Colonial Institutions and Socioeconomic Development: The Case of Latin America." *Journal of Development Economics*, 124: 22–40.

Angeles, Luis. 2007. "Income Inequality and Colonialism." *European Economic Review*, 51: 1155–1176.

Arruñada, Benito. 2010. "Protestants and Catholics: Similar Work Ethic, Different Social Ethic." *The Economic Journal*, 120(547): 890–918.

Ashraf, Quamrul, and Oded Galor. 2011. "Cultural Diversity, Geographical Isolation, and the Origin of the Wealth of Nations." The National Bureau of Economic Research Working Paper 17640.

Ashraf, Quamrul, and Stelios Michalopoulos. 2015. "Climatic Fluctuations and the Diffusion of Agriculture." *The Review of Economics and Statistics*, 97(3): 589–609.

Ashraf, Quamrul, Oded Galor, and Omer Ozak. 2010. "Isolation and Development." *Journal of the European Economic Association*, 8(2–3): 401–412.

Assiotis, Andreas, and Kevin Sylwester. 2014. "Do the Effects of Corruption upon Growth Differ between Democracies and Autocracies?" *Review of Development Economics*, 18(3): 581–594.

Aurangzeb, Zeb, and Thanasis Stengos. 2012. "Economic Policies and the Impact of Natural Disasters on Economic Growth: A Threshold Regression Approach." *Economics Bulletin*, 32(1): 229–241.

Bairoch, Paul. 1993. *Economics and World History: Myths and Paradoxes*. Chicago: University of Chicago Press.

Baldwin, Kate, and John Huber. 2010. "Economic versus Cultural Differences: Forms of Ethnic Diversity and Public Goods Provision." *American Political Science Review*, 104(4): 644–662.

Banerjee, Abhijit, and Esther Duflo. 2003. "Inequality and Growth: What Can the Data Say?" *Journal of Economic Growth*, 8(3): 267–299.

Bardhan, Pranab. 1997. "Corruption and Development: A Review of Issues." *Journal of Economic Literature*, 35(3): 1320–1346.

Barrios, Salvador, Luisito Bertinelli, and Eric Strobl. 2010. "Trends in Rainfall and Economic Growth in Africa: A Neglected Cause of the African Growth Tragedy." *The Review of Economics and Statistics*, 92(2): 350–366.

Barro, Robert, and Rachel McCleary. 2003. "Religion and Economic Growth across Countries." *American Sociological Review*, 68(5): 760–781.

Barro, Robert, and Rachel McCleary. 2006. "Religion and Political Economy in an International Panel." *Journal for the Scientific Study of Religion*, 45(2): 149–175.

Barro, Robert. 1996. "Institutions and Growth, an Introductory Essay." *Journal of Economic Growth*, 1: 145–148.

Barro, Robert. 2000. "Inequality and Growth in a Panel of Countries." *Journal of Economic Growth*, 5: 5–32.

Barro, Robert. 2006. "Democracy and Growth." *Journal of Economic Growth*, 1: 1–27.

Baten, Joerg, and Dácil Juif. 2014. "A Story of Large Landowners and Math Skills: Inequality and Human Capital Formation in Long-Run Development, 1820–2000." *Journal of Comparative Economics*, 42: 375–401.

Baum, Matthew, and David Lake. 2003. "The Political Economy of Growth: Democracy and Human Capital." *American Journal of Political Science*, 47(2): 333–347.

Bayley, David. 1966. "The Effects of Corruption in a Developing Nation." *The Western Political Quarterly*, 19(4): 719–732.

Becker, Sascha, and Ludger Woessmann. 2008. "Luther and the Girls: Religious Denomination and the Female Education Gap in Nineteenth-Century Prussia." *The Scandinavian Journal of Economics*, 110(4): 777–805.

Becker, Sascha, and Ludger Woessmann. 2009. "Was Weber Wrong? A Human Capital Theory of Protestant Economic History." *The Quarterly Journal of Economics*, 124(2): 531–596.

Becker, Sascha, and Ludger Woessmann. 2010. "The Effect of Protestantism on Education before the Industrialization: Evidence from 1816 Prussia." *Economics Letters*, 107: 224–228.

Beck-Johnson, Lindsay, William Nelson, Krijn Paaijmans, Andrew Read, Matthew Thomas, and Ottar Bjørnstad. 2013. "The Effect of Temperature on Anopheles Mosquito Population Dynamics and the Potential for Malaria Transmission." *PLOS*, 8(11): 1–12.

Beker, Sascha, Steven Pfaff, and Jared Rubin. 2016. "Causes and Consequences of the Protestant Reformation." *Explorations in Economic History*, 62: 1–25.

Belloc, Marianna, Francesco Drago, and Roberto Galbiati. 2016. "Earthquakes, Religion, and Transition to Self-Government in Italian Cities." *The Quarterly Journal of Economics*, 131(4): 1875–1926.

Bénabou, Roland, Davide Ticchi, and Andrea Vindigni. 2015. "Forbidden Fruits: The Political Economy of Science, Religion, and Growth." National Bureau of Economic Research Working Paper 21105.

Bénabou, Roland, Davide Ticchi, and Andrea Vindigni. 2015. "Religion and Innovation." *American Economic Review: Papers and Proceedings*, 105(5): 346–351.

Bentzen, Jeanet, Nicolai Kaarsen, and Asger Wingender. 2017. "Irrigation and Autocracy." *Journal of the European Economic Association*, 15(1): 1–53.

Bentzen, Jeanet. 2012. "How Bad Is Corruption? Cross Country Evidence of the Impact of Corruption on Economic Prosperity." *Review of Development Economics*, 16(1): 167–184.

Bentzen, Jeanet. 2019. "Acts of God? Religiosity and Natural Disasters across Subnational World Districts." *Economic Journal*, 129(622): 2295–2321.

Berggren, Niclas, and Christian Bjørnskov. 2013. "Does Religiosity Promote Property Rights and the Rule of Law?" *Journal of Institutional Economics*, 9(2): 161–185.

Bergreen, Laurence. 2004. *Over the Edge of the World: Magellan's Terrifying Circumnavigation of the Globe*. New York: Perennial / Harper Collins.

Bergreen, Laurence. 2012. *Columbus: The Four Voyages, 1492–1504*. Penguin Books.

Bergreen, Laurence. 2021. *In Search of a Kingdom: Francis Drake, Elizabeth I, and the Perilous Birth of the British Empire*. New York: Custom House.

Bergrren, Niclas, and Christian Bjornskov. 2011. "Is the Importance of Religion in Daily Life Related to Social Trust? Cross-country and Cross-State Comparisons." *Journal of Economic Behavior & Organization*, 80: 459–480.

Bergrren, Niclas, and Mikael Elinder. 2012. "Is Tolerance Good or Bad for Growth?" *Public Choice*, 150: 283–308.

Bergrren, Niclas, Sven-Olov Daunfelt, and Jorgen Hellstrom. 2014. "Social Trust and Central-Bank Independence." *European Journal of Political Economy*, 34: 425–439.

Bergrren, Niclas, Sven-Olov Daunfelt, and Jorgen Hellstrom. 2016. "Does Social Trust Speed up Reforms? The Case of Central-Bank Independence." *Journal of Institutional Economics*, 12(2): 395–415.

Berkowitz, Daniel, Katharina Pistor, and Jean-Francois Richard. 2003. "Economic Development, Legality, and the Transplant Effect." *European Economic Review*, 47: 165–195.

Berman, Nicolas, Mathieu Couttenier, Dominic Rohner, and Mathias Thoenig. 2017. "This Mine is Mine! How Minerals Fuel Conflicts in Africa." *American Economic Review*, 107(6): 1564–1610.

Berrebi, Claude, and Jordan Ostwald. 2011. "Earthquakes, Hurricanes, and Terrorism: Do Natural Disasters Incite Terror?" *Public Choice*, 149(3/4): 383–403.

Bertocchi, Graziella, and Fabio Canova. 2002. "Did Colonization Matter for Growth? An Empirical Exploration into the Historical Causes of Africa's Underdevelopment." *European Economic Review*, 46: 1851–1871.

Besley, Timothy, and Stephen Coate. 1997. "An Economic Model of Representative Democracy." *The Quarterly Journal of Economics*, 112(1): 85–114.

Besley, Timothy, and Stephen Coate. 1998. "Sources of Inefficiency in a Representative Democracy: A Dynamic Analysis." *The American Economic Review*, 88(1): 139–156.

Bettendorf, Leon, and Elbert Dijkgraaf. 2010. "Religion and Income: Heterogeneity between Countries." *Journal of Economic Behavior & Organization*, 74: 12–29.

Beugelsdijk, Sjoerd, and Ton van Schaik. 2005. "Differences in Social Capital between 54 Western European Regions." *Regional Studies* 39: 1053–1064.

Beugelsdijk, Sjoerd, and Ton van Schaik. 2005. "Social Capital and Growth in European Regions: An Empirical Test." *European Journal of Political Economy*, 21: 301–324.

Bezemer, Dirk, Jutta Bolt, and Robert Lensink. 2014. "Slavery, Statehood, and Economic Development in Sub-Saharan Africa." *World Development*, 57: 148–163.

Bjørnskov, Christian, and Andreas Bergh. 2011. "Historical Trust Levels Predict the Current Size of the Welfare State." *Kyklos*, 64(1): 1–19.

Bjørnskov, Christian, and Andreas Bergh. 2014. "Trust, Welfare States and Income Equality: Sorting out the Causality." *European Journal of Political Economy*, 35: 183–199.

Bjørnskov, Christian, and Gert Tinggaard Svendsen. 2013. "Does Social Trust Determine the Size of the Welfare State? Evidence using Historical Identification." *Public Choice*, 157(1–2): 269–286.

Bjørnskov, Christian. 2010. "How Does Social Trust lead to Better Governance? An Attempt to Separate Electoral and Bureaucratic Mechanisms." *Public Choice*, 144: 323–346.

Bjørnskov, Christian. 2011. "Combating Corruption: On the Interplay between Institutional Quality and Social Trust." *The Journal of Law & Economics*, 54(1): 135–159.

Blackburn, Keith, and Jonathan Powell. 2011. "Corruption, Inflation and Growth." *Economics Letters*, 113: 225–227.

Bleaney, Michael, and Arcangelo Dimico. 2011. "Biogeographical Conditions, the Transition to Agriculture and Long-Run Growth." *European Economic Review*, 55: 943–954.

Bleaney, Michael, and Arcangelo Dimico. 2016. "State History, Historical Legitimacy and Modern Ethnic Diversity." *European Journal of Political Economy*, 43: 159–170.

Bloom, David, Jeffrey Sachs, Paul Collier, and Christopher Udry. 1998. "Geography, Demography, and Economic Growth in Africa." *Brookings Papers on Economic Activity*, (2): 207–295.

Bockstette, Valerie, Areendam Chanda, and Louis Putterman. 2002. "States and Markets: The Advantage of an Early Start." *Journal of Economic Growth*, 7: 347–369.

Bomhoff, Eduard, and Grace Hooi Yean Lee. 2012. "Tolerance and Economic Growth Revisited: A Note." *Public Choice*, 153(3–4): 487–494.

Boppart, Timo, Josef Falkinger, and Volker Grossman, Ulrich Woitek, and Gabriela Wüthrich. 2013. "Under Which Conditions Does Religion Affect Educational Outcomes?" *Explorations in Economic History*, 50: 242–266.

Boppart, Timo, Josef Falkinger and Volker Grossman. 2014. "Protestantism and Education: Reading (The Bible) and Other Skills." *Economic Inquiry*, 52(2): 874–895.

Borcan, Oana, Ola Olsson, and Louis Putterman. 2018. "State History and Economic Development: Evidence from Six Millennia." *Journal of Economic Growth*, 23: 1–40.

Brecht, Bertolt. 1935. "When Evil-Doing Comes Like Falling Rain [Wenn die Untat kommt, wie der Regen fällt]." Translated by John Willett. Web.

Broms, Rasmus. 2017. "Colonial Revenue Extraction and Modern-Day Government Quality in the British Empire." *World Development*, 90: 269–280.

Brückner, Markus, and Antonio Ciccone. 2011. "Rain and the Democratic Window of Opportunity." *Econometrica*, 79(3): 923–947.

Brückner, Markus, and Rabah Arezki. 2011. "Oil Rents, Corruption, and State Stability: Evidence from Panel Data Regressions." *European Economic Review*, 55(7): 955–963.

Brückner, Markus, Antonio Ciccone, and Andrea Tesei. 2012. "Oil Price Shocks, income, and Democracy." *The Review of Economics and Statistics*, 94(2): 389–399.

Bruckner, Markus. 2010. "Natural Resource Dependence, Non-Tradables, and Economic Growth." *Journal of Comparative Economics*, 38: 461–471.

Bruhn, Miriam, and Francisco Gallego. 2012. "Good, Bad, and Ugly Colonial Activities: Do They Matter for Economic Development?" *The Review of Economics and Statistics*, 94(2): 433–461.

Brunnschweiler, Christa, and Erwin Bulte. 2008. "The Resource Curse Revisited and Revised: A Tale of Paradoxes and Red Herrings." *Journal of Environmental Economics and Management*, 55: 248–264.

Brunnschweiler, Christa, and Erwin Bulte. 2009. "Natural Resources and Violent Conflict: Resource Abundance, Dependence, and the Onset of Civil Wars." *Oxford Economic Papers*, 61(4): 651–674.

Brunnschweiler, Christa. 2008. "Cursing the Blessings? Natural Resource Abundance, Institutions, and Economic Growth." *World Development*, 36(3): 399–419.

Buggle, Johannes, and Ruben Durante. 2021. "Climate Risk, Cooperation, and the Co-Evolution of Culture and Institutions." *The Economic Journal*, 131(637): 1947–1987.

Buggle, Johannes. 2020. "Growing Collectivism: Irrigation, Group Conformity and Technological Divergence." *Journal of Economic Growth*, 25: 147–193.

Bulte, Erwin, Richard Damania, and Robert Deacon. 2005. "Resource Intensity, Institutions, and Development." *World Development*, 33(7): 1029–1044.

Burgess, Robin, Remi Jedwab, Edward Miguel, Ameet Morjaria, and Gerard Padró i Miquel. 2015. "The Value of Democracy: Evidence from Road Building in Kenya." *American Economic Review*, 105(6): 1817–1851.

Burke, Marshall, Solomon Hsiang, and Edward Miguel. 2013. "Quantifying the Influence of Climate on Human Conflict." *Science*, 341(6151).

Burke, Marshall, Solomon Hsiang, and Edward Miguel. 2015. "Climate and Conflict." *Annual Review of Economics*, 7: 577–617.

Butkiewicz, James, and Halit Yanikkaya. 2006. "Institutional Quality and Economic Growth: Maintenance of the Rule of Law or Democratic Institutions, or Both?" *Economic Modelling*, 23: 648–661.

Campante, Filipe, and David Yanagizawa-Drott. 2015. "Does Religion Affect Economic Growth and Happiness? Evidence from Ramadan." *The Quarterly Journal of Economics*, 130(2): 615–658.

Campante, Filipe, Davin Chor and Quoc-Anh Do. 2009. "Instability and the Incentives for Corruption." *Economics and Politics*, 21(1): 42–92.

Campos, Edgardo, Donald Lien, and Sanjay Pradhan. 1999. "The Impact of Corruption on Investment: Predictability Matters." *World Development*, 27(6): 1059–1067.

Campos, Nauro, Ahmad Saleh, and Vitaliy Kuzeyev. 2011. "Dynamic Ethnic Fractionalization and Economic Growth." *The Journal of International Trade and Economic Development*, 20(2): 129–152.

Campos, Nauro, and Jeffrey Nugent. 2003. "Aggregate Investment and Political Instability: An Econometric Investigation." *Economica*, 70: 533–549.

Campos, Nauro, and Jeffrey Nugent.2002. "Who is Afraid of Political Instability?" *Journal of Development Economics*, 67: 157–172.

Campos, Nauro, and Vitaliy Kuzeyev. 2007. "On the Dynamics of Ethnic Fractionalization." *American Journal of Political Science*, 51(3): 620–639.

Cantoni, Davide, Jeremiah Dittmar, and Noam Yuchtman. 2018. "Religious Competition and Reallocation: The Political Economy of Secularization in the Protestant Reformation." *The Quarterly Journal of Economics*, 133(4): 2037–2096.

Carpantier, Jean-Francois, and Anastasia Litina. Forthcoming. "Dissecting the Act of God: An Exploration of the Effect of Religiosity on Economic Activity." *The B.E. Journal of Macroeconomics*.

Carroll, Christopher. 2000. "Why do the Rich Save So Much?" In *Does Atlas Shrug?: Economic Consequences of Taxing the Rich*, edited by J. Slemrod. Cambridge: Cambridge University Press.

Carstensen, Kai, and Erich Gundlach. 2006. "The Primacy of Institutions Reconsidered: Direct Income Effects of Malaria Prevalence." *The World Bank Economic Review*, 20(3): 309–339.

Caruso, Germán Daniel. 2017. "The Legacy of Natural Disasters: The Intergenerational Impact of 100 Years of Disasters in Latin America." *Journal of Development Economics*, 127: 209–233.

Caselli, Francesco, Massimo Morelli, and Dominic Rohner. 2015. "The Geography of Interstate Resources Wars." *The Quarterly Journal of Economics*, 130(1): 267–315.

Cashdan, Elizabeth. 2001. "Ethnic Diversity and Its Environmental Determinants: Effects of Climate, Pathogens, and Habitat Diversity." *American Anthropologist*, 103(4): 968–991.

Cavallo, Eduardo, Sebastian Galiani, Ilan Noy, and Juan Pantano. 2013. "Catastrophic Natural Disasters and Economic Growth." *The Review of Economics and Statistics*, 95(5): 1549–1561.

Cervellati, Matteo, Elena Esposito, and Uwe Sunde. 2017. "Long Term Exposure to Malaria and Development: Disaggregate Evidence for Contemporaneous Africa." *Journal of Demographic Economics*, 83: 129–148.

Cervellati, Matteo, Giorgio Chiovelli, and Elena Esposito. 2019. "Bite and Divide: Malaria and Ethnolinguistic Diversity." Center for Economic and Policy Research Discussion Paper DP13437.

Cervellati, Matteo, Piergiuseppe Fortunato and Uwe Sunde. 2014. "Violence during Democratization and the Quality of Democratic Institutions." *European Economic Review*, 66: 226–247.

Chanda, Areendam, and Louis Putterman. 2007. "Early Starts, Reversals and Catch-up in the Process of Economic Development." *Scandinavian Journal of Economics*, 109(2): 387–413.

Chanda, Areendam, Justin Cook, and Loius Putterman. 2014. "Persistence of Fortune: Accounting for Population Movements, There Was No Post-Columbian Reversal." *American Economic Journal: Macroeconomics*, 6(3): 1–28.

Chen, Baizhu, and Yi Feng. 1996. "Some Political Determinants of Economic Growth: Theory and Empirical Implications." *European Journal of Political Economy*, 12(4): 609–627.

Chen, Keith. 2013. "The Effect of Language on Economic Behavior: Evidence from Savings Rates, Health Behaviors, and Retirement Assets." *American Economic Review*, 103(2): 690–731.

Churchill, Sefa, and Russell Smyth. 2017. "Ethnic Diversity and Poverty." *World Development*, 95: 285–302.

Ciccone, Antonio. 2011. "Economic Shocks and Civil Conflict: A Comment." *American Economic Journal: Applied Economics*, 3: 215–227.

Ciccone, Antonio. 2013. "Estimating the Effect of Transitory Economic Shocks on Civil Conflict." *Review of Economics and Institutions*, 4(2): 1–14.

Cieslik, Andrzej, and Łukasz Goczek. 2018. "Control of Corruption, International Investment, and Economic Growth—Evidence from Panel Data." *World Development*, 103: 323–335.

Clarke, George. 1995. "More Evidence on Income Distribution and Growth." *Journal of Development Economics*, 47: 403–427.

Clemens, Michael, and Jeffery Williamson. 2004. "Why did the Tariff–Growth Correlation Change after 1950?" *Journal of Economic Growth*, 9(1): 5–46.

Cliff, Nigel. 2011. *Holy War: How Vasco da Gama's Epic Voyages Turned the Tide in a Centuries-Old Clash of Civilizations*. New York: Harper.

Cliff, Nigel. 2012. *The Last Crusade: The Epic Voyages of Vasco da Gama*. New York: Harper Perennial.

Cline, Brandon, and Claudia Williamson. 2017. "Individualism, Democracy, and Contract Enforcement." *Journal of Corporate Finance*, 46: 284–306.

Clingingsmith, David, Asim Ijaz Khwaja, and Michael Kremer. 2009. "Estimating the Impact of the Hajj: Religion and Tolerance in Islam's Global Gathering." *The Quarterly Journal of Economics*, 124(3): 1133–1170.

Coase, Ronald. 2005. "The Institutional Structure of Production." In *The Handbook of Institutional Economics*, edited by Claude Menard and Mary Shirley. New York: Springer.

Coleman, James. 1990. *Foundations of Social Theory*. Cambridge, MA: Belknap Press.

Collier, Paul, and Anke Hoeffler. 1998. "On Economic Causes of Civil War." *Oxford Economic Papers*, 50(4): 563–573.

Collier, Paul, and Anke Hoeffler. 2004. "Greed and Grievance in Civil War." *Oxford Economic Papers*, 56(4): 563–595.

Collier, Paul, and Dominic Rohner. 2008. "Democracy, Development, and Conflict." *Journal of the European Economic Association*, 6(2–3): 531–540.

Collier, Paul. 2000. "Ethnicity, Politics, and Economic Performance." *Economics and Politics*, 12(3): 225–245.

Comin, Diego, and Bart Hobijn. 2010. "An Exploration of Technology Diffusion." *American Economic Review*, 100: 2031–2059.

Comin, Diego, William Easterly, and Erick Gong. 2010. "Was the Wealth of Nations Determined in 1000 BC?" *American Economic Journal: Macroeconomics*, 2: 65–97.

Cook, Justin. 2014. "Potatoes, Milk, and the Old-World Population Boom." *Journal of Development Economics*, 110: 123–138.

Cook, Justin. 2014. "The Role of Lactose Persistence in Pre-colonial Development." *Journal of Economic Growth*, 19: 369–406.

Cook, Steven. 2012. "Corruption and the Arab Spring." *The Brown Journal of World Affairs*, 18(2): 21–28.

Cook, Steven. 2012. *The Struggle for Egypt: From Nasser to Tahrir Square*. Oxford: Oxford University Press.

Cotet, Anca, and Kevin Tsui. 2013. "Oil and Conflict: What Does the Cross-Country Evidence Really Show?" *American Economic Journal: Macroeconomics*, 5(1): 49–80.

Couttenier, Mathieu, and Raphael Soubeyran. 2014. "Drought and Civil War in sub-Saharan Africa." *Economic Journal*, 124(575): 201–244.

Crosby, Alfred. 2004. *Ecological Imperialism: The Biological Expansion of Europe, 900–1900*. Cambridge: Cambridge University Press.

Cukierman, Alex, Sebastian Edwards, and Guido Tabellini. 1992. "Seigniorage and Political Instability." *The American Economic Review*, 82(3): 537–55.

Curtin, Philip. 1989. *Death by Migration: Europe's Encounter with the Tropical World in the Nineteenth Century*. Cambridge: Cambridge University Press.

Curtin, Philip. 1998. *Disease and Empire: The Health of European Troops in the Conquest of Africa*. Cambridge: Cambridge University Press.

Dahlum, Sirianne, and Carl Henrik Knutsen. 2017. "Do Democracies Provide Better Education? Revisiting the Democracy–Human Capital Link." *World Development*, 94: 186–199.

Daniel Yergin. 1992. *The Prize: The Epic Quest for Oil, Money and Power*. Washington, DC: Free Press.

Daniele, Gianmarco, and Benny Geys. 2015. "Interpersonal Trust and Welfare State Support." *European Journal of Political Economy*, 39: 1–12.

Darling, Linda. 2007. "Social Cohesion ('Asabiyya') and Justice in the Late Medieval Middle East." *Comparative Studies in Society and History*, 49(2): 329–357.

Davis, Lewis, and Claudia Williamson. 2016. "Culture and the Regulation of Entry." *Journal of Comparative Economics*, 44(4): 1055–1083.

Davis, Lewis, and Farangis Abdurazokzoda. 2016. "Language, Culture and Institutions: Evidence from a New Linguistic Dataset." *Journal of Comparative Economics*, 44: 541–561.

Davis, Lewis, and Megan Reynolds. 2018. "Gendered Language and the Educational Gender Gap." *Economics Letters*, 168: 46–48.

Davis, Lewis. 2016. "Individual Responsibility and Economic Development: Evidence from Rainfall Data." *Kyklos*, 69(3): 426–470.

de Montesquieu, Charles. 1989. *The Spirit of the Laws*. Cambridge: Cambridge University Press.

Dearmon, Jacob, and Kevin Grier. 2009. "Trust and Development." *Journal of Economic Behavior & Organization*, 71(2): 210–220.

Dearmon, Jacob, and Robin Grier. 2011. "Trust and the Accumulation of Physical and Human Capital." *European Journal of Political Economy*, 27(3): 507–519.

Deininger, Klaus, and Lyn Squire. 1998. "New Ways of Looking at Old Issues: Inequality and Growth." *Journal of Development Economics*, 57: 259–287.

Dell, Melissa, Benjamin Jones, and Benjamin Olken. 2009. "Temperature and Income: Reconciling New Cross-Sectional and Panel Estimates." *American Economic Review: Papers and Proceedings*, 99(2): 198–204.

Denoon, Donald. 1983. *Settler Capitalism: The Dynamics of Dependent Development in the Southern Hemisphere*. Oxford: Oxford University Press.

Depetris-Chauvin, Emilio, and David Weil. 2018. "Malaria and Early African Development: Evidence from the Sickle Cell Trait." *The Economic Journal*, 128(610): 1207–1234.

Depetris-Chauvin, Emilio. 2016. "State History and Contemporary Conflict: Evidence from Sub-Saharan Africa." Documentos de Trabajo 475, Instituto de Economia, Pontificia Universidad Católica de Chile.

Des Forges, Alison. 1999. *Leave None to Tell the Story: Genocide in Rwanda*. Human Rights Watch.

Desmet, Klaus, Ignacio Ortuño-Ortín, and Romain Wacziarg. 2017. "Culture, Ethnicity, and Diversity." *The American Economic Review*, 107(9): 2479–2513.

Devereux, Michael, and Jean-François Wen. 1998. "Political Instability, Capital Taxation, and Growth." *European Economic Review*, 42(9): 1635–1651.

Diamond, Jared. 2001. "Why Did Human History Unfold Differently on Different Continents for The Last 13,000 Years?" The Haskins Lectureship on Science Policy.

Diamond, Jared. 2005. *Guns, Germs, and Steel: The Fates of Human Societies*. New York: W. W. Norton & Company.

Dickens, Andrew. 2018. "Ethnolinguistic Favoritism in African Politics." *American Economic Journal: Applied Economics*, 10(3): 370–402.

Dills, Angela, and Rey Hernández-Julián. 2014. "Religiosity and State Welfare." *Journal of Economic Behavior & Organization*, 104: 37–51.

Djankov, Simeon, Caralee McLiesh, and Rita Maria Ramalho. 2006. "Regulation and Growth." *Economics Letters*, 92: 395–401.

Djankov, Simeon, Rafael La Porta, Florencio Lopez-de-Silanes, and Andrei Schleifer. 2003. "Courts." *The Quarterly Journal of Economics*, 118(2): 453–517.

Djankov, Simeon, Rafael La Porta, Florencio Lopez-de-Silanes, and Andrew Schleifer. 2002. "The Regulation of Entry." *The Quarterly Journal of Economics*, 117(1): 1–37.

Dollar, David, and Aart Kraay. 2003. "Institutions, Trade, and Growth." *Journal of Monetary Economics*, 50: 133–162.

Dollar, David, and Aart Kraay. 2004. "Trade, Growth, and Poverty." *The Economic Journal*, 114: F22–F49.

Driskell, Robyn, Elizabeth Embry, and Larry Lyon. 2008. "Faith and Politics: The Influence of Religious Beliefs on Political Participation." *Social Science Quarterly*, 89(2): 294–314.

Durlauf, Steven, Andros Kortellos, and Chih Ming Tan. 2012. "Is God in the Details? A Reexamination of the Role of Religion in Economic Growth." *Journal of Applied Econometrics*, 27(7): 1059–1075.

Easterly, William, and Ross Levine. 1997. "Africa's Growth Tragedy: Policies and Ethnic Divisions." *The Quarterly Journal of Economics*, 112(4): 1203–1250.

Easterly, William, and Ross Levine. 2003. "Tropics, Germs and Crops: How Endowments Influence Economic Development." *Journal of Monetary Economics*, 50: 3–39.

Easterly, William, and Ross Levine. 2016. "The European Origins of Economic Development." *Journal of Economic Growth*, 21(3): 225–257.

Easterly, William, Roberta Gatti, and Sergio Kurlat. 2006. "Development, Democracy, and Mass Killings." *Journal of Economic Growth*, 11: 129–156.

Easterly, William. 2001. "Can Institutions Resolve Ethnic Conflict?" *Economic Development and Cultural Change*, 49(4): 687–706.

Easterly, William. 2001. "The Middle-Class Consensus and Economic Development." *Journal of Economic Growth*, 6(4): 317–335.

Easterly, William. 2007. "Inequality Does Cause Underdevelopment: Insights from a New Instrument." *Journal of Development Economics*, 84: 755–776.

El Bahnasawy, Nasr, Michael Ellis, and Assandé Désiré Adom. 2016. "Political Instability and the Informal Economy." *World Development*, 85:31–42.

Elgin, Ceyhun, Turkmen Goksel, Mehmet Gurdal, and Cuneyt Orman. 2013. "Religion, Income Inequality, and the Size of the Government." *Economic Modelling*, 30: 225–234.

Ellsworth, Huntington. 2013. *Civilization and Climate*. Los Angeles: HardPress Publishing.

Eltis, David, David Richardson, David Blight, and David Davis. 2015. *Atlas of the Transatlantic Slave Trade*. New Haven: Yale University Press.

Ember, Carol, and Elvin Ember. 2007. "Climate, Econiche, and Sexuality: Influences on Sonority in Language." *American Anthropologist*, 109(1): 180–185.

Engerman, Stanley, and Kenneth Sokoloff. 2000. "Institutions, Factor Endowments, and Paths of Development in the New World." *Journal of Economic Perspectives*, 14(3): 217–232.

Engerman, Stanley, and Kenneth Sokoloff. 2002. "Factor Endowments, Inequality, and Paths of Development among New World Economies." National Bureau of Economic Research Working Paper 9259.

Engerman, Stanley, and Kenneth Sokoloff. 2005. "Colonialism, Inequality, and Long Run Paths of Development." National Bureau of Economic Research Working Paper 11057.

Engerman, Stanley, and Kenneth Sokoloff. 2013. "Five Hundred Years of European Colonization: Inequality and Paths of Development." In *Settler Economies in World History*, edited by Christopher Lloyd, Jakob Metzer, and Richard Sutch. Netherlands: BRILL.

Ertan, Arhan, Louis Putterman and Martin Fiszbein. 2016. "Who Was Colonized and When? A Cross-Country Analysis of Determinants," *European Economic Review*, 83: 165–184.

Esteban, Joan, Laura Mayoral, and Debraj Ray. 2012. "Ethnicity and Conflict: An Empirical Study." *The American Economic Review*, 102(4): 1310–1342.

Everett, Caleb Everett. 2013. "Evidence for Direct Geographic Influences on Linguistic Sounds: The Case of Ejectives." *PLOS One* 8(6). https://doi.org/10.1371/journal.pone.0065275.

Fairgrieve, James. 2013. "Geography and World Power." TheClassics.us.

Farhadi, Minoo, Rabiul Islam, and Solmaz Moslehi. 2015. "Economic Freedom and Productivity Growth in Resource-rich Economies." *World Development*, 72: 109–126.

Fearon, James, and David Laitin. 2003. "Ethnicity, Insurgency, and Civil War." *American Political Science Review*, 97(1): 75–90.

Fearon, James, Kimuli Kasara, and David Laitin. 2007. "Ethnic Minority Rule and Civil War Onset." *American Political Science Review*, 101(1): 187–193.

Fehr, Ernest. 2009. "On the Economics and Biology of Trust." *Journal of the European Economic Association*, 7(2/3): 235–266.

Felbermayr, Gabriel, and Jasmin Gröschl. 2014. "Naturally Negative: The Growth Effects of Natural Disasters." *Journal of Development Economics*, 111: 92–106.

Feng, Yi. 1997. "Democracy, Political Stability and Economic Growth." *British Journal of Political Science*, 27(3): 391–418.

Feng, Yi. 2001. "Political Freedom, Political Instability, and Policy Uncertainty: A Study of Political Institutions and Private Investment in Developing Countries." *Institutional Studies Quarterly*, 45(2): 271–294.

Fenske, James, and Namrata Kala. 2015. "Climate and Slave Trade." *Journal of Development Economics*, 112: 19–32.

Fenske, James, and Namrata Kala. 2017. "1807: Economic Shocks, Conflict and the Slave Trade." *Journal of Development Economics*, 126: 66–76.

Fenske, James. 2015. "African Polygamy: Past and Present." *Journal of Development Economics*, 117: 58–73.

Ferguson, Niall. 2007. *The War of the World: Twentieth-Century Conflict and the Descent of the West.* New York: Penguin Books.

Ferguson, Niall. 2013. *The Great Degeneration: How Institutions Decay and Economies Decay.* New York: Penguin Press.

Ferguson, Niall. 2017. *The Square and the Tower.* New York: Penguin Books.

Feyrer, James, and Bruce Sacerdote. 2009. "Colonialism and Modern Income: Islands as Natural Experiments." *The Review of Economics and Statistics*, 91(2): 245–262.

Figlio, David, Paola Giuliano, Umut Özek, and Paola Sapienza. 2019. "Long-Term Orientation and Educational Performance." *American Economic Journal: Economic Policy*, 11(4): 272–309.

Fincher, Corey, Randy Thornhill, Damian Murray, and Mark Schaller. 2008. "Pathogen Prevalence Predicts Human Cross-cultural Variability in Individualism/Collectivism." *Proceedings of the Royal Society*, 275(1640): 1279–85.

Florida, Richard. 2003. "Cities and the Creative Class." *City and Community*, 2(1): 3–19.

Fomby, Thomas, Yuki Ikeda, and Norman Loayza. 2012. "The Growth Aftermath of Natural Disasters." *Journal of Applied Econometrics*, 28: 412–434.

Forbes, Kristin. 2000. "A Reassessment of the Relationship between Inequality and Growth." *The American Economic Review*, 90(4): 869–887.

Franck, Raphael, and Ilia Rainer. 2012. "Does the Leader's Ethnicity Matter? Ethnic Favoritism, Education, and Health in Sub-Saharan Africa." *American Political Science Review*, 106(2): 294–325.

Frankel, Jeffery, and David Romer. 1999. "Does Trade Cause Growth?" *The American Economic Review*, 89(3): 379–399.

Frankel, Jeffrey. 2010. "The Natural Resource Curse: A Survey." The National Bureau of Economic Research Working Paper 15836.

Fukuyama, Francis. 2014. "At the 'End of History' Still Stands Democracy." *The Wall Street Journal*, June 6.

Fukuyama, Francis. 2012. *The Origins of Political Order: From Prehuman Times to the French Revolution*. New York: Farrar, Straus and Giroux.

Fuller, Lon. 1965. "Irrigation and Tyranny." *Stanford Law Review*, 17(6): 1021–1042.

Gallup, John, and Jeffery Sachs. 2001. "The Economic Burden of Malaria." *American Journal of Tropical Medicine and Hygiene*, 64(1–2): 85–96.

Gallup, John, and Jeffrey Sachs. 2000. "Agriculture, Climate, and Technology: Why are the Tropics Falling Behind." *American Journal of Agricultural Economics*, 82(3): 731–737.

Gallup, John, Jeffrey Sachs, and Andrew Mellinger. 1999. "Geography and Economic Development." *International Regional Science Review*, 22(2): 179–232.

Galor, Oded, and Omer Moav. 2004. "From Physical to Human Capital Accumulation: Inequality and the Process of Development." *Review of Economic Studies*, 71: 1001–1026.

Gates, Warren. 1967. "The Spread of Ibn Khaldun's Ideas on Climate and Culture." *Journal of the History of Ideas*, 28(3): 415–422.

Gay, Victor, Daniel Hicks, Estefania Santacreu-Vasut and Amir Shoham. 2018. "Decomposing Culture: An Analysis of Gender, Language, and Labor Supply in the Household." *Review of Economics of the Household*, 16(4): 879–909.

Gay, Victor, Estefania Santacreu-Vasut, and Amir Shoham. 2013. "Do Female/Male Distinctions in Language Matter? Evidence from Gender Political Quotas." *Applied Economics Letters*, 20(5): 495–498.

Gennaioli, Nicola, and Ilia Rainer. 2007. "The Modern Impact of Precolonial Centralization in Africa." *Journal of Economic Growth*, 12: 185–234.

Giddens, Anthony. 1991. *The Consequences of Modernity*. Cambridge, MA: Polity Press.

Gilbert, James Stanley. 2016. *The Fall of Panamá: And Other Isthmian Rhymes and Sketches*. New York: Palala Press.

Givati, Yehonatan, and Ugo Troiano. 2012. "Law, Economics, and Culture: Theory of Mandated Benefits and Evidence from Maternity Leave Policies." *The Journal of Law & Economics*, 55(2): 339–364.

Glaeser, Edward, Rafael La Porta, Florencio Lopez De-Salinas, and Andrei Schleifer. 2004. "Do Institutions Cause Growth." *Journal of Economic Growth*, 9: 271–303.

Glaeser, Edward. 2005. "The Political Economy of Hatred." *The Quarterly Journal of Economics*, 120(1): 45–86.

Glasgow, John Philip. 1963. *The Distribution and Abundance of Tsetse*. Oxford: Pergamon Press.

Glazer, Amihai. 1989. "Politics and the Choice of Durability." *The American Economic Review*, 79(5): 1207–1213.

Gorodnichenko, Yuriy, and Gerard Roland. 2011. "Which Dimensions of Culture Matter for Long Run Growth." *The American Economic Review: Papers and Proceedings*, 101(3): 492–498.

Gorodnichenko, Yuriy, and Gerard Roland. 2015. "Culture, Institutions, and Democratization." National Bureau of Economic Research Working Paper 21117.

Gorodnichenko, Yuriy, and Gerard Roland. 2017. "Culture, Institutions, and the Wealth of Nations." *Review of Economics and Statistics*, 99(3): 402–416.

Greenaway, David, Wyn Morgan, and Peter Wright. 1997. "Trade Liberalization and Growth in Developing Countries: Some New Evidence." *World Development*, 25(11): 1885–1892.

Greenaway, David, Wyn Morgan, and Peter Wright. 2002. "Trade Liberalisation and Growth in Developing Countries." *Journal of Development Economics*, 67: 229–244.

Greif, Avner. 1993. "Contract Enforceability and Economic Institutions in Early Trade: The Maghribi Traders' Coalition." *American Economic Review* 83: 525–48.

Greif, Avner. 1994. "Cultural Beliefs and the Organization of Society: A Historical and Theoretical Reflection on Collectivist and Individualist Societies." *Journal of Political Economy*, 102(5): 912–50.

Grier, Robin. 1999. "Colonial Legacies and Economic Growth." *Public Choice*, 98(3/4): 317–335.

Grossman, Gene, and Elhanan Helpman. 1991. "Trade, Knowledge Spillovers, and Growth." *European Economic Review*, 35(2–3): 517–526.

Grossman, Herschell. 1991. "A General Equilibrium Model of Insurrections." *The American Economic Review*, 81: 912–921.

Guiliano, Paola, and Nathan Nunn. 2021. "Understanding Cultural Persistence and Change." *Review of Economic Studies*, 88(4): 1541–1581.

Guiso, Luigi, Paola Sapienza and Luigi Zingales. 2010. "Civic Capital as the Missing Link." National Bureau of Economic Research Working Paper 15845.

Guiso, Luigi, Paola Sapienza, and Luigi Zingales. 2003. "People's Opium? Religion and Economic Attitudes." *Journal of Monetary Economics*, 50: 225–282.

Guiso, Luigi, Paola Sapienza, and Luigi Zingales. 2009. "Cultural Biases and Economic Exchange." *The Quarterly Journal of Economics*, 124(3): 1095–1131.

Gupta, Sanjeev, Hamid Davoodi, and Rosa Alonso-Terme. 2002. "Does Corruption Affect Income Inequality and Poverty?" *Economics of Governance*, 3: 23–45.

Gyimah-Brempong, Kwabena. 2002. "Corruption, Economic Growth, and Income Inequality in Africa." *Economics of Governance*, 3: 183–209.

Gylfason, Thorvaldur. 2001. "Natural Resources, Education, and Economic Development." *European Economic Review*, 45: 847–859.

Haber, Stephen, and Victor Menaldo. 2011. "Do Natural Resources Fuel Authoritarianism? A Reappraisal of the Resource Curse." *American Political Science Review*, 1–26.

Haber, Stephen, and Victor Menaldo. 2011. "Rainfall, Human Capital, and Democracy." Manuscript, Stanford University.

Habibur Rahman, Muhammad, Nejat Anbarci, Prasad Sankar Bhattacharya and Mehmet Ali Ulubaşoğlu. 2017. "Can Extreme Rainfall Trigger Democratic Change? The Role of Flood-induced Corruption." *Public Choice*, 171: 331–358.

Habibur Rahman, Muhammad, Nejat Anbarci, Prasad Sankar Bhattacharya and Mehmet Ali Ulubaşoğlu. 2017. "The Shocking Origins of Political Transitions: Evidence from Earthquakes." *Southern Economic Journal*, 83(3): 796–823.

Hall, Robert, and Charles Jones. 1999. "Why Do Some Countries Produce so much more Output Per Worker than Others?" *Quarterly Journal of Economics*, 114(1): 83–116.

Hariri, Jacob. 2015. "Foreign Aided: Why Democratization Brings Growth when Democracy Does Not." *British Journal of Political Science*, 45(1): 53–71.

Heckscher, Eli, and Bertil Ohlin. 1991. *Heckscher-Ohlin Trade Theory*. Cambridge: MIT Press.

Helliwell, John. 1994. "Empirical Linkages between Democracy and Economic Growth." *British Journal of Political Science*, 24: 225–248.

Henderson, Vernon, Adam Storeygard, and David Weil. 2011. "A Bright Idea for Measuring Economic Growth." *American Economic Review: Papers & Proceedings*, 101(3): 194–199.

Henderson, Vernon, Adam Storeygard, and David Weil. 2012. "Measuring Economic Growth from Outer Space." *The American Economic Review*, 102(2): 994–1028.

Herzer, Dierk, and Holger Strulik. 2017. "Religiosity and Income: A Panel Cointegration and Causality Analysis." *Applied Economics*, 49(3): 2922–2938.

Hodge, Andrew, Sriram Shankar, Prasado Rao, and Alan Duhs. 2011. "Exploring the Links between Corruption and Growth." *Review of Development Economics*, 15(3): 474–490.

Hodler, Roland, Sorawoot Srisuma, Alberto Vesperoni, and Noémie Zurlinde. 2020. "Measuring Ethnic Stratification and its Effect on Trust in Africa." *Journal of Development Economics*, 146: 102–475.

Hofstede, Geert. 2003. *Culture's Consequences: Comparing Values, Behaviors, Institutions and Organizations across Nations*. Washington, DC: SAGE Publications.

Horbury, William. 1999. *The Cambridge History of Judaism: Volume 3, The Early Roman Period*. Cambridge: Cambridge University Press.

Hornbeck, Richard. 2012. "The Enduring Impact of the American Dust Bowl: Short-and Long-Run Adjustments to Environmental Catastrophe." *American Economic Review*, 102(4): 1477–1507.

Horváth, Roman. 2013. "Does Trust Promote Growth?" *Journal of Comparative Economics*, 41(3): 777–788.

Hsiang, Solomon, Kyle Meng, and Mark Cane. 2011. "Civil Conflicts are Associated with the Global Climate." *Nature*, 476: 438–441.

http://db.nelsonmandela.org/speeches/pub_view.asp?pg=item&ItemID=NMS919.

http://www.who.int/topics/tropical_diseases/en/.

https://foreignpolicy.com/2011/02/10/mubaraks-70-billion-nest-egg/.

https://founders.archives.gov/documents/Adams/99-02-02-6371.

https://georgewbush-whitehouse.archives.gov/news/releases/2001/09/20010916-2.html.

https://list.uvm.edu/cgi-bin/wa?A2=POETRY;39dfb3d5.1902.
https://news.un.org/en/story/2021/09/1098662.
https://www.britannica.com/science/Plasmodium-protozoan-genus#ref200404.
https://www.britannica.com/topic/checks-and-balances.
https://www.britannica.com/topic/rule-of-law.
https://www.cnn.com/2019/01/20/business/oxfam-billionaires-davos/index.html.
https://www.washingtonpost.com/news/wonk/wp/2013/04/23/george-w-bushs-presidency-in24-charts/.

Hubner, Malte, and Gonzague Vannoorenberghe. 2015. "Patience and Long-Run Growth." *Economics Letters*, 137: 163–167.

Hugon, Anne. 1993. *The Exploration of Africa: From Cairo to the Cape*. London: Thames and Hudson.

Huillery, Elise. 2009. "History Matters: The Long-Term Impact of Colonial Public Investments in French West Africa." *American Economic Journal: Applied Economics*, 1(2): 176–215.

Huntington, Samuel. 1968. *Political Order in Changing Societies*. New Haven: Yale University Press.

Iannacone, Laurence. 1998. "Introduction to the Economics of Religion." *Journal of Economic Literature*, 36(3): 1465–1495.

Ibn Khaldun. 2014. *Al Muqqadimah: Prolegomena*. Jiahu Books.

Ingelhart, Ronald, and Wayne Baker. 2000. "Modernization, Cultural Change, and the Persistence of Traditional Values." *American Sociological Review*, 65: 19–51.

Irwin, Douglas, and Marko Tervio. 2002. "Does Trade Raise Income? Evidence from the Twentieth Century." *Journal of International Economics*, 58: 1–18.

Iyigun, Murat, Nathan Nunn, and Nancy Qian. 2017. "The Long Run Effects of Agricultural Productivity on Conflict, 1400–1900." National Bureau of Economic Research Working Paper 24066.

Iyigun, Murat, Nathan Nunn, and Nancy Qian. 2017. "Winter is Coming: The Long Run Effects of Climate Change on Conflict: 1400–1900." National Bureau of Economic Research Working Paper 23033.

Jaffee, Adam, and Manuel Trajtenberg. 1999. "International Knowledge Flows: Evidence from Patent Citations." *Economics of Innovation and New Technology*, 8: 105–136.

Jaffee, Adam, Manuel Trajtenberg, and Rebecca Henderson. 1993. "Geographic Localization of Knowledge Spillovers as Evidenced by Patent Citations." *Quarterly Journal of Economics*, 108(3): 577–598.

James, Robert Rhodes (ed.). 1974. *Winston Churchill: His Complete Speeches, 1897–1963*. New York: Chelsea House Publishers.

Jared Diamond. *Guns, Germs, and Steel: The Fate of Human Societies*. New York: W. W. Norton & Company, 1999.

Jellema, Jon, and Gerard Roland. 2011. "Institutional Clusters and Economic Performance." *Journal of Economic Behavior & Organization*, 79: 108–132.

Jensen, Nathan, and Leonard Wantchekon. 2004. "Resource Wealth and Political Regimes in Africa." *Comparative Political Studies*, 37: 816–41.

Jones, Benjamin, and Benjamin Olken. 2010. "Climate Shocks and Exports." *American Economic Review: Papers and Proceedings*, 100: 454–459.

Jones, Eric. 2003. *The European Miracle: Environments, Economies and Geopolitics in the History of Europe and Asia*. Cambridge: Cambridge University Press.

Jones, Patricia. 2013. "History Matters: New Evidence on the Long Run Impact of Colonial Rule on Institutions." *Journal of Comparative Economics*, 41(1): 181–200.

Jong-A-Pin, Richard. 2009. "On the Measurement of Political Instability and its Impact on Economic Growth." *European Journal of Political Economy*, 25(1): 15–29.

Jowett, Benjamin. 1921. *Politica*. Oxford: Oxford University Press.

Kahn, Matthew. 2005. "The Death Toll from Natural Disasters: The Role of Income, Geography, and Institutions." *The Review of Economics and Statistics*, 87(2): 271–284.

Kaplan, Robert. 2012. *The Revenge of Geography*. New York: Random House.

Kashima, Emiko, and Yoshihisa Kashima. 1998. "Culture and Language: The Case of Cultural Dimensions and Personal Pronoun Use." *Journal of Cross-Cultural Psychology*, 29(3): 461–486.

Kashima, Emiko, and Yoshihisa Kashima. 2005. "Erratum to Kashima and Kashima (1998) and Reiteration." *Journal of Cross-Cultural Psychology*, 36(3): 396–400.

Keefer, Phillip, and Stephen Knack. 2002. "Polarization, Politics and Property Rights: Links Between Inequality and Growth." *Public Choice*, 111: 127–154.

Khalifa, Sherif, and Sherine El Hag. 2010. "Income Disparities, Economic Growth and Development as a Threshold." *Journal of Economic Development*, 35(2): 23–36.

Khalifa, Sherif. 2015. *Egypt's Lost Spring: Causes and Consequences*. Westport, CT: Praeger.

Khalifa, Sherif. 2016. "Trust, Landscape, and Economic Development." *Journal of Economic Development*, 41(1): 19–32.

Kim, Dong-Hyeon Kim, Ting-Cih Chen, and Shu-Chin Lin. 2020. "Does Oil Drive Income Inequality? New panel Evidence." *Structural Change and Economic Dynamics*, 55: 37–152.

Kipling, Rudyard. 1999. *The Collected Poems of Rudyard Kipling*. Hertfordshire, UK: Wordsworth Editions Ltd.

Klasing, Mariko. 2013. "Cultural Dimensions, Collective Values and their Importance for Institutions." *Journal of Comparative Economics*, 41(2): 447–467.

Klomp, Jeroen. 2017. "Flooded with Debt." *Journal of International Money and Finance*, 73: 93–103.

Knack, Stephen, and Paul Zak. 2003. "Building Trust: Public Policy, Interpersonal Trust, and Economic Development." *Supreme Court Economic Review*, 10, *The Rule of Law, Freedom, and Prosperity*: 91–107.

Knack, Stephen, and Philip Keefer. 1995. "Institutions and Economic Performance: Cross Country Tests Using Alternative Institutional Measures." *Economics and Politics*, 7(3): 207–225.

Knack, Stephen, and Philip Keefer. 1997. "Why Don't Poor Countries Catch Up?: A Cross National Test of an Institutional Explanation." *Economic Inquiry*, 35: 590–602.

Knack, Stephen, and Philip Keefer. 1997. "Does Social Capital Have an Economic Payoff? A Cross Country Investigation." *The Quarterly Journal of Economics*, 112(40): 1251–1288.

Kodila-Tedika, Oasis, and Sherif Khalifa. 2020. "Long-Term Vision and Economic Development." *The World Economy*, 43(11): 3088–3102.

Kotschy, Rainer, and Uwe Sunde. 2017. "Democracy, Inequality, and Institutional Quality." *European Economic Review*, 91: 209–228.

Kourtellos, Andros, Ioanna Stylianou and Chih Ming Tan. 2013. "Failure to Launch? The Role of Land Inequality in Transition Delays." *European Economic Review*, 62: 98–113.

Krieger, Tim, and Daniel Meierrieks. 2016. "Political Capitalism: The Interaction between Income Inequality, Economic Freedom and Democracy." *European Journal of Political Economy*, 45: 115–132.

Kuran, Timur. 2003. "The Islamic Commercial Crisis: Institutional Roots of Economic Underdevelopment in the Middle East." *The Journal of Economic History*, 63(2): 414–446.

Kuran, Timur. 2004. "Why the Middle East is Economically Underdeveloped: Historical Mechanisms of Institutional Stagnation." *Journal of Economic Perspectives*, 18(3): 71–90.

Kurer, Oskar. 1993. "Clientelism, Corruption, and the Allocation of Resources." *Public Choice*, 77(2): 259–273.

Kuznets, Simon. 1955. "Economic Growth and Income Inequality." *The American Economic Review*, 45: 1–28.

Kydland, Finn, and Edward Prescott. 1977. "Rules Rather Than Discretion: The Inconsistency of Optimal Plans." *Journal of Political Economy*, 85(3): 473–491.

Kyriacou, Andreas. 2016. "Individualism–Collectivism, Governance and Economic Development." *European Journal of Political Economy*, 42: 91–104.

La Porta, Rafael, Florencio Lopez-de-Silanes, and Andrei Schleifer. 2008. "The Economic Consequences of Legal Origins." *Journal of Economic Literature*, 46(2): 285–332.

La Porta, Rafael, Florencio Lopez-de-Silanes, Cristian Pop-Eleches, and Andrei Schleifer. 2004. "Judicial Checks and Balances." *Journal of Political Economy*, 112(2): 445–470.

Lambsdorff, Johann. 2002. "Corruption and Rent-Seeking." *Public Choice*, 113: 97–125.

Landes, David. 1969. *The Unbound Prometheus: Technological Change and Industrial Development in Western Europe from 1750 to the Present*. Cambridge: Cambridge University Press.

Landes, David. 1999. *The Wealth and Poverty of Nations: Why Some Are So Rich and Some So Poor*. New York: W.W. Norton & Company.

Lange, Matthew. 2004. "British Colonial Legacies and Political Development." *World Development*, 32(6): 905–922.

Lanzafame, Matteo. 2014. "Temperature, Rainfall and Economic Growth in Africa." *Empirical Economics*, 46(1): 1–18.

Le Billon, Phillipe. 2001. "The Political Ecology of War: Natural Resources and Armed Conflicts." *Political Geography*, 20(5): 561–84.

Leff, Nathaniel. 1964. "Economic Development through Bureaucratic Corruption." *American Behavioral Scientist*, 8(3): 8–14.

Lei, Yu-Hsiang, and Guy Michaels. 2014. "Do Giant Oilfield Discoveries Fuel Internal Armed Conflicts?" *Journal of Development Economics*, 110: 139–157.

Levathes, Louise. 1997. *When China Ruled the Seas: The Treasure Fleet of the Dragon Throne, 1405–1433*. Oxford: Oxford University Press.

Lien, Da-Hsiang Donald. 1990. "Corruption and Allocation Efficiency." *Journal of Development Economics*, 33(1): 153–164.

Litina, Anastasia. 2014. "The Geographical Origins of Early State Formation." Center for Research in Economics and Management Paper 28.

Ljunge, Martin. 2014. "Social Capital and Political Institutions: Evidence that Democracy Fosters Trust." *Economics Letters*, 122: 44–49.

Loayza, Norman, Eduardo Olaberria, Jamele Rigolini, and Luc Christiansen. 2012. "Natural Disasters and Growth: Going Beyond the Averages." *World Development*, 40(7): 1317–1336.

Lui, Francis. 1985. "An Equilibrium Queuing Model of Bribery." *Journal of Political Economy*, 93(4): 760–781.

Lule, Jack. 2018. *Globalization and Media: Global Village of Babel*. Lanham, MD: Rowman and Littlefield.

Lydon, Ghislaine. 2009. "A Paper Economy of Faith without Faith in Paper: A Reflection on Islamic Institutional History." *Journal of Economic Behavior & Organization*, 71(3): 647–659.

M'bokolo, Elikia. "The Impact of the Slave Trade on Africa." *Le Monde Diplomatique*, April 1998.

Maaravi, Yossi, Aharon Levy, Tamar Gur, Dan Confino, and Sandra Segal. 2021. "The Tragedy of the Commons: How Individualism and Collectivism Affected the Spread of the COVID-19 Pandemic." *Front Public Health*, 9: 1–6.

Mace, Ruth, and Mark Pagel. 1995. "A Latitudinal Gradient in the Density of Human Languages in North America." *Proceedings of the Royal Society: Biological Sciences*, 261(1360): 117–21.

Mace, Ruth, and Thomas Currie. 2012. "The Evolution of Ethnolinguistic Diversity." *Advances in Complex Systems*, 15(1–2): 1–20.

Mackinder, Halford. 2015. *Democratic Ideals and Reality*. Oxford, UK: Waxkeep Publishing, 2015.

Madsen, Jakob, Paul Raschky and Ahmed Skali. 2015. "Does Democracy Drive Income in the World, 1500–2000?" *European Economic Review*, 78: 175–195.

Maffi, Luisa. 2005. "Linguistic, Cultural and Biological Diversity." *Annual Review of Anthropology*, 34(1): 599–617.

Masseland, Robert. 2018. "Is Colonialism History? The Declining Impact of Colonial Legacies on African Institutional and Economic Development." *Journal of Institutional Economics*, 14(2): 259–287.

Masters, William, and Margaret McMillan. 2001. "Climate and Scale in Economic Growth." *Journal of Economic Growth*, 1: 167–186.

Masters, William, Mesbah Motamed, and Raymond Florax. 2014. "Agriculture, Transportation and the Timing of Urbanization: Global analysis at the Grid Cell Level." *Journal of Economic Growth*, 19(3): 339–368.

Matranga, Andrea. 2017. "The Ant and the Grasshopper: Seasonality and the Invention of Agriculture." Manuscript.

Mauro, Paolo. 1995. "Corruption and Growth." *The Quarterly Journal of Economics*, 110(3): 681–712.

Mauro, Paul. 1998. "Corruption and the Composition of Government Expenditure." *Journal of Public Economics*, 69: 263–279.

Mavisakalyan, Astghik, and Clas Weber. 2018. "Linguistic Structures and Economic Outcomes." *The Journal of Economic Surveys*, 32(3): 916–939.

Maviskalyan, Astghik. 2015. "Gender in Language and Gender in Employment." *Oxford Development Studies*, 43(4): 403–424.

Mayshar, Joram, Omer Moav, Zvika Neeman and Luigi Pascali. 2017. "Cereals, Appropriability and Hierarchy." Manuscript.

Mazar, Nina and Pankaj Aggarwal. 2011. "Greasing the Palm: Can Collectivism Promote Bribery?" *Psychological Science*, 22(7): 843–84.

McArthur, John, and Jeffrey Sachs. 2001. "Institutions and Geography: Comment on Acemoglu, Johnson and Robinson (222)." National Bureau of Economic Research Working Paper 8114.

McChesney, Fred. 1987. "Rent Extraction and Rent Creation in the Economic Theory of Regulation." *The Journal of Legal Studies*, 16(1): 101–118.

McCullough, David. 2001. *The Path between the Seas: The Creation of the Panama Canal, 1870–1914*. New York: Simon and Schuster.

McNeill, William. 2009. *The Rise of the West: A History of Human Community*. Chicago: University of Chicago Press.

Mehlum, Halvor, Karl Moene and Ragnar Torvik. 2006. "Institutions and the Resource Curse." *The Economic Journal*, 116: 1–20.

Meltzer, Milton. 1993. *Slavery: A World History*. Burlington, VT: Da Capo Press.

Mendez, Fabio, and Facundo Sepulveda. 2006. "Corruption, Growth, and Political Regimes: Cross Country Evidence." *European Journal of Political Economy*, 22: 82–98.

Meon, Pierre Guillaume, and Khalid Sekkat. 2005. "Does Corruption Grease or Sand the Wheels of Growth?" *Public Choice*, 122(1/2): 69–97.

Meon, Pierre Guillaume, and Laurent Weill. 2010. "Is Corruption an Efficient Grease?" *World Development*, 38(3): 244–259.

Michael Ross. 2013. *The Oil Curse: How Petroleum Wealth Shapes the Development of Nations*. Princeton: Princeton University Press.

Michalopolous, Stelios, and Elias Papaioannou. 2013. "Pre-Colonial Ethnic Institutions and Contemporary African Development." *Econometrica*, 81(1): 113–152.

Michalopolous, Stelios. 2012. "The Origins of Ethnolinguistic Diversity." *American Economic Review*, 102(4): 508–1539.

Michalopoulos, Stelios, and Elias Papaioannou. 2014. "National Institutions and Subnational Development in Africa." *The Quarterly Journal of Economics*, 151–213.

Michalopoulos, Stelios, and Elias Papaioannou. 2016. "The Long-Run Effects of the Scramble for Africa." *The American Economic Review*, 106(7): 1802–1848.

Miguel, Edward, and Shanker Satyanath. 2011. "Re-examining Economic Shocks and Civil Conflict." *American Economic Journal: Applied Economics*, 3: 228–232.

Miguel, Edward, Shanker Satyanath and Ernest Sergenti. 2004. "Economic Shocks and Civil Conflict: An Instrumental Variables Approach." *Journal of Political Economy*, 112(4): 725–753.

Mill, John Stuart. 2004. *Principles of Political Economy*. Buffalo, NY: Prometheus Books.

Mo, Pak Hung. 2001. "Corruption and Economic Growth." *Journal of Comparative Economics*, 29: 66–79.

Montalvo, Jose, and Marta Reynal-Querol. 2003. "Religious Polarization and Economic Development." *Economics Letters*, 80: 201–210.

Montalvo, Jose, and Marta Reynal-Querol. 2005. "Ethnic Diversity and Economic Development." *Journal of Development Economics*, 76: 293–323.

Montalvo, Jose, and Marta Reynal-Querol. 2010. "Ethnic Polarization and the Duration of Civil Wars." *Economics of Governance*, 11(2): 123–143.

Montalvo, Jose, and Marta Reynal-Querol. 2019. "Earthquakes and Terrorism: The Long-Lasting Effect of Seismic Shocks." *Journal of Comparative Economics*, 47(3): 541–561.

Moore, Joslin, Lisa Manne, Thomas Brooks, Neil Burgess, Robert Davies, Carsten Rahbek, Paul Williams, and Andrew Balmford. 2002. "The Distribution of Cultural and Biological Diversity in Africa." *Proceedings of the Royal Society: Biological Sciences*, 269 (1501): 1645–53.

Moore, Sarah. 2017. "Mosquitoes, Malaria, and Cold Butter: Discourses of Hygiene and Health in the Panama Canal Zone in the Early Twentieth Century." *Panorama: Journal of the Association of Historians of American Art*, 3(2), https://doi.org/10.24926/24716839.1603.

Morand, Serge, and Bruno Walther. 2018. "Individualistic Values are related to an Increase in the Outbreaks of Infectious Diseases and Zoonotic Diseases." *Scientific Reports, Nature*, 8(3866). https://doi.org/10.1038/s41598-018-22014-4

Morelli, Massimo, and Dominic Rohner. 2015. "Resource Concentration and Civil Wars." *Journal of Development Economics*, 117: 32–47.

Morris, Ian. 2014. *War! What Is It Good For? Conflict and the Progress of Civilization from Primates to Robots.* New York: Farrar, Straus and Giroux.

Murphy, Kevin, Andrei Schleifer, and Robert Vishny. 1993. "Why is Rent-seeking So Costly to Growth." *American Economic Review*, 83: 409–14.

Murphy, Kevin, Andrei Shleifer, and Robert Vishny. 1991. "The Allocation of Talent: Implications for Growth." *The Quarterly Journal of Economics*, 106(2): 503–530.

Murphy, Kevin, Andrei Shleifer, and Robert Vishny. 1993. "Why Is Rent-Seeking So Costly to Growth?" *American Economic Review Papers and Proceedings*, 83(2): 409–414.

Nagasawa, Eiji. 2006. "Inventing the Geography of Egyptian Nationalism: A Review of Gamal Hamdan's The Personality of Egypt and his Personal History." *Mediterranean World*, 18(3): 271–318.

Nettle, Daniel. 1998. "Explaining Global Patterns of Language Diversity." *Journal of Anthropological Archaeology*, 17(4): 354–74.

Ngoma, Abubakar Lawan, and Normaz Wana Ismail. 2013. "The Determinants of Brain Drain in Developing Countries." *International Journal of Social Economics*, 40(8): 744–754.

North, Douglas. 1990. *Institutions, Institutional Change and Economic Performance*. Cambridge: Cambridge University Press.

North, Douglass. 1981. *Structure and Change in Economic History*. New York: W. W. Norton & Co.

North, Douglass. 1990. *Institutions, Institutional Change, and Economic Performance*. Cambridge: Cambridge University Press.

Noy, Ilan. 2009. "The Macroeconomic Consequences of Disasters." *Journal of Development Economics*, 88: 221–231.

Nunn, Nathan, and Diego Puga. 2012. "Ruggedness: The Blessing of Bad Geography in Africa." *The Review of Economics and Statistics*, 94(1): 20–36.

Nunn, Nathan, and Leonard Wantchekon. 2011. "The Slave Trade and the Origins of Mistrust in Africa." *The American Economic Review*, 101: 3221–3252.

Nunn, Nathan, and Nancy Qian. 2011. "The Potato's Contribution to Population and Urbanization: Evidence from a Historical Experiment." *The Quarterly Journal of Economics*, 126: 593–650.

Nunn, Nathan. 2008. "The Long-Term Effects of Africa's Slave Trade." *The Quarterly Journal of Economics*, 123(1): 139–176.

Nunziata, Luca, and Lorenzo Rocco. 2016. "A Tale of Minorities: Evidence on Religious Ethics and Entrepreneurship." *Journal of Economic Growth*, 21: 189–224.

Oishi, Shigihiro, and Asuka Komiya. 2017. "Natural Disaster Risk and Collectivism." *Journal of Cross-Cultural Psychology*, 48(8): 1263–1270.

Olsson, Ola, and Christopher Paik. 2016. "Long-Run Cultural Divergence: Evidence from the Neolithic Revolution." *Journal of Development Economics*, 122: 197–213.

Olsson, Ola, and Christopher Paik. 2020. "A Western Reversal Since the Neolithic? The Long-Run Impact of Early Agriculture." *The Journal of Economic History*, 80(1): 100–135.

Olsson, Ola, and Douglas Hibbs. 2004. "Geography, Biogeography, and Why Some Countries are Rich, and others are Poor." *Proceedings of the National Academy of Science PNAS*, 101(10): 3715–3720.

Olsson, Ola, and Douglas Hibbs. 2005. "Biogeography and Long-Run Economic Development." *European Economic Review*, 49: 909–938.

Olsson, Ola. 2009. "On the Democratic Legacy of Colonialism." *Journal of Comparative Economics*, 37(4): 534–551.

O'Rourke, Kevin. 2000. "Tariffs and Growth in the Late Nineteenth Century." *The Economic Journal*, 110(463): 456–483.

Osafo-Kwaako, Philip, and James Robinson. 2013. "Political Centralization in Pre-Colonial Africa." *Journal of Comparative Economics*, 41: 6–21.

Ozak, Omer. 2018. "Distance to the Pre-industrial Technological Frontier and Economic Development." *Journal of Economic Growth*, 23(2): 175–221.

Pagden, Anthony. 2008. *Worlds at War: The 2,500 Year Struggle between East and West*. New York: Random House.

Paik, Christopher. 2010. "Historical Underpinnings of Institutions: Evidence from the Neolithic Revolution." Manuscript.

Papaioannou, Elias, and Gregorios Siourounis. 2008. "Democratisation and Growth." *The Economic Journal*, 118: 1520–1551.

Parcero, Osiris and Elissaios Papyrakis. 2016. "Income Inequality and the Oil Resource Curse." *Resource and Energy Economics*, 45: 159–177.

Parker, Miles. 2018. "The Impact of Disasters on Inflation." *Economics of Disasters and Climate Change*, 2(1): 21–48.

Paxton, Pamela. 2002. "Social Capital and Democracy: An Interdependent Relationship." *American Sociological Review*, 67(2): 254–277.

Peiró-Palomino, Jesús, and Emili Tortosa-Ausina. 2013. "Can Trust Effects on Development be Generalized? A Response by Quantile." *European Journal of Political Economy*, 32: 377–390.

Peiró-Palomino, Jesús, Emili Tortosa-Ausina, and Anabel Forte. 2015. "Does Social Capital Matter for European Regional Growth?" *European Economic Review*, 77: 47–64.

Perotti, Roberto. 1996. "Growth, Income Distribution, and Democracy: What the Data Say." *Journal of Economic Growth*, 1: 149–187.

Persson, Torsten, and Guido Tabellini. 1994. "Is Inequality Harmful for Growth?" *The American Economic Review*, 84(3): 600–621.

Persson, Torsten, and Guido Tabellini. 2009. "Democratic Capital: The Nexus of Political and Economic Change." *American Economic Journal: Macroeconomics*, 1(2): 88–126.

Persson, Torsten, and Lars Svensson. 1989. "Why a Stubborn Conservative would run a Deficit: Policy with Time-Inconsistent Preferences." *The Quarterly Journal of Economics*, 104(2): 325–345.

Persson, Torsten. 2005. "Forms of Democracy, Policy and Economic Development." National Bureau of Economic Research Working Paper 11171.

Petersen, Michael Bang, and Svend-Erik Skaaning. 2010. "Ultimate Causes of State Formation: The Significance of Biogeography, Diffusion, and Neolithic Revolutions." *Historical Social Research*, 35(133): 200–226.

Popp, Aaron. 2006. "The Effects of Natural Disasters on Long Run Growth." *Major Themes in Economics*, 8(1): 61–82.

Posner, Richard. 1974. "Theories of Economic Regulation." *The Bell Journal of Economics and Management Science*, 5(2): 335–358.

Proust, Marcel. 1924. *Within a Budding Grove*. New York: Thomas Seltzer.

Putnam, Robert. 1994. *Making Democracy Work: Civic Traditions in Modern Italy*. Princeton: Princeton University Press.

Putnam, Robert. 2000. *Bowling Alone: The Collapse and Revival of American Community*. New York: Simon & Schuster.

Putterman, Louis. 2008. "Agriculture, Diffusion and Development: Ripple Effects of the Neolithic Revolution." *Economica*, 75: 729–748.

Rabiul Islam, Md. 2018. "Wealth Inequality, Democracy and Economic Freedom." *Journal of Comparative Economics*, 46(4): 920–935.

Reynal-Querol, Marta, and Jose Montalvo. 2008. "Discrete Polarization with an Application to the Determinants of Genocide." *The Economic Journal*, 118: 1835–1865.

Reynal-Querol, Marta. 2002. "Ethnicity, Political Systems, and Civil Wars." *Journal of Conflict Resolution*, 46(1): 29–54.

Ricardo, David. 2015. *On the Principles of Political Economy and Taxation*. British Columbia, Canada: Andesite Press.

Robinson, Amanda Lea, Simon Ejdemyr and Eric Kramon. 2018. "Segregation, Ethnic Favoritism, and the Strategic Targeting of Local Public Goods." *Comparative Political Studies*, 51(9): 1111–1143.

Robinson, Amanda Lea. 2020. "Ethnic Diversity, Segregation and Ethnocentric Trust in Africa." *British Journal of Political Science*, 50(1): 217–239.

Rock, Michael, and Heidi Bonnett. 2004. "The Comparative Politics of Corruption: Accounting for the East Asian Paradox in Empirical Studies of Corruption, Growth and Investment." *World Development*, 32(6): 999–1017.

Rodrick, Dani, and Arvind Subramanian. 2003 (June). "The Primacy of Institutions." *Finance and Development*, 31–34.

Rodrick, Dani, Arvind Subramanian, and Francesco Trebbi. 2004. "Institutions Rule: The Primacy of Institutions over Geography and Integration in Economic Development." *Journal of Economic Growth*, 9: 131–165.

Rodrick, Dani. 2000. "Institutions for High-Quality Growth: What They Are and How to Acquire Them." *Studies in Comparative International Development*, 35(3): 3–31.

Romer, Paul. 1990. "Endogenous Technological Change." *Journal of Political Economy*, 98: 71–102.

Ross, Michael. 1999. "The Political Economy of the Resource Curse." *World Politics*, 51(2): 297–322.

Ross, Michael. 2001. "Does Oil Hinder Democracy?" *World Politics*, 53: 325–61.

Ross, Michael. 2004. "How Do Natural Resources Influence Civil War? Evidence from Thirteen Cases." *International Organization*, 58: 35–67.

Ross, Michael. 2004. "What Do We Know About Natural Resources and Civil War?" *Journal of Peace Research*, 41(3): 337–356.

Ross, Michael. 2006. "A Closer Look at Oil, Diamonds, and Civil War." *Annual Review of Political Science*, 9: 265–300.

Ross, Michael. 2015. "What Have We Learned about the Resource Curse?" *Annual Review of Political Science*, 18: 239–259.

Rubin, Jared. 2010. "Bills of Exchange, Interest Bans, and Impersonal Exchange in Islam and Christianity." *Explorations in Economic History*, 47(2): 213–227.

Rubin, Jared. 2011. "Institutions, the Rise of Commerce and the Persistence of Laws: Interest Restrictions in Islam and Christianity." *The Economic Journal*, 121: 1310–1339.

Sacerdote, Bruce, and Edward Glaeser. 2008. "Education and Religion." *Journal of Human Capital*, 2(2): 188–215.

Sachs, Jeffery, and Andrew Warner. 1995. "Economic Reform and the Process of Global Integration." *Brookings Papers on Economic Activity*, 1: 1–118.

Sachs, Jeffrey, and Andrew Warner. 1995. "Natural Resource Abundance and Economic Growth." National Bureau of Economic Research Working Paper 5398.

Sachs, Jeffrey, and Andrew Warner. 1997. "Sources of Slow Growth in African Economies." *Journal of African Economies*, 6(3): 335–76.

Sachs, Jeffrey, and Andrew Warner. 1999. "The Big Push, Natural Resource Booms and Growth." *Journal of Development Economics*, 59: 43–76.

Sachs, Jeffrey, and Andrew Warner. 2001. "The Curse of Natural Resources." *European Economic Review*, 45: 827–838.

Sachs, Jeffrey. 2001. "Tropical Underdevelopment." National Bureau of Economic Research Working Paper 8119.

Sachs, Jeffrey. 2003. "Institutions Don't Rule: Direct Effects of Geography on Per Capita Income." National Bureau of Economic Research Working Paper 9490.

Saramago, José. 2010. *The Notebook*. New York: Verso.

Sartre, Jean-Paul. 2001. *Colonialism and Neocolonialism*. East Sussex, UK: Psychology Press.

Schenkler, Wolfram, Anthony Fisher, Michael Hanemann, and Michael Roberts. 2012. "The Economic Impacts of Climate Change: Evidence from Agricultural Output and Random Fluctuations in Weather: Comment." *American Economic Review*, 102(7): 3749–3760.

Schenkler, Wolfram, David Lobell and Justin Costa-Roberts. 2010. "Climate Trends and Global Crop Production since 1980." *Science*, 333(6042): 616–620.

Schenkler, Wolfram, Jonathan Eyer and Michael Roberts. 2013. "Agronomic Weather Measures in Econometric Models of Crop Yield with Implications for Climate Change." *American Journal of Agricultural Economics*, 95(2): 236–243.

Schenkler, Wolfram, Michael Hanemann and Anthony Fisher. 2006. "The Impact of Global Warming on U.S. Agriculture: An Econometric Analysis of Optimal Growing Conditions." *Review of Economics and Statistics*, 88(1): 113–125.

Schenkler, Wolfram, and Michael Roberts. 2006. "Nonlinear Effects of Weather on Corn Yields." *Review of Agricultural Economics*, 28(3): 391–398.

Schmid, Boris, Ulf Büntgen, W. Ryan Easterday, Christian Ginzler, Lars Walløe, Barbara Bramanti, and Nils Tenseth. 2015. "Climate-Driven Introduction of the Black Death and Successive Plague Reintroductions into Europe." *Proceedings of the National Academy of Sciences PNAS*, 112(10): 3020–3025.

Schularick, Moritz, and Solomos Solomou. 2011. "Tariffs and Economic Growth in the First Era of Globalization." *Journal of Economic Growth*, 16(1): 33–70.

Science and Imperial Affairs. 1932. *Nature*, 129, 1–3. https://doi.org/10.1038/129001a0.

Scully, Gerald. 1988. "The Institutional Framework and Economic Development." *Journal of Political Economy*, 96(3): 652–662.

Shirer, William. 2011. *The Rise and Fall of the Third Reich: A History of Nazi Germany*. New York: Simon & Schuster.

Shleifer, Andrei, and Robert Vishny. 1993. "Corruption." *The Quarterly Journal of Economics*, 108: 599–618.

Skidmore, Mark, and Hideki Toya. 2002. "Do Natural Disasters Promote Long Run Growth?" *Economic Inquiry*, 40(4): 664–687.

Smith, Adam. 1811. *An Inquiry into the Nature and Causes of the Wealth of Nations*. New York: Peter Gleason & Co. Printers.

Smith, Adam. 1818. *Inquiry into the Nature and Causes of the Wealth of Nations*. Washington, DC: Cooke & Hale.

Smith, Adam. 1937. *The Wealth of Nations*. New York: The Modern Library.

Smith, Adam. 1979. *An Inquiry into the Nature and Causes of the Wealth of Nations*. Edited by Roy H. Campbell, Andrew S. Skinner, and W. B. Todd. Oxford: Clarendon.

Soares, Rodrigo, Juliano Assunção, and Tomás Goulart. 2012. "A Note on Slavery and the Roots of Inequality." *Journal of Comparative Economics*, 40: 565–580.

Spykman, Nicholas. 1938. "Geography and Foreign Policy." *The American Political Science Review*, 32(1): 28–50.

Spykman, Nicholas. 2007. *America's Strategy in World Politics: The United States and the Balance of Power*. New York: Routledge.

Stigler, George. 1971. "The Theory of Economic Regulation." *The Bell Journal of Economics and Management Science*, 2(1): 3–21.

Strobl, Eric, and Preeya Mohan. 2017. "A Hurricane Wind Risk and Loss Assessment of Caribbean Agriculture." *Environment and Development Economics*, 22(1): 84–106.

Strobl, Eric, Luisito Bertinelli and Preeya Mohan. 2016. "Hurricane Damage Risk Assessment in the Caribbean: An Analysis Using Synthetic Hurricane Events and Nightlight Imagery." *Ecological Economics*, 124(C): 135–144.

Strobl, Eric, Preeya Mohan and Bazoumana Ouattara. 2018. "Decomposing the Macroeconomic Effects of Natural Disasters: A National Income Accounting Perspective." *Ecological Economics*, 146(C): 1–9.

Strobl, Eric. 2012. "The Economic Growth Impact of Natural Disasters in Developing Countries: Evidence from Hurricane Strikes in the Central American and Caribbean Regions." *Journal of Development Economics*, 97: 130–141.

Stromberg, David. 2007. "Natural Disasters, Economic Development, and Humanitarian Aid." *Journal of Economic Perspectives*, 21(3): 199–222.

Strulik, Holger. 2016. "Secularization and Long-Run Economic Growth." *Economic Inquiry*, 54: 177–200.

Sturm, Jan-Egbert, and Jakob De Haan. 2015. "Income Inequality, Capitalism, and Ethno-linguistic Fractionalization." *The American Economic Review: Papers and Proceedings*, 105(5): 593–97.

Sunde, Uwe, and Matteo Cervellati. 2014. "Civil Conflict, Democratization, and Growth: Violent Democratization as Critical Juncture." *The Scandinavian Journal of Economics*, 116(2): 482–505.

Sunde, Uwe, and Matteo Cervellati. 2014. "Democratizing for Peace? The Effect of Democratization on Civil Conflicts." *Oxford Economic Papers*, 66: 774–797.

Sylwester, Kevin. 2000. "Income Inequality, Education Expenditures, and Growth." *Journal of Development Economics*, 63: 379–398.

Sylwester, Kevin. 2005. "Decolonization and Economic Growth: The Case of Africa." *Journal of Economic Development*, 30(2): 87–102.

Tabellini, Guido. 2010. "Culture and Institutions: Economic Development in the Regions of Europe." *Journal of the European Economic Association*, 8(4): 677–716.

Tan, Chih Ming. 2010. "No One True Path: Uncovering the Interplay between Geography, Institutions, and Fractionalization in Economic Development." *Journal of Applied Econometrics*, 25: 1100–1127.

Tanzi, Vito and Hamid Davoodi. 1998. "Corruption, Public Investment, and Growth." In *The Welfare State, Public Investment, and Growth*, edited by H. Shibata and T. Ihori. Tokyo: Springer.

Tebaldi, Edinaldo, and Bruce Elmslie. 2008. "Institutions, Innovation and Economic Growth." *Journal of Economic Development*, 33(2): 1–27.

Tebaldi, Edinaldo, and Bruce Elmslie. 2013. "Does Institutional Quality Impact Innovation? Evidence from Cross-country Patent Grant Data." *Applied Economics*, 45(7): 887–900.

Toya, Hideki, and Mark Skidmore. 2007. "Economic Development and the Impacts of Natural Disasters." *Economics Letters*, 94: 20–25.

Toynbee, Arnold. 1949. *Civilization on Trial*. Oxford: Oxford University Press.

Toynbee, Arnold. 1987. *A Study of History*. Oxford: Oxford University Press.

Tsui, Kevin, and Anca Cotet. 2013. "Oil, Growth, and Health: What Does the Cross-Country Evidence Really Show?" *The Scandinavian Journal of Economics*, 115(4): 1107–1137.

Tsui, Kevin. 2011. "More Oil, Less Democracy: Evidence from Worldwide Crude Oil Discoveries." *The Economic Journal*, 121: 89–115.

Turchin, Peter. 2007. *War and Peace and War: The Rise and Fall of Empires*. New York: Plume.

Turchin, Peter. 2009. *Secular Cycles*. Princeton: Princeton University Press.

Turchin, Peter. 2015. *Ultrasociety: How 10,000 Years of War Made Humans the Greatest Cooperators on Earth*. Chaplin, CT: Beresta Books.

Turchin, Peter. 2018. *Historical Dynamics: Why States Rise and Fall*. Princeton: Princeton University Press.

Tyerman, Christopher. 2006. *God's War*. Cambridge: The Belknap Press of Harvard University Press.

van Hoorn, André, and Robbert Maseland. 2013. "Does a Protestant Work Ethic Exist? Evidence from the Well-being Effect of Unemployment." *Journal of Economic Behavior & Organization*, 91: 1–12.

Van Wijnbergen, Sweder. 1984. "The 'Dutch Disease': A Disease After All?" *The Economic Journal*, 94(373): 41.

Venables, Anthony and Frederick van der Ploeg. 2012. "Natural Resource Wealth: The Challenge of Managing a Windfall." *Annual Review of Economics*, 4: 315–337.

Venables, Anthony. 2016. "Using Natural Resources for Development: Why has it proven so Difficult?" *Journal of Economic Perspectives*, 30(1): 161–184.

Vick, Karl. 2014. "ISIS Militants Declare Islamist 'Caliphate.'" *Time*, June 29.

Vogel, Gretchen. 2013. "The Forgotten Malaria." *Science*, 342(6159): 684–687.

Voigt, Stefan, and Jerg Gutmann. 2013. "Turning Cheap Talk into Economic Growth: On the Relationship between Property Rights and Judicial Independence." *Journal of Comparative Economics*, 41: 66–73.

Voigt, Stefan, and Lars Feld. 2003. "Economic Growth and Judicial Independence: Cross-country Evidence Using a New Set of Indicators." *European Journal of Political Economy*, 19: 497–527.

Voigt, Stefan, Jerg Gutmann, and Lars Feld. 2015. "Economic Growth and Judicial Independence, a Dozen Years On: Cross-Country Evidence using an Updated Set of Indicators." *European Journal of Political Economy*, 38: 197–211.

Vu, Trung. 2021. "Climate, Diseases, and the Origins of Corruption." *Economics of Transition and Institutional Change*, 29(4): 621–649.

Wacziarg, Romain, and Fabrice Murtin. 2014. "The Democratic Transition." *Journal of Economic Growth*, 19: 141–181.

Wacziarg, Romain, and Jose Tavares. 2001. "How Democracy Affects Growth." *European Economic Review*, 45: 1341–1378.

Wacziarg, Romain, and Karen Welch. 2008. "Trade Liberalization and Growth: New Evidence." *The World Bank Economic Review*, 22(2): 187–231.

Wantchekon, Leonard. 2002. "Why Do Resource Dependent Countries Have Authoritarian Governments?" *Journal of African Finance and Economic Development*, 2: 57–77.

Watson, Alan. 1993. *Legal Transplants: An Approach to Comparative Law*. Athens: University of Georgia Press.

Watson, Alan. 2003. *Legal Origins and Legal Change*. London: Bloomsbury Academic.

Weber, Max. 2002. *The Protestant Ethic and the Spirit of Capitalism and Other Writings*. New York: Penguin Books.

Wei, Shang-Jin. 2000. "How Taxing is Corruption on International Investors?" *Review of Economics and Statistics*, 82: 1–11.

Weingast, Barry. 1995. "The Economic Role of Political Institutions: Market-Preserving Federalism and Economic Development." *Journal of Law, Economics, & Organization*, 11(1): 1–31.

Weingast, Barry. 1997. "The Political Foundations of Democracy and the Rule of Law." *The American Political Science Review*, 91(2): 245–263.

Weiss, Harvey, and Raymond Bradley. 2001. "What Drives Societal Collapse?" *Science*, 291(5504): 609–610.

Whatley, Warren, and Rob Gillezeau. 2011. "The Impact of the Transatlantic Slave Trade on Ethnic Stratification in Africa." *American Economic Review: Papers & Proceedings*, 101(3): 571–576.

Whitbeck, Ray Hughes. 1921. "Geography and Man at Panama." *Bulletin of the Geographical Society of Philadelphia*, 19: 8.

Williamson, Claudia. 2009. "Informal Institutions Rule: Institutional Arrangements and Economic Performance." *Public Choice*, 139(3/4): 371–387.

Wittfogel, Karl. 1957. *Oriental Despotism: A Comparative Study of Total Power.* New Haven: Yale University Press.

Witvliet, Margot, Anton Kunst, Onyebuchi Arah and Karien Stronks. 2013. "Sick Regimes and Sick People: A Multilevel Investigation of the Population Health Consequences of Perceived National Corruption." *Tropical Medicine and International Health*, 18(10): 1240–1247.

www.cdc.gov/parasites/leishmaniasis/epi.html.

www.cdc.gov/parasites/lymphaticfiliariasis/epi.html.

www.cdc.gov/parasites/onchocerciasis/epi.html.

www.cdc.gov/parasites/schistosomiasis/epi.html.

www.cdc.gov/parasites/sleepingsickness/epi.html.

Yanikkaya, Halit. 2003. "Trade Openness and Economic Growth: A Cross-Country Empirical Investigation." *Journal of Development Economics*, 72: 57–89.

Yergin, Daniel. 1992. *The Prize: The Epic Quest for Oil, Money and Power.* New York: Free Press.

Yu, Shu, Sjoerd Beugelsdijk, and Jakob de Haan. 2015. "Trade, Trust and the Rule of Law." *European Journal of Political Economy*, 37: 102–115.

Zac, Paul, and Stephen Knack. 2001. "Trust and Growth." *The Economic Journal*, 111(470): 295–321.

Zuleta, Hernando. 2012. "Seasonal Fluctuations and Economic Growth." *Journal of Economic Development*, 37(4): 1–27.

Index

About the Author

Sherif Khalifa is professor of economics at California State University, Fullerton. Khalifa is a former diplomat who holds a doctorate degree in economics from Johns Hopkins University. His scholarly work comes at the intersection of development economics, political economy, and political science. His research focuses on the deep determinants of economic development, and the economic consequences of income inequality, cultural values, democratic transitions, and globalization. His published articles appeared on various academic outlets such as *Review of Development Economics*, *Journal of Economic Development*, *Journal of International Development*, the *World Economy*, and others. He also published several opinion articles in *Foreign Policy Journal*, a well-known outlet for foreign policy analysis in the United States, and AlJazeera.net, the website of the Aljazeera news channel. The author completed his first book titled *Egypt's Lost Spring: Causes and Consequences* in 2015.

www.ingramcontent.com/pod-product-compliance
Lightning Source LLC
Chambersburg PA
CBHW071412290326
41932CB00047B/2607

* 9 7 8 1 6 6 6 9 0 0 5 4 5 *